Fodor's

E X P L O R I N G

FODOR'S TRAVEL PUBLICATIONS, INC.
NEW YORK • TORONTO • LONDON • SYDNEY • AUCKLAND

WWW.FODORS.COM

Cover (front): Santiago
de Cuba festival
Above: in Guantánamo
Page 3: Trinidad, from
bell tower
Page 4: Varadero beach
Page 5: Capitolio,
Havana
Pages 6–7: Sierra
Maestra
Page 6 (bottom):
sugar-cane cutter
Page 7 (bottom):
Havana University,
Vedado
Page 8: in Pinar del Rio
Page 9 (a): Memorial
José Martí, Plaza de la
Revolución, Havana
Page 9 (b): drinking
coconut milk in
Maguana
Page 37 (a): The
Malecón, Havana
Page 37 (b): dancers at
the Tropicana in 1954

Published in the United States by Fodor's Travel
Publications, Inc.
Published in the United Kingdom by AA Publishing.

ISBN 0-679-00268-5
First Edition

Fodor's Exploring Cuba

Author: **Fred Mawer**
Joint Series Editor: **Josephine Perry**
Copy Editor: **Sue Gordon**
Original Photography: **Clive Sawyer**
Cartography: **The Automobile Association**
Cover Design: **Louise Fili, Fabrizio La Rocca**
Front Cover Silhouette: **Nik Wheeler**

Special Sales

Printed and bound in Italy by Printer Trento srl
10 9 8 7 6 5 4 3 2 1

How to use this book

This book is divided into five main sections:

❏ Section 1: *Cuba Is*

discusses aspects of life and living today, from communism to rum

❏ Section 2: *Cuba Was*

places the country in its historical context and explores past events whose influences are still felt

❏ Section 3: *A to Z Section*

covers places to visit, arranged by region, with suggested walks and drives. Within this section are the Focus-on articles, which consider a variety of topics in greater detail

❏ Section 4: *Travel Facts*

contains the strictly practical information that is vital for a successful trip

❏ Section 5:
Hotels and Restaurants

lists recommended establishments in Cuba, giving a brief overview of what they offer

How to use the star rating
Most places described in this book have been given a separate rating:

▶▶▶ **Do not miss**

▶▶ **Highly recommended**

▶ **Worth seeing**

  Not essential viewing

Map references
To make the location of a particular place easier to find, every main entry in this book is given a map reference, such as 53C2. The first number (53) indicates the page on which the map can be found; the letter (C) and the second number (2) pinpoint the square in which the main entry is located. The maps on the inside front and inside back covers are referred to as IFC and IBC respectively.

Admission charges
Standard admission charges are categorized in this book as follows:

Inexpensive	$1–2
Moderate	$3–4
Expensive	$5 or over

Contents

Quick reference

This quick-reference guide highlights the elements of the book you will use most often: the maps; the introductory features; the Focus-on articles; the walks; and the drives.

My Cuba by Fred Mawer

I've been lucky enough to have visited Cuba three times in the 1990s. The first trip, in 1992, was a "study tour", where our group was shown how Cuban communism worked. We were introduced to Committees for the Defense of the Revolution and shown around hospitals, farms, and schools. But what I remember most is how communism was not working: the massive lines, lack of food, the department stores empty but for shuttlecocks and plastic flowers.

On my second trip, I traveled independently. Away from the resorts and main cities, I was often a fish in a goldfish bowl, the only foreigner who had dropped by for weeks. I took furtive, illegal rides in Cadillacs (and regretted it when we broke down on the way to the airport for our flight home) and I rented a car: in Cuba everyone hitches, and I met literally hundreds of Cubans by giving people lifts.

My third journey covered the whole length of the island, reaching spellbinding corners such as Viñales and Baracoa. Cuba had altered vastly since my first visit, primarily because tourism had taken off. Cubans were becoming more streetwise. A teacher I had met in 1992 now spent most of his time touting cigars to tourists. Sightseeing would all too often be brought to a grinding halt by pressing offers and requests. Did I want a taxi? Could I come around that evening with some sausages? Varadero, Cuba's main resort, had virtually doubled in size, and now there were legalized private restaurants and rooms for rent everywhere. Nonetheless, one night I became embroiled in a police raid on a home that was clandestinely serving lobster to tourists. The owners threw the lobster shells out of the bedroom window to hide the evidence. Only in Cuba.

It sounds corny, but I'm in love with Cuba. I am seduced by its baffling ways, its funky tropical charms. It can be maddeningly bureaucratic (just getting a journalist's visa has always proved a nightmare).But, being in love, I forgive its faults.

The island is on a roller coaster of change. Visit now, before it becomes just another sanitized vacation destination, while it is still trying to dance to a tune composed by Karl Marx.

Fred Mawer is a London-based travel journalist who, having given up a career in teaching after four weeks, became a researcher with Holiday Which? magazine. Since then he has gone on to write or contribute to over a dozen guidebooks. He also contributes articles regularly to the Daily Telegraph, the Sunday Telegraph, and the Mail on Sunday.

CUBA IS

■ **Cuba offers the classic Caribbean landscapes of palms and beaches, along with a multilayered, musical culture that is both African and Latin in its roots. Intertwined with this heady mix are the laws and practices imposed by one of the world's last communist regimes.** ■

A vacation island Cuba manages to deliver all the clichéd images beloved of travel brochures, and without stinting. The beaches do consist of dazzling white sand and are fringed with palms and transparent turquoise waters. You can indulge to your heart's content in plentiful rum-based cocktails and the very best home-produced cigars. The *salsa* and *rumba* rhythms are sensational and ubiquitous (expect to be serenaded on and off your plane); glorious colonial architecture awaits; the people are friendly, beautiful, sexy.

Tourism has taken off in the last decade. Mostly it is of the fun-in-the-sun kind, but Cuba is far too fascinat-

One-room living, typical of many a Cuban home

ing to spend all your time bronzing on the beach with a rum and coke at your side. What, above all, makes it so absorbing is that since Fidel Castro came to power in 1959 and turned the country onto a communist course, the island has been isolated from much of the world. Someone, it seems, has pressed the "pause" button on Cuba's history: Western commercialization is noticeably absent; horse-and-buggies and grandiose, octane-guzzling 1950s American automobiles ply the roads, and oxen till the fields.

In judgment Modern-day Cuba is a radical social and political experiment that begs judgment—whether favorable or not depends against which nations it is compared. There is little

10

of the misery and squalor found in other undeveloped countries. The United Nations regards Cuba as excellent for its egalitarian distribution of income, national health care programs, and free and universal education system. Yet the well-being of Cubans rates poorly against Western countries' standards. Cuba is an economic and physical mess. This is partly due to its own failings, but also because of both the collapse of empathetic political systems in Eastern bloc countries since 1989 and the decades-long U.S. trade embargo against the island. Admittedly, free-market reforms introduced in the last few years have improved the country's economy, but for most Cubans life is a question of survival—of empty shops, lengthy lines, meager rations, dealing on the black market, and bartering with neighbors. Even housewives press tourists for a dollar, a bar of soap, or the T-shirt off their back. It's all about *resolviendo*, a catchall word Cubans use to describe somehow—by fair means or foul—getting by.

The future Many commentators wrongly predicted communist Cuba would collapse after 1989. Yet, in true Darwinian fashion, it has adapted to survive. The capitalist

Long, grilled windows are ideal for neighborly gossip

tinkerings with the economy are proving a qualified success, and the question now is how far they will go. Presently, Castro is at pains to stress that his government will keep the economy under firm state control and his people will be called communists while he is around. And most Cuba-watchers surmise that his regime will be around so long as the U.S. imposes its embargo. While the lifting of sanctions is probably the only act that would end Cuba's economic woes, ironically it would probably also bring about the downfall of the government, since its scapegoat, the U.S., would disappear. In the meantime, Castro is able to rally his people behind him against the big bad American wolf: "Never will the dragon be allowed to slay the lamb," he proclaims.

Cubans, it is said, are too preoccupied with day-to-day subsistence to have any energy left to rise up against Castro. Accustomed to waiting endlessly in line for everything from buses to bread, they are also simply waiting for something to happen to change their country, for someone to press the "play" button on their history.

Fidel Castro

■ **Born in 1927 in eastern Cuba as the son of a well-off Galician landowner, this guerrilla-fighter turned statesman is both the prime creator and the embodiment of communist Cuba. Undoubtedly one of the 20th century's most intelligent and charismatic leaders, Fidel Castro is also presently one of the world's longest-ruling heads of state. ■**

Names Castro has many titles— President of the Councils of State and Ministers, First Secretary of the Communist Party, Commander-in-Chief of the Armed Forces—and is often referred to as *El Comandante* or *El Jefe Máximo* (the Maximum Leader). But his subjects more commonly call him just Fidel, normally in semi-affectionate overtones. His nicknames include the Horse (*El Caballo*), a reference to his alleged sexual prowess; the Flight Attendant, since he's always asking his people to tighten their belts; and the Bearded One (*El Barbudo*). When people want to refer to Castro silently, they often just stroke their chin.

Personality Castro's capabilities are legendary. At school he won a prize for Cuba's best all-round school athlete. He is said to have an encyclopedic knowledge of everything from biochemistry to cheese crackers. Though he now rarely occupies a platform for long, in his prime he delivered speeches of preposterous length in his uniquely fiery yet chatty style, unaided by notes: 14 hours is his record. It is the prime way he communicates with his people, rousing them to herculean new endeavors, explaining what the government is doing, and even lambasting it when not up to scratch.

In his favored olive-green military fatigues Castro has always cut a rather ascetic image. But little is known about his private life: in order to maintain his mystique no pictures are allowed of him doing everyday activites. He actively discourages any personality cult of himself (or any other living Cuban leader). But while there are no statues of him nor streets named after him, his portrait adorns the wall of many a living room and office throughout the country.

Popularity His friend, the Columbian novelist Gabríel Gárcia Marquez, has called him "one of the great idealists of our time." Yet Cuban exiles in Miami drive around with "No Castro

Castro, the very personification of Cuba

no problem" bumper stickers on their cars. Opinion is as divided in Cuba. Many admire and even worship Castro as the man who has restored Cuba's national pride by taking on the United States and the one who has provided free education and health care for all. However, an increasing number resent Castro's despotism, and have had enough of the endless personal hardships he forces them to face. This feeling is summed up in a recent Cuban joke. A man is so fed up waiting in line for hours for a loaf of bread he says he's going to kill Castro. Next day he returns to the bread line and his neighbors ask him if he did it. No, he replies, the line was too long.

❏ Rumour has it that the CIA has carried out more than 30 assassination attempts on Castro. He has reportedly been given exploding cigars and has had his diver's wetsuit contaminated with a virulent strain of tuberculosis. It is even alleged that a plot was hatched to make him take a poison that would make his beard fall out. Castro is said to have dozens of safehouses around the island—so, Cubans joke, that he can attend to all his lovers. ❏

Castro's future Although he is now in his seventies, with a graying beard and occasionally slurred speech, no serious questions have been raised about Castro's health. There is little talk of resignation: "It would be like deserting the front line in the heat of

battle," he says. The country's ongoing economic changes clearly indicate his ambition to retain power at all costs. Given that his people are so in awe of him and that there is an absence of an outstanding, obvious successor waiting in the wings, it is unlikely he will be ousted.

Few offices are without a portrait of El Jefe Máximo

■ **Overpoweringly sensual, extraordinarily warm, resourceful, and long-suffering, Cuba's citizens, numbering just under 11 million, are the country's best asset. Somehow their *joie de vivre* remains intact, despite the hardships they are presently undergoing. Sex, music, and dancing, they like to say, are their greatest pleasures, since none are rationed and all are free.** ■

Cuba is one of the friendliest places in the world. Admittedly, some of the Cubans who greet you only want to sell you something or sponge a dollar or two; most, however, simply want your friendship. Cubans deluge foreigners with invitations to visit their houses, where they ply them with what little food and drink they have and always insist they take the best seat in the house. The home is an excellent place to observe Cuban

Smiling in the face of adversity

resourcefulness, maybe in a doorbell made from an old telephone or a coffee filter fashioned from a coat hanger and piece of fabric. Cubans, it has been said, suffer from a shortage of everything—except ingenuity.

Race Cuba is the most ethnically diverse country in the Caribbean, so there are few clear-cut ethnic groups. Official Cuban figures indicate that two-thirds of the population are white (mainly Hispanic). In reality, it is probably the case that about two-thirds of Cubans are either black, largely descendants of slaves from West Africa and emigrants from other Caribbean countries (especially Jamaica), or mulatto. Owing to emigration to the U.S., it is the white population that has dwindled the most since the revolution.

Prior to 1959, black Cubans suffered appalling prejudice, not only in the workplace but also in whites-only beaches and hotels. While the black population has undoubtedly benefited from the revolution, the government's claim that racism has been eradicated is unfounded. Despite a marked improvement in their employment prospects, blacks are very underrepresented in the higher echelons of Cuban society.

Women Employment prospects for women have improved tremendously under the Castro regime, with excellent representation in traditional male bastions such as medicine and education, if not in the political élite. However, machismo is still deeply ingrained in the male psyche, despite enlightened pieces of legislation such as the Family Code, introduced

Banter and dominoes – both could be regarded as national pastimes

in 1974, which calls for men and women to share responsibilities for rearing the children, and even the housework, equally. The majority of Cuban families still celebrate their daughter's passage to womanhood with a lavish party on her 15th birthday called *quince primaveras*.

Homosexuality Immediately after the revolution, homosexuality was seen as an evil of a decadent capitalist society, and gay people were even sent to labor camps for "reeducation." While homophobia is still rife, matters have improved. Castro has gone on record as saying he is opposed to discrimination against homosexuals, and the law against public displays of homosexuality was scrapped in 1987. In Havana, gay people hold large-scale parties in their homes called *fiestas de diez pesos*—traditionally they cost 10 pesos to get in, and anyone can go.

Special people Cuba's angelic children create an indelible impression. Generally well nourished and well dressed—especially in neat school uniforms colored maroon for primary school and saffron for secondary school—they are a fine advertisement for the country's

health and education systems. In the countryside keep an eye out for the legendary *guajiro*, the Cuban peasant or farmer. Straw-hatted, machete dangling at his side, he plods along the lanes on horseback, drives his oxen in the fields, and tends the crops around his *bohío*, a wooden hut thatched with palm leaves, similar to pre-Columbian structures.

❑ Cubans are incredibly patriotic, regardless of whether they approve of their government. José Triana, a Cuban playwright living in exile in Paris, wrote in 1995: "I have never mistaken the government for the people. Powerful virtues make Cubans stand out in the concert of humanity; among them I would point out as paradigmatic patience and generosity...I believe that no government has ever represented our people. All governments have, instead, taken advantage of that patience and generosity." ❑

Landscape and wildlife

■ **Often likened in shape to a scythe or an alligator, Cuba is by far the biggest Caribbean island, roughly the size of the state of Pennsylvania and nearly as large as England. Some 776 miles from head to tail, it has 3,726 miles of coastline that includes some 300 catalogued beaches and is surrounded by between 1,200 and 4,000 islets—depending on how many of the small ones are counted.** ■

The lay of the land Administratively, Cuba consists of 14 provinces, plus the "special municipality" of the Isla de la Juventud, the largest offshore island and one of the few to be inhabited. Topographically, flat low-lying plains, mostly covered by sugarcane, account for about two-thirds of the country, with mountains taking up the rest. The north coast is rocky and sandy, while the south coast is generally swampy. But the most obvious way to think of Cuba is in three parts. The west, the alligator's tail, is characterized by tobacco plantations and the long spine of the Guaniguanico mountain range, which splits into the Sierra de los Organos and Sierra del Rosario. Central Cuba, the alligator's long thin body, is relentlessly flat save for the Sierra del Escambray. The alligator's head, eastern Cuba, is far more dramatic, particularly in the grand Sierra Maestra, whose mountains rise to Cuba's highest point at the Pico Turquino, at 6,465 feet.

Flora Cuba has been called the Galápagos of the Caribbean for its number and variety of plant and animal species. Of its 6,700 types of plants, around half are endemic. Two hundred years ago the island was almost entirely covered in trees; now most have been felled for agricultural land, lumber, and fuel. The mountain ranges, however, are still forested, and contain tiny pockets of tropical

rain forest. Cuba boasts wonderful specimens of banyans and *jagüeys*, with their strange aerial roots, and an incredible number of palms (some 70 million, it is said), the rarest being the cork palm, a cycad found in western Cuba that dates from prehistoric times. While mangroves and *Uvas caletas*, or sea grapes, lie along the coasts, the fertile interior is cultivated for sugarcane, tobacco, rice, coffee, and every type of fruit, from oranges and grapefruits to pineapples and bananas. Meanwhile, flushes of bougainvillea, hibiscus, oleander, and frangipani bring roads, gardens, and courtyards to life.

Fauna Cuba has some interesting animals, but don't expect to see many of them.

A turkey vulture—one of Cuba's more easily spottable birds

Endemic species include the *jutía*, a large ratlike creature which, though protected, appears secretly on dinner plates in Pinar del Río Province, and the *polymita*, a snail with a fabulous multicolored shell. Some crocodiles that live and are farmed in the Zapata and Isla de la Juventud swamps are a subspecies called rhombifers, found only in these areas. Though the manatee has almost disappeared from Cuba's waters, turtles nest on beaches (on Cayo Largo, for example), and iguanas are common on offshore cays. As for other reptiles, Cuba claims to have the world's smallest frog, the *Eleutherodactylus-limbatus*. There are no poisonous snakes on the island.

Much of Cuba's abundant birdlife, however, is more visible. The island is home to around 350 species of birds, some 60 percent of which migrate from North America for the winter. The Península de Zapata is the best place to observe them,

Crocodiles were a dwindling species, but they are now farmed in swampy regions

along with almost all Cuba's indigenous birds and flocks of pink flamingos (which can also be spotted around Cayo Coco and Playa Santa Lucía). Wherever you are in Cuba, you will come across wheeling turkey vultures and white cattle egrets, often perched on the back of a cow.

❑ Cuba's national bird is the Cuban trogon, or *tocororo*, (named because of its cry): it has the same colors as the national flag—red, white, and blue. The national flower is the butterfly jasmine or white mariposa, and the national tree is the royal palm, which can grow to a stately height of 98 feet. ❑

■ **Politics** encroaches on some of the most intimate details of daily life. People call each other *compañero* or *compañera* (comrade); giant billboards exhort Cubans to work harder and be patriotic, publicizing such rallying cries as *socialismo o muerte* (socialism or death). In schools, children as young as five are sworn in as communist pioneers and start the day chanting: "We will be like Che!" ■

Party and government Castro claims that Cuban democracy is far superior to "so-called Western democracy, which has nothing to do with real democracy. It's complete garbage." Cuba is a single-party state governed by the Partido Comunista de Cuba (PCC) or Cuban Communist Party. Membership is highly selective, and virtually all the government's leaders belong to the party's Central Committee and the smaller, more powerful Political Bureau. Every five years the party congress convenes, effectively to rubber-stamp the leadership's decisions.

The party's pronouncements and the daily administration of the country are carried out by the Organs of People's Power, at municipal and provincial levels and through the National Assembly of People's Power. Cubans directly elect the

Images of Che Guevara and José Martí appear everywhere

national assembly's 589 members, but have only one candidate per seat from which to choose. The assembly meets just twice a year. At other times its powers are exercised by the Council of State, whose members are elected by the national assembly, and the Council of Ministers, chosen by Castro. As head of the Council of State and the Communist Party, Castro is all-powerful.

Mass organizations Support for the party and the government is mobilized through politicized mass organizations. Membership of these groups, to which about four-fifths of the population sign up, is a prerequisite for a successful life in Cuba. Children between the ages of five and 14 are enlisted as "pioneers," and are then encouraged to join the Union of Young Communists. Workers may be members of trade unions (though strikes have been illegal since the early days of the revolution), and women may join the Federation of Cuban Women.

In the early 1960s, Committees for the Defense of the Revolution (CDRs) were formed to ferret out counterrevolutionaries. Now, as well as reporting on anything from overfriendliness with a foreigner to drunkenness, CDRs organize community service, placing guards at the local market, for instance, and sweeping the streets. Every neighborhood in every town has its own CDR: there are said to be more than 100,000 across the country, to which over 90 percent of the population belongs.

Cuba's army (headed by Castro and his brother Raúl) has around 200,000 troops. There is compulsory military service for all but university students, lasting three years. In addition, millions of civilians, men and women alike, undergo regular military training as part of the country's militias.

Freedom of speech The Communist Party is the country's only legal political organization. The state controls all media; Castro has even been known to write unsigned editorials for *Granma*, the main newspaper. Anyone who undermines the principles of the revolution may be imprisoned. While happy to discuss their economic hardships, Cubans are very wary about directly criticizing the regime. Cuba has a very sophisticated system of surveillance at grassroots levels through the CDRs and other mass organizations. Many Cubans feel they are constantly being watched, not least by plain clothes agents from the Ministry of the Interior (MININT).

The most common expression of dissatisfaction is to leave the country. The government forces many dissidents to leave, and prosecutes others under such charges as "dangerousness" and "enemy propaganda" in trials that fall far short of international standards of fair play. In 1996, the Concilio Cubano, a coalition of some 140 peaceful opposition organizations, intended to hold a conference, but it was banned and its leaders were imprisoned. Amnesty International publicizes the plight of prisoners of conscience held in Cuban jails; it estimates there are presently around 600.

A giant billboard encourages "steadfastness and courage"

■ Cuba's economy nosedived at the beginning of the 1990s. The catalyst for this was the demise of politically like-minded countries abroad. However, the economy has also long been beset by chronic inefficiency and the U.S. trade embargo, which Castro estimates has cost Cuba $40 billion and describes as "an attempt at genocide." ■

A snapshot Cuba's economy is chiefly agriculturally based, the main products being tobacco, coffee, citrus fruits and, above all, sugar. The island also possesses about a third of the world's nickel reserves and has a small-scale oil industry that creates around 1.5 million tons of oil annually. Recently, it has invested heavily in biotechnological and pharmaceutical industries, developing meningitis and Hepatitis B vaccines, and in tourism, now the country's top foreign currency earner.

Problems Following the collapse of the communist regimes in eastern Europe and the subsequent breakup of the Soviet Union in 1991, Cuba lost 80 percent of its trade and US$5 billion a year in subsidies. Vital commodities such as grain and oil, and Soviet-made consumer products such as cars, refrigerators and TVs, were no longer available to Cuba at giveaway prices. As a result, Castro declared the Special Period in Time of Peace. Severe food rationing was imposed; power cuts lasted for up to 16 hours a day; factories closed down due to lack of fuel, working machinery, and raw materials. Gasoline was rationed, too, the bicycle and horse-and-buggy became regular means of transportation and oxen were used in the fields as much as tractors. These

Makeshift, overcrowded public transport is a clear sign of Cuba's economic problems

conditions still apply, though the economy has gradually improved (see pages 22–23).

A belligerent anti-American message faces Havana's US Interests Section

Inefficiency There are other reasons for the economic crisis. Cuba has had a paucity of consumer goods and food ever since the beginning of the revolution. Its centralized, state-run economy has long been poorly managed and underproductive. Moreover, Cuba has always relied far too heavily on its sugar industry: while the large and very fertile island could be self-sufficient in food, most land is given over to sugarcane.

The embargo The Cuban authorities claim all their woes stem from the trade embargo, or blockade as they call it, that the U.S. has imposed against the island for over 35 years. The embargo was tightened in 1992 with the Torricelli Bill, which forbade even foreign subsidiaries of U.S. companies to trade with Cuba, and in 1996 by the Helms-Burton Act. This threatens to allow foreign companies who "traffic" in U.S. property expropriated by Castro after 1959 to be sued in U.S. courts, and to deny company executives and their families U.S. entry. Violating international law, the bill has provoked a worldwide furor, and President Clinton has therefore postponed implementing its most controversial clauses. Castro

sardonically says: "Supporters of Helms-Burton want 100 percent socialism in Cuba—they want no one to invest." So far most companies have ignored the bill, though some have pulled out of the island.

Washington claims it would lift the embargo were the island to adopt multiparty democracy and respect human rights. But in reality, the embargo has more to do with America's wounded pride in having been defied by its smaller neighbor for so long, and a desire to appease its million-strong, largely anti-Castro, American-Cuban community. World opinion is highly critical, arguing that the U.S. trades with countries such as China whose regimes it does not condone, and pointing out that the embargo is not working and is punishing the Cuban people rather than their government. The United Nations General Assembly condemns the embargo annually—in 1996 by 137 votes to three (namely the U.S., Israel, and Uzbekistan). Former U.S. President Carter judges it to be the "worst mistake" a U.S. administration has ever made, and reckons it gives Castro "an undeserved excuse for his own economic and political failures."

■ **Since 1993, Cuba's government has been performing a precarious balancing act in an effort to rescue its economy. It is trying to remain communist while at the same time abandoning long-held political beliefs by introducing large dollops of capitalism. So far the reforms have been reasonably successful in stopping the economy from hemorrhaging any further.** ■

Foreign investment Cuba has been forced to seek new foreign trading partners to replace its former communist ones. Presently, Canada is the most important, then Spain, Mexico, Italy, France, Germany, and the U.K. Foreign companies are being invited to invest in Cuba, and many see it as a golden opportunity to establish themselves while their U.S. competitors are excluded from the action by the trade embargo. The many so-called "joint venture" offers (dubbed "joint adventures"—no one knows how things will turn out) to be seen in Cuban business magazines, where Cuban firms seek partnerships with foreign companies, read like ads in a lonely hearts' column. By 1996, some 250 ventures were

Filling cigarette lighters is one of the permissible self-employed activities

under way, and the latest step is to allow foreign companies to operate in Cuba independently.

It is tourism that has opened up the most to foreign investment, followed by nickel mining, oil exploration and drilling and, most recently, sugar production. In Varadero, the country's largest resort, Spanish, German, and Canadian flags fly over brand-new hotel complexes, while the maple leaf also flutters over the resort's oil wells. In addition, half-a-dozen Canadian companies are prospecting for gold and silver, and there are even foreign retail outlets such as Benetton —unheard of a few years ago.

Capitalism arrives The Cuban government is also gingerly opening up the country to capitalist market forces. The process was kick-started in 1993 when, in order to bring the millions swilling around the black market into the official economy, the U.S. dollar was made legal tender— previously it had been a criminal offense to possess greenbacks. Automatically enriching those with access to dollars, it is a controversially divisive measure.

Meanwhile, to boost production, the government converted three-quarters of state farms into co-operatives, allowing them a substantial element of autonomy. Since 1994, farmers have also been permitted, once they have met government quotas, to sell surplus food directly to consumers in "farmers' markets." Prices, determined by supply and demand, can be astronomically high, but it has meant more food being available for those who can afford it.

A limited amount of other private trade is also now allowed. At the last count there were 157 permissible self-employed activities, from crafts seller to "driver of children's carriage drawn by minor animals." The self-employed are not allowed to employ others, except in private restaurants where only family members can be put to work, and professionals cannot work within their own profession (so a doctor can become a taxi driver but not practice medicine privately). The self-employed make far more money than the rest of the state-employed population, who are no longer guaranteed jobs. To make sure private enterprise does not become too enterprising, however, the government makes the self-employed buy an expensive trading

license (around 200,000 have been issued) and pay a high rate of income tax—something not seen in Cuba for over 30 years.

Effect of changes In 1996, the country's GDP grew by nearly 8 percent, the sugar harvest increased by a third (though it is still well below 1980s levels), gross earnings from tourism reached $1.3 billion. Cuba's foreign debt, however, stands at $11 billion. The island is creeping toward a freer economic system, but at a snail's pace, with the leadership adamant that it must avoid at all costs the economic changes that undermined the Soviet Union and other communist countries. Castro flatly rejects calls to democratize Cuba's political apparatus: the only reason why capitalism is being introduced at all is to allow the communist regime to

Billboards en route to Varadero's airport advertise Western products

■ **Two parallel economies now function in Cuba—one through the local currency, the peso, the other through the American dollar. Cuba has become a country of haves (those with dollars) and have nots (those without), an estimated 80 percent of the population, for whom life is a constant struggle, with a paucity of food, clothes, and transportation.** ■

Rich and poor Prior to Cuba's capitalist reforms, more or less everyone in Cuba had roughly the same standard of living. Now there is a small yet conspicuous number of new rich, who prance around with mobile phones and in fast cars, while at the other end of the spectrum there are outright beggars, unseen on Cuba's streets since the bad old days of the 1950s.

The peso economy Pesos are used to buy government-subsidized goods with a *libreta*, or ration card; all Cubans have one card for food and one for clothing and other essentials. Rationing has existed for decades, but since the Special Period the list of rationed items has grown dramatically and the quantity and availability of goods has radically dwindled. Typical rations per person for a month are 5.5 pounds of rice, 2 pounds of beans, a pound of fish, eight eggs, plus one pair of shoes and trousers per year; milk allowances are available only for young children and pregnant women. Pesos can be also used in shops marked "*libre venta*" ("free sale"), noticeable for the fact that they have either nothing in them at all or nothing worth buying, and in farmers' markets. Though these are filled with fruit, vegetables, and meat, prices are astronomical: an onion can cost a day's wages.

The dollar economy "Dollars or death." Cubans quip, with reference to the state's most famous slogan "socialism or

The libreta *or ration card*

death." Virtually anything worth buying—a TV, cooking oil, soap—is available only in special "dollar shops" or on the all-pervasive *bolsa negra*, or black market, where greenbacks are the preferred currency. With U.S. dollars, you can procure medicines, car parts, perfume, lobster—whatever you want—on the *bolsa negra*, which is inextricably linked with petty corruption. Workers steal goods in vast quantities from state enterprises, and there are even clandestine factories producing consumer goods and cigars.

Yet though Cubans need dollars to get by, the irony is that almost everyone is paid in pesos: the average wage is around 200 pesos a month, and an old person's pension is around 80 pesos a month. Many Cubans feel forced to convert their pesos into dollars through recently opened exchange bureaus or on the black market. The exchange rate—as high as 140 pesos to the dollar in 1994, down to

*Picking up the daily allowance
from a ration shop*

around 23 pesos to the dollar in early
1998—makes all dollar purchases
prohibitively expensive for Cubans.
Many have relatives abroad who send
them dollars to buy necessities, a
process estimated to invest $500–
800 million into the Cuban economy
annually. At the same time, jobs that
pay in dollars have become dispropor-
tionately desirable. Waiters and
barmen in hotels often turn out to be
professors and doctors: the dollar tips
they earn in an evening can easily
exceed a month of their former salary.

Other hardships A universal fact of
life for Cubans is *la cola*, waiting in
line. Outside a restaurant or ice-
cream parlor, or a shop where a
delivery of cooking oil is rumored, a
line can engulf a whole street. Often
you come across massive roadside
crowds, like extras in a Hollywood
epic, waiting for a bus. When one
does arrive, it is so packed that
heads protrude from windows, not
only for air but also because there is
no room for them inside, and athletic
types hang on to the outside by their
fingertips. Any vehicle is loaded to
capacity—ten in an old Chevrolet,
five on a motorbike with a sidecar,
and three on a bike. Hundreds of
thousands of bicycles have been
introduced to combat fuel shortages.

*Cubans often have to line up to
enter a dollar shop*

■ **Cubans have universal access to free health and education systems that are the pride of the revolution, surpassing any in Latin America and in some respects as good as many in so-called First World countries. Cuba's health care, for example, is so technologically advanced that thousands of foreigners annually visit special clinics for medical treatment such as plastic surgery. ■**

Health Cuba proudly boasts infant mortality rates (7.2 per 1,000 in 1997) and average life expectancy rates (76 years in 1997) that match most developed countries. It has the highest proportion of doctors per head of

Many Cubans, particularly in Old Havana, get by in tough conditions

population in Latin America; even in the remotest parts of the country medics make house calls, traveling by mule. Diseases such as malaria and tuberculosis have been eradicated. Not surprisingly, therefore, Cuba has a strict AIDS policy with HIV sanitoriums in every province and the island has a far lower rate of incidence than the rest of the Caribbean, where the disease is rife. Since the beginning of the 1990s Cubans' daily calorie intake has dropped by a third and there has been a drastic shortage of conventional medicines, due to the U.S. embargo, resulting in a return to herbal remedies.

Education The Cuban government claims to have virtually eliminated illiteracy and has three million students and 300,000 teachers in an educational system that includes 40 universities. However, much education takes place within a clearly defined ideological framework. The Argentinian journalist Jacobo Timerman comments: "If it is true that every Cuban knows how to read and write, it is likewise true that every Cuban has nothing to read and must be very cautious about what he writes."

Housing While shanty towns are absent, Cubans often live in tumbledown, overcrowded conditions. A third are without running water, and three generations may live together in one small apartment. Privacy is such a problem that many couples visit *posadas*, or love hotels, to rent a room for an hour of intimacy.

■ **The revolution made a point of ridding Cuba of vices such as prostitution and gambling, and a mere decade ago tourism was condemned as capitalist decadence. Now, in pursuit of dollars, ideological principles are bent every which way to cater to foreigners, and Cuba has become the Caribbean's fastest-growing vacation destination.** ■

Massive growth In the 1960s and 1970s, many of Cuba's tourists were from Eastern bloc countries or left-wingers on international brigades helping with the sugarcane harvest. Now most come from western Europe and Canada for fun in the sun. In 1997, 1.2 million visitors arrived, over three times as many as in 1989 and a number the authorities hope nearly to double by the year 2000.

Tourism apartheid The Cuban constitution enshrines the right for all its citizens to have access to all public places, but in practice Cubans are excluded from the island's best beaches, hotels, nightclubs, and restaurants. While they survive on rations and wait hours for a bus or a seat at a restaurant, tourists gorge themselves on fabulous buffets, are pushed to the front of restaurant lines and whizz around in rented Jeeps. Castro reckons "only a *petit bourgeois* dandy is unable to under-stand why Cubans can't use these hotel rooms." Cubans do appreciate their country's need for hard currency. Yet many resent the fact that, having extolled the revolution's egalitarianism for so long, Castro now seems to care more for the welfare of foreigners than of his own citizens. As for the tourists, they often find these arrangements guilt-inducing.

Hassle Some Cubans, called *jineteros/jineteras*, see tourists as walking banks, there to be separated from their dollars. They include pros-titutes, who hang around outside hotels and nightclubs, and who even phone hotel rooms at random hoping to catch a lonely foreigner. In response to this, the police have begun a rather belated and often heavy-handed attempt to crack down on prostitution by making a number of arrests.

A lavish buffet in a Varadero hotel —for tourists only

Exodus and exile

■ Florida, a luxurious utopia in the eyes of most Cubans, lies enticingly close—Key West is 90 miles away from Cuba's north coast. Since 1959, over a million *gusanos*, or worms, as Castro calls them, have escaped the hardships of their homeland by emigrating to the United States in search of a better life. ■

Emigration The 200,000 who left in the first years after 1959, and the 250,000 more who departed between 1965 and 1971 in what was called the Freedom Flights Program, tended to be well-off Cubans who had most to lose under communism. On the one hand, their departure benefited Castro as it exported the discontented and any potential figureheads of political opposition, but it also drained Cuba of skilled and professional people. In 1980, Castro opened the floodgates again, and a further 125,000 Cubans fled; they were picked up by Floridian boats from the port of Mariel, west of Havana. The so-called *marielitos* included an estimated 25,000 Cubans whom Castro decided to off-load from his prisons.

Balseros Over the decades, many thousands of Cubans have sneaked off the island illegally in boats and on makeshift rafts or by swimming across to the U.S. Guantánamo Naval Base in southeastern Cuba. In 1994, some 30,000 *balseros*, or rafters, left for Florida on flimsy craft made from cork, wood, and inner tubes as Castro deliberately relaxed his grip on emigration again. But, so as to avoid another Cuban influx of Mariel proportions, and piqued at having U.S. immigration policy determined by Castro, President Clinton, in 1995, decided to cancel the long-standing U.S. policy of granting automatic asylum to Cubans who reached U.S. shores. Most *balseros* were intercepted by the U.S. Coast Guard and taken to Guantánamo Naval Base, but after being held there in trying conditions for many months, they have eventually been accepted into the U.S.

The U.S. now regards Cubans trying to reach the country illegally as

A street festival in Miami, Florida, where there is a large Cuban emigrant population

economic migrants rather than political refugees, and returns them to Cuba (at a rate of, on average, one a day). Also, it has made a promise, which it has so far kept, to grant visas to 20,000 Cubans per year who wish to emigrate through official channels.

Cuban-Americans Early exiles were the richest in their country rather than the poorest, setting them apart from almost any other U.S. immigrants. Many found new wealth and power. One such person is Jorge Mas Canosa, who began washing dishes and became a millionaire and self-appointed president in exile as head of the Cuban-American National Foundation before he died in 1997. CANF, known as "the most effective lobbying force" in Washington, has a massive influence on U.S.–Cuban policy. Other active Miami-based anti-Castro groups include paramilitary organizations such as Alpha 66, which has a training camp in the Everglades, carries out occasional armed attacks on Cuban installations, and has terrorized U.S. businesses and individuals believed to be sympathetic to Castro. Brothers to the Rescue, dedicated to helping Cuban refugees at sea and dropping propaganda leaflets on Havana,

Many balseros *have drowned, died of thirst, or even been savaged by sharks as they try to reach Florida*

sparked an international crisis in 1996 when two of its planes accused of flying inside Cuban airspace were shot down by the Cuban airforce.

Yet many Cuban-Americans are simply concerned with the welfare of the relatives they have left behind and visit them regularly (until recently, flights connected Miami and Havana specifically for this purpose). Moreover, many second-generation exiles now regard themselves as more American than Cuban.

❏ Most Cubans living abroad reside in the U.S.—in New Jersey, Tampa and, above all, Miami, a metropolis they now dominate numerically, economically, politically, and culturally. In Little Havana, the Cuban heart of the city, restaurants offer Cuban specialties and shops sell statuettes from Afro-Cuban religions. The annual Cuban carnival is the largest Hispanic celebration in the U.S. and bigger than any carnival in Cuba itself. ❏

■ **Cuba is simply one of the world's most musical places: its people seem to be born with perfect rhythm and an ability to dance sensationally. Its musical genres are the fullest expression of the country's mixed African and Spanish heritage, famously called "the love affair of the African drum and the Spanish guitar."** ■

The European-African mix African influences—above all drum rhythms used in Afro-Cuban worship—form the essential pulse of Cuban music. With the abolition of slavery coming so late in Cuba, these influences are more pronounced here than on any other island in the Caribbean. The purest African musical form, whose dances come directly from cult rituals, is the *rumba*, which in the late 19th century emanated from Havana's and Matanzas's black townships. Cuba's most famous *rumba* band is Los Muñequitos de Matanzas.

Europeans contributed stringed and brass instruments, melody and harmony to the "Creole symphony." In the 1800s *trovas*, or ballads, were sung to the accompaniment of the guitar, and in dance salons the *bolero*, *habanera*, and above all, by the early 20th century, the classical-style *danzón* were all the rage. But

African and European styles really fused in the early 1900s in *son*, the most influential genre in Latin-American music. Originating from eastern Cuba's working classes as a simple guitar and African percussion combination, it infiltrated the repertoire of danzón orchestras, and became the classic big band sound. Its most famous exponent was Beny Moré, El Bárbaro del Ritmo—the Wild Man of Rhythm.

In the 1940s and 1950s, *mambo* and *chachachá* (so called because of the sound people's feet made when they danced to it) evolved from son and danzón. Around the same time, jazz came to Cuba from the U.S., evolving into Latin jazz with the incorporation of Cuban sounds. Cuba's top contemporary jazz group, Irakere, plays a fantastic combination

Street musicians play anything from trova to danzón and son

of modern and classical jazz, rock, and Afro-Cuban rhythms.

Salsa and *nueva trova* *Salsa* is a catchall name for contemporary Latin-American music that took off in the Latin *barrios* of New York in the 1970s. Cuban exile Celia Cruz, the Queen of salsa, says it is "Cuban music with another name. It's mambo, chachachá, rumba, son…". So inextricable are son and salsa that the music of many of Cuba's top bands is described as both. They include the long-established Los Van Van, Sierra Maestra, funky NG La Banda, and the latest hit, El Médico de la Salsa (The Salsa Doctor). All have an enormous following in Cuba, not least for often employing lyrics that subtly criticize the regime.

The only important postrevolution-ary musical movement to come from Cuba, which was effectively culturally cut off from the world after 1959, is *nueva trova*. The best-known singers of its highly politicized ballads are Silvio Rodríguez, Pablo Milanés, and Carlos Varela.

Tracking down Cuban music Every town has a *casa de la trova*, a very laid-back open-house club for all types of music, and a *casa de la cultura*, used for more formal performances. Most towns also boast a dance club on their main square that opens at weekends: the clubbers' graceful movements can be quite transfixing. Top Cuban bands perform mainly at Havana's major venues (see pages 90–91); a show's heady atmosphere, and the rapport between performers and audience, can be exhilarating. Professional musicians are all employed by the government (there are some 500 salaried groups), and there is only one record company, EGREM. Its tapes and CDs are available in hotel and ARTEX shops.

❏ Instruments that invest Cuban music with its unique sounds include: African drums such as the *batá*, *bongo*, and *conga*; *claves*, two short sticks beaten together; the *güiro*, a hollowed gourd with grooves that is scraped with a drumstick; maracas, small gourds contain-ing seeds, stones, or bits of metal; and the *tres*, a guitar with three sets of double strings. ❏

Any excuse for a party: dancing in the streets is a facet of everyday life in Cuba

■ **Cuba attaches great importance to sporting prowess, not least to enhance its international prestige, and its baseball players and boxers rank among the world's best. Most participatory activities are water based, with outstanding diving and deep-sea fishing heading the bill.** ■

Sporting excellence Top Cuban athletes, like those in the former Eastern bloc countries, train in special sports schools and, although they have amateur status, are paid by the state. In 1991, Cuban athletes won more medals than any other nation (including the U.S.) at the Pan American Games—which Cuba hosted in a vast complex built on the edge of Havana at great expense, despite the country being at its lowest financial ebb. In the 1996 Atlanta Olympics, Cuba came eighth in the medal tables, with nine golds: four in boxing, and one each in baseball, judo, volleyball, weight-lifting, and wrestling. However, the Atlanta games also witnessed high-profile defections of two weightlifters and the country's leading baseball pitcher.

Ask around in any city and you should find the local boxing gymnasium, chess club (Cuban José Raúl y Graupera Capablanca was world champion from 1921 to 1927), and gymnastics academy. But above all,

People cycle everywhere in Cuba (but most are not normally dressed like this)

don't miss the chance to watch a baseball game in one of the massive stadiums. Championship games run from November to March, and you should be able to get in for a few pesos.

Baseball, imported from North America in the late 19th century, is the country's national game (and obsession): impromptu games are played on any open piece of ground with a makeshift stick and ball. Cuba's best players used to be poached by U.S. teams before the revolution (the Washington Senators even made overtures to one Fidel Castro). With its 1987 to 1996 record of played 94, won 93, the national team (the Equipo de Sueño or Dream Team) is arguably the world's best. Cuba's four top baseball teams are Industriales of Havana, Santiago, Pinar del Río, and Villa Clara.

Watersports Centers in the main resorts offer everything from wind-surfing to canoeing and jet-skiing to water-skiing. The centers are normally affiliated with hotels but, unless the hotels are all-inclusive, they take anyone. Yachting is also possible from Varadero, Cayo Largo, and Havana's Marina Hemingway. However, where Cuba really excels is in its diving, offered at rates that are the cheapest in the Caribbean. A string of coral reefs surrounds most of the Cuban archipelago. Some sites have caves and shipwrecks, but the biggest attraction is the profusion of tropical marine life and the reefs themselves, with sponges, gorgonian fans, and sometimes prized black coral. Virtually every resort has at least one diving center. Outstanding are: Playa Santa Lucía, Playa Girón, where the diving is directly from the shore, and the specialist centers of María La Gorda and, with top billing, the Hotel Colony on Isla de la Juventud. These last two are not well geared to beginners, but most resorts offer courses for all levels of ability, with internationally recognized certification. Remember not to dive less than 24 hours prior to flying.

Fishing Ernest Hemingway, in his novel *The Old Man and the Sea*,

Cuba has some of the Caribbean's least explored and most exciting diving sites

immortalized deep-sea fishing in the Gulf Stream, which runs along Cuba's northwest coast, describing it as "the great deep blue river...that has the finest fishing I have ever known." The best time of year to catch big marlin, tuna, and swordfish is July and August. Trips, which cost anything from $200 to $350 for six hours per boat (four people), depart from Varadero and Havana's Hemingway Marina. The latter holds a marlin fishing tournament every May; it was started by Hemingway in 1950 and won by Castro in 1960. Inland fishing trips can be taken from any resort, while lakes Hanabanilla, Zaza (near Sancti Spíritus), and La Redonda (near Morón) are renowned for their trophy-sized largemouth bass.

Food and drink

■ "If Cuba means to earn millions of tourist dollars, it will have to make a culinary Revolución," wrote Hemingway's wife Martha Gellhorn after visiting the island in the mid-1980s. Food is better and more plentiful than it was a few years ago (particularly for tourists), but don't expect many memorable gastronomic experiences. ■

34

Cuba's cuisine, which reflects Spanish and African influences, has never been fancy: essentially, it is hearty but bland country fare. More important, although the country is incredibly fertile, it cannot feed its people: most vegetables and fruits are shipped abroad in exchange for much-needed hard currency. Food shortages, which have existed since the revolution, became acute in the early 1990s, but have recently been somewhat lessened by foreign investment and private enterprise. In any case, tourists are largely cocooned from any deprivations.

Where to eat The country's best supplies are reserved for tourist hotels. Their breakfast buffets usually run to fruit, pancakes, croissants, and bacon and eggs, and evening buffets encompass mountains of cakes and roast meats. These meals are included in half-board package rates; if you are not staying at the hotel, you can pay for them separately.

Otherwise, there are two broad types of state-run restaurants: those geared to foreigners, where the food is relatively plentiful and you pay in dollars, and those intended for peso-paying Cubans, who stand in line for ages for food that often runs out. In some establishments, tourists pay in dollars and Cubans in pesos (which makes the tourist bill over 20 times higher).

In most state restaurants, service is notoriously slow and offhand. *Paladares*, which translates literally as "palates," are invariably friendlier and offer cheaper and reliably better food. These mini private restaurants

Famously good ice cream is served in Havana's Coppelia parlor and in many hotels

typically occupy the front room of a home. Regulations limit the number of diners to 12, forbid the serving of lobster or beef, and allow only family members to be employed. Paladares also have to pay heavy taxes, so many operate outside the law.

For a snack, try one of the dollar cafés that are cropping up all over the island, particularly the El Rápido chain. They serve fried chicken, *bocadillos* (sandwiches, invariably filled with ham and cheese), and little else. Private enterprise has also spawned a plethora of hole-in-the-wall pizza joints and markets where you can buy fruit and vegetables in pesos.

What to eat Tourist hotels serve international fare. Elsewhere, expect *comida criolla*, or traditional Cuban Creole cuisine. The national dish is rice and beans, most commonly *moros y cristianos* (literally "Moors and Christians"), which is rice and black beans, but also, especially in eastern Cuba, *congrí*, rice and kidney beans. You will also be served white rice accompanied by a separate bowl of black beans mixed with pork fat. The most ubiquitous meat dishes are *pollo asado* (roast chicken) and *cerdo asado* (roast pork). Better restaurants may serve *bistec* (beefsteak), *picadillo* (minced beef), and *ajiaco crillo*, a meat and vegetable stew. *Pescado*, fish, is usually simply grilled; *langosta* (lobster) is often available, at a price. Apart from rice and beans and salads, the most common side dishes are *yuca* (cassava), *malanga* (a sweet potato),

35

and *plátanos* (plantains), served either as *tostones* (french fries) or *fufú* (boiled and mashed). The only dessert worth bothering with is the fabled, tangy and creamy Cuban-made Coppelia ice cream.

Drinks Local soft-drink specialties include *guarapo*, or sugarcane juice, and *granizado*, flavored water-ice served from street carts. Cubans love their coffee. *Café cubano* is served strong in a small cup, traditionally with an improbably large amount of sugar; *café americano* is weaker and larger. National brands of beer (Hatuey, Mayabe, Cristal, Bucanero) are very palatable. Wines, usually Spanish or Argentinian, are only available in restaurants. For cocktails, see page 36.

Paladares, *or private restaurants, were legalized in 1995*

■ Once a drink for sailors and slaves called kill-devil or rumbullion, rum (*ron* in Spanish) is now Cuba's universal social lubricant. Drink it neat or in cocktails; the local custom on a night out is to order a whole bottle along with a pile of ice and cans of soft drinks as mixers. ■

The production process Rum is made from molasses, the dark brown residue that remains after crystallized sugar has been removed from sugarcane. The molasses is fermented with yeast, then diluted with distilled water in copper tanks, and the resulting liquid is aged in barrels for anything from one to 15 years before it is bottled. The tannin from the barrels provides rum with its distinctive amber hue (caramel is often added, too).

The Bacardí story Don Facundo Bacardí, a Catalan migrant, established a rum factory in Santiago in 1838; by the 1860s he had made himself a millionaire. Bacardí rum was synonymous with Cuba until the family fled to Puerto Rico in 1959, where Bacardí rum is now made. International patent laws forbid Cuban rum to be sold under the Bacardí label: Cuba's top-selling rum is now Havana Club, though Ron Caney is closer to the original Bacardí spirit.

What to drink White, lightly flavored one- to three-year-old rums are used in cocktails. The most popular are the ironic-sounding *Cuba Libre* (rum and Coca-Cola), the *mojito* (rum, sugar, lime juice, mint leaves, and soda water), and the *daiquiri* (rum, sugar, lime juice, and maraschino blended with crushed ice), described by Hemingway in his novel *Islands in the Stream* as like "the way downhill glacier skiing feels running through powdered snow." For drinking on its own or on the rocks, choose a dark rum at least five years old. In dives you are offered raw, unaged rum called *aguardiente*, "firewater," the alcohol content of which can be so high that a sip can make you feel dizzy.

From left to right: a mojito, *a* daiquiri, *and a* Cuba Libre

CUBA WAS

Discovery & colonization

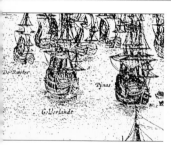

■ **Little is known about Cuba before its discovery by the Italian navigator Christopher Columbus, who was employed in 1492 by the Spanish Crown to seek a quicker trade route to Asia. The subsequent Spanish colonization was a brutal, slow affair, and Cuba—Havana excepted—remained a largely underpopulated, unwanted colonial outpost through the middle of the 18th century.** ■

Pre-Columbian Cuba Primitive, seminomadic Ciboney Indians began to settle along Cuba's central and western coasts around 1000 BC. They later settled in eastern Cuba, too, but were dislodged after about AD 1100 by more sophisticated Arawak or Taíno Indians, who came from South America. They lived in the fertile uplands in *bohíos*, or thatched huts, and cultivated crops such as beans, maize, and tobacco. There were estimated to be around 110,000 Indians in Cuba at the end of the 15th century, 90 percent being Taíno.

Columbus arrives On October 28, 1492, Columbus landed near Gibara on Cuba's north coast, and described the land he saw as "the most lovely that eyes have ever seen" (his diaries are full of hyperbole). After looking around for five weeks he left to discover Hispaniola, returning again to Cuba in 1493 in a massive expedition of 17 ships and more than 12,000 men. This time he reconnoitered the south coast as far west as Batabanó, unsuccessfully searching for gold, great centers of population and, believing Cuba to be part of Cathay (mainland China), the court of Marco Polo's Great Khan. He even made his crew swear an affadavit that Cuba was a peninsula—no island could be so large, he thought. It wasn't until it was circumnavigated

Cuba's place in the New World, as depicted on a map dated 1540

by Sebastián de Ocampo in 1508 that Cuba was understood to be an island.

Conquest Colonization began in 1511 with a 300-strong expeditionary force under Diego de Velázquez, a wealthy soldier and landowner from neighboring Hispaniola. By 1515, seven villas or fortified settlements were established, first Baracoa in 1512, then Bayamo, Trinidad, Sancti Spíritus, Puerto Príncipe (to become Camagüey), Santiago de Cuba, and Havana (then on the south coast).

The conquest of Cuba was swift and ruthless. Indians who dared to resist were massacred, while others died from infections and diseases introduced by the conquistadors. Whole villages were even reported to have committed suicide and, as the Indians were the principal source of labor in the new colony, yet more were literally worked to death in the fields and mines (the Spaniards had discovered a little gold). Fray Bartolomé de las Casas, a Spanish priest who became an advocate for the Indian cause, reported that the colonists employed a system of oppression "seldom paralleled in the annals of mankind." By the mid-1550s, there were estimated to be less than 3,000 Indians left on Cuba.

Decline and rise In other respects, colonization was not progressing well. The island fell into severe economic decline in the 1520s and 1530s, as settlers headed off to seek their fortune in the Spanish conquests of Mexico and Peru; the numbers leaving were so great that the Spanish authorities forbade unau-

The French sacked Havana frequently during the 16th century

thorized departure upon threat of death. By the mid-16th century, Cuba was an abandoned backwater with no more than 700 Spanish settlers.

But riches on the American continents proved to be Cuba's salvation, too. From the mid-16th century onward, Havana, which ousted Santiago as Cuba's capital in 1553, became the prime stopping-off point for Spanish flotillas laden with New World treasure. Each year two fleets of merchant vessels and armed galleons congregated in Havana's port to carry out repairs and be loaded with supplies before making the long Atlantic crossing back to Spain. Often ransacked by French, Dutch, and English navies under official privateers such as Sir Francis Drake, and by independent pirates from lawless communities on outlying keys, Havana and the island's other settlements began to fortify themselves.

Sugar and slaves

■ **During the mid-18th century, Cuba began to evolve from an underdeveloped island of small holdings and cattle ranches to a booming land of large sugar plantations with an enormous labor force of slaves. A hundred years later it had become the world's top sugar producer.** ■

Causes for change In 1762, the English captured Havana. Even though they stayed for only 10 months, they opened the island to world trade (previously all commerce had to be with Spain), making the expansion of Cuba's nascent sugar industry profitable. Equally significant was a slave rebellion in 1791 in the nearby French colony of St. Domingue that resulted not only in the creation of independent Haiti but also in the destruction of its developed sugar and coffee economy. Cuban producers benefited from increased prices and demand as well as an influx of experienced planters from St. Domingue. Cuba almost immediately took over as the Caribbean's top sugar manufacturer. By 1868, there were 1,400 sugar mills producing a third of the world's sugar.

A share certificate in one of Cuba's burgeoning sugar companies

Slavery Slaves were first brought to Cuba from Africa in the mid-16th century, replacing the Indians whom the Spanish were killing off. The harvesting of sugarcane was heavily dependent on physical labor, so with the sugar boom at the end of the 18th century, the numbers of African slaves increased dramatically—from around 60,000 in 1763 to 500,000 in 1841, making up a third of the island's population. Though Spain signed a treaty with Britain to end the slave trade as early as 1817, it was not until 1886 that slavery was finally abolished in Cuba.

Slaves who were lucky enough to survive the horrors of the sea voyage had an average life expectancy in Cuba of seven years. Owners openly discussed whether it was more advantageous to look after slaves or work them to death. So barbaric was life, there were frequent uprisings and even mass suicides.

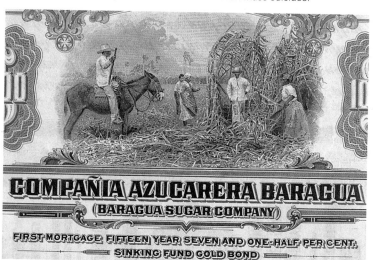

COMPAÑIA AZUCARERA BARAGUA

(BARAGUA SUGAR COMPANY)

FIRST MORTGAGE FIFTEEN YEAR SEVEN AND ONE-HALF PER CENT.

SINKING FUND GOLD BOND

■ **Politics and trade in 19th-century Cuba were controlled by a Spanish-born élite called *peninsulares*, while local economic power lay in the hands of *criollos*, landowners of Spanish descent who were born in Cuba. Eventually the criollos rebelled, and the heroes from the ensuing wars are some of the country's most revered patriots today. ■**

Seeds of discontent Many *criollos* wanted less Spanish taxation and more autonomy; after all, Cuba was the only remaining Spanish possession in the New World apart from Puerto Rico. Yet they were also terrified that quarreling with Spain would lead to a slave revolt, as had been the case in St. Domingue. Many hoped annexation by the United States would protect the slave trade that was so elemental to sugar production. However, their hopes were dashed in 1865 when the southern states' defeat in the American Civil War brought an end to U.S. slavery.

Ten Years' War (1868–1878) The cause of independence was taken up by poorer plantation owners in less developed eastern Cuba. On October 10, 1868, Carlos Manuel de Céspedes freed his slaves and issued a call for independence known as the "Grito de Yara." The war against Spain that followed was fought primarily by the landowning class, but many freed blacks also took up arms. The rebels, under much venerated generals Máximo Gómez, Calixto García, and Antonio Maceo, used effective guerrilla tactics and at times controlled much of eastern Cuba. Spain employed 100,000 troops and resorted to such measures as digging a defensive ditch across the island's middle. Spain won, however, largely because the rebels were divided and support

was low in more prosperous western Cuba. Overall, at least 200,000 combatants died in the fighting.

Second War of Independence (1895–1898) This time the rebels were more cohesive, under the ideology of José Martí (see page 42). Martí was soon killed, but the so-called *mambises* under generals Gómez, García, and Maceo overran most of the island. While they laid plantations waste, the Spanish burned crops and herded peasants into prison camps. After three years of fighting, the Spanish were on the brink of capitulating.

(see page 42)

41

Top: the bell at Demajagua rung by Céspedes when he freed his slaves
Right: fighting in the Second War of Independence

José Martí

■ **Poet, journalist, political philosopher, military activist, Martí articulated the voice for Cuban independence. Described as "the only guy in the world both Washington and Havana have the hots for," he heads the pantheon of Cuban heroes at home and abroad. Every Cuban town has a Martí square or street and a bust showing off his trademark moustache, while Cuban-Americans have christened anti-Castro TV and radio stations after him.** ■

His life Born in 1853, the father of Cuban independence was sentenced to six years' hard labor in 1870 for writing a letter denouncing a fellow student for supporting Spain in the Ten Years' War. After six months he was released and deported to Spain, where he studied law. Having worked as a journalist and teacher in Mexico and Guatemala, he returned to Cuba in 1878, but was again deported for conspiracy in 1879. In 1881, he settled in New York, where he worked as a newspaper correspondent while campaigning tirelessly for Cuban independence. He succeeded in uniting the many disparate elements in the Cuban exile community, founded nationalistic newspapers and, in 1892, formed the Cuban Revolutionary Party. Having masterminded the start of the Second War of Independence, tragically he was shot dead on his first day of armed conflict on May 19, 1895. Had he lived, he would almost certainly have become Cuba's first president.

His views Martí was an idealist and his copious writings—his poetry and essays fill 70 volumes—broadened the struggle for Cuban independence into one that also sought social justice, racial equality, and economic well-being for all. Put simply, he turned rebellion into revolution. As the years passed, he became increasingly concerned about the United States' growing imperialist traits in the Americas and toward Cuba in particular, issuing many prophetic warnings about the "colossus to the north." Among the famous last words he wrote were: "I know the monster [i.e., the U.S.] because I have lived in its lair."

José Martí's first home (top) and (left) one of the many statues of him in Cuba, here in Matanzas

■ Throughout the 19th century, the United States debated how best to control and exploit Cuba. There were three disastrous expeditionary assaults on the island, and four American presidents tried to buy it. Finally, just as Cuba was on the verge of liberating itself from Spanish rule, the Americans intervened: Cuba swapped one imperialist power for another. ■

The *Maine* The United States' pretext for wholesale interference came on February 15, 1898, when the battleship USS *Maine* exploded in Havana harbor, causing the deaths of 262 American sailors. There was no evidence that the Spanish had blown up the ship, but it gave American warmongers the excuse they needed. The *New York Journal* coined the famous battle cry "Remember the *Maine*, to hell with Spain"; its owner, William Randolph Hearst, later admitted he wanted war simply to improve his newspaper's circulation.

Spanish–American War War was duly declared against Spain. Through three years of bloody conflict up to 1898, the Cuban rebels had already done all the hard work in evicting the Spanish. They initially believed U.S. intervention would benefit their cause. However, though the U.S. presented its involvement as a selfless act to secure Cuban independence, many American investors and politicians believed that by liberating Cuba, annexation to the U.S. would follow. The "splendid little war," as it was described by the U.S. Secretary of State, had a foregone conclusion. With only one significant encounter—the Battle of San Juan Hill near Santiago—it lasted just three months. The Cuban contribution, though significant, was largely ignored, as is reflected in the war's misleading name. The Cuban army was regarded as a rabble—"a collec-

A cartoonist's view of U.S. intervention: Columbus (at rear) says: "Had I foreseen it, I would never have discovered America."

tion of real tropic savages," in the words of one U.S. reporter.

After a treaty signed in December 1898 that ended Spanish domination, a U.S. military government ruled Cuba until 1902. It began to restore prosperity—years of fighting had reduced the population by 200,000 and had devastated the economy—but it also imposed terms that severely limited Cuban independence.

■ **Cuba became a republic in 1902, but it was a false dawn. Up to 1959, the fledgling democracy was racked by fraud, political gangsterism, and corruption. In essence it was a U.S. protectorate, with the reins of economic and political power, exercised through puppet presidents and dictators, being held by Washington and the American ambassador. Hence Cuban history books call the period the "pseudo republic."** ■

The Platt Amendment With the appointment in 1902 of Cuba's first president, Tomás Estrada Palma, U.S. troops began to leave the island. But they returned as soon as 1906, after political disruption at elections, and the country was ruled by a U.S. governor until 1909. This was possible due to the Platt Amendment, introduced in 1901. This appendix to the Cuban constitution gave the U.S. the right to intervene on the island "for the maintenance of a government adequate for the protection of life, property, and individual liberties" There were demonstrations across Cuba against the amendment, with a Cuban leader judging that it "reduced the independence and sovereignty of the Cuban republic to a myth." However, Cuba had no choice but to accept the amendment, since the U.S. government made it clear that the island could be either a protected republic or no republic at all. The amendment was abrogated in 1934, except for the clause that allowed the U.S. to retain its naval base at Guantánamo.

U.S. economic control Cuba also became increasingly tied to the U.S. economically. The Reciprocity Treaty in 1903 meant the U.S. could buy Cuban sugar at preferential rates in return for North American imports being accepted onto the island on favorable duty and tax terms, thus swamping the island with U.S. goods. Moreover, many of Cuba's sugarcane factories were U.S. owned, as were electricity generation, the railways, and

Two dictators: Batista takes the oath of office in 1940 (top, on the far right), and (right) presses the flesh; and Machado (above, on the left)

❏ By the 1950s, middle-class Cubans were among the wealthiest in Central and South America. Yet over a quarter of the population, mainly those who lived in the countryside, lived in abject poverty, with no running water, electricity, education, or health facilities. ❏

the telephone company. By the 1950s, 80 percent of Cuba's imports came from the U.S., and the country was the most Americanized place in the world outside North America.

The dictators Up to the mid-1920s, Cuba had been governed weakly and often corruptly. Worse was yet to

come. General Gerardo Machado's presidency, which began in 1924, became in 1928 an unelected dictatorship characterized by terror, censorship, and military courts to preserve his power.

Following a general strike and through American connivance, Machado was forced to resign in 1933. Power soon passed to another military figure, Fulgencio Batista. A mulatto army sergeant of working-class background who had risen to colonel in a week, he was to rule Cuba with U.S. backing, directly or indirectly, for much of the next quarter of a century. Up to 1940, he governed as a strongman behind the scenes, fronted by tokenist presidents; from 1940 to 1944, he ruled as elected president himself; then, after a coup, from 1952 to 1959 he was outright dictator. Though his name has now become a byword for venality and cruelty, Batista was initially considered by many to be a man of the people, and he did introduce some good measures. For example, he legalized trade unions and the Communist Party, and he introduced land distribution and welfare reform. However, it later became apparent that he simply wanted to amass a fortune for himself and his cronies (some $300 million by 1959), and was willing to employ any means, however ruthless, to do so.

❏ From the 1930s, Havana developed a reputation as the capital of a banana republic where Americans came to get drunk and to seek carnal pleasures, earning itself the nickname "an offshore Las Vegas." The city's many casinos and brothels were funded by organized crime leaders who, reportedly, filled Batista's bank accounts with millions of dollars in return for allowing their business activities on the island to go unfettered. ❏

The road to revolution

■ The dramatic tale of how Castro and his motley band of "Los Barbudos" ("the Bearded Ones") came to power against all odds sounds utterly implausible. That they succeeded was due to commitment and heroism—and the fact that the group emerged as a symbol of liberation and social justice from Batista's deeply unpopular and barbarous regime. ■

Castro's emergence Castro became a political animal at Havana University, from where he graduated in law in 1951. In 1952, he was a congressional candidate for the popular Ortodoxos Party, whose leader, Eduardo Chibás, had the previous year committed suicide in the middle of a radio broadcast. In the end, however, no elections were held as Batista seized control of the country in a coup. From this point, Castro turned his back on constitutional politics and committed himself to armed struggle, gathering other discontented Cubans to his cause.

Moncada The road to revolution began with what seemed like a desperate and foolhardy assault on the Moncada Barracks in Santiago. With just 125 rebels pitched against over 1,000 soldiers, the assault, launched on carnival night on July 26, 1953, needed but failed to have complete surprise. Some 70 assailants died in the action or were put to death immediately after; Castro was captured but his life was spared. Put on trial, he gave his first

The Barbudos were greeted as heroes when they entered Havana in 1959 (top), and Moncada (below)

great speech, proclaiming a program for Cuba's regeneration. His five-hour oration ended with the famous words: "Condemn me if you will! History will absolve me!" The attack on Moncada and the trial had been a public relations triumph, creating martyrs and establishing Castro as Batista's main opposition figure. His speech effectively became the manifesto for the newly formed 26 July Movement, committed to violent insurrection.

From the Isle of Pines to the Sierra Maestra For his part in Moncada Castro was given a 15-year prison sentence on the Isle of Pines (now the Isla de la Juventud), but he and his 25 incarcerated comrades served only 19 months. In mid-1955 Batista, feeling secure in power and wanting to appear benevolent, granted an amnesty to all political prisoners, a decision he was sorely to regret. Forbidden from making public speeches, Castro and his followers went to Mexico, where they were joined by Che Guevara (see pages 50–51), and trained in guerrilla warfare. On December 2, 1956, Castro and a force of 82 rebels landed in eastern Cuba on the *Granma*, a boat designed to carry only 20 passengers. Batista's troops had got wind of their arrival, and few of the rebels survived the landing. For five days Castro and two colleagues hid in cane fields, sucking cane stalks for sustenance.

From the Sierra Maestra to Havana Castro, with a tiny corps of 13 survivors, retreated to the safety of the inaccessible Sierra Maestra mountains. There they gained support from the local peasantry, thanks partly to Castro's promise of agrarian reform and partly to the brutal treatment being meted out by Batista's soldiers to those reckoned to be sheltering the rebels. The rebels' numbers swelled, and within a year the mountains had effectively become a liberated area. At the same time, across the country the urban arm of the 26 July Movement was carrying out thousands of acts of sabotage and terrorism. A force of a

Che led much of the fighting against Batista's forces

mere few thousand guerrillas was winning simply because they were well led and highly motivated—in stark contrast to the Batistianos, who became ever more unpopular as they employed such drastically brutal methods as torturing guerrilla suspects and hanging their bodies in the streets. They murdered an estimated 20,000 Cubans in the 1950s.

In May 1958, Batista's forces surrounded the Sierra Maestra with 10,000 troops but made no inroads against Castro's band of a mere 300 fighters. From then on the dictator's fate was sealed. The guerrilla war spread east to the Sierra del Cristal, north to Bayamo, then, under Che Guevara, west into central Cuba. On New Year's Day 1959, Batista fled for the Dominican Republic and Castro made a triumphant entry into first Santiago, then, a week later, Havana.

■ **After the revolution, Cuba switched allegiance from the United States to the Soviet Union, and the country's rallying cry changed from *"patria o muerte"* ("homeland or death") to *"socialismo o muerte"* ("socialism or death"). Gains in equality and social welfare were offset by a lack of economic growth and restrictions on civil liberties. ■**

48

From nationalism to communism

Castro's triumph was greeted with jubilance and nationalist pride by the vast majority of Cubans. However, while radical social reforms and the reestablishment of democracy had been promised from the Sierra Maestra, no one was sure what the new masters, entirely without experience in running a country, would actually do. Lower rents, higher wages, and land reform were quickly introduced: under the Agrarian Reform Act estates over 988 acres passed to the state and provided

Castro relaxing in 1965 in familiar territory—the Sierra Maestra

secure jobs for laborers. However, Castro said free elections were unnecessary since the people manifestly supported the revolution.

The government soon fell foul of the United States, and the first overt declaration that it was on a socialist/communist course came during the Bay of Pigs invasion in 1961 (see page 52). Despite Castro's claim that he had been a Marxist-Leninist since university days, most historians argue that he swung to the left simply to provide Cuba with Soviet economic help and military protection. Without Soviet backing, the revolution would have died. The Cuban–Soviet alliance was, according to one historian, "a marriage of convenience, with Castro the eager bride and the Soviet Union the suspicious, initially reluctant groom."

Revolutionizing the system

The Cuban political system was reorganized along Soviet lines, headed by the Cuban Communist Party. The government centralized the economy and nationalized virtually everything in sight, from the utility companies to country clubs and all private businesses (except small farms): by the end of the 1960s, you couldn't get a haircut or even a hot dog without dealing with the state.

Unemployment was abolished— and replaced by inefficiency and underemployment. The communist ethos was epitomized in the concept of the *Hombre Nuevo*, or the New Man, who works not for material reward but selflessly, for the good of the community. In practical terms, this meant mass mobilization of "voluntary" labor. Elements of a free

market economy were introduced in the 1980s, but canceled after a few years in a process called the Rectification of Errors.

Cuba's economy, which prior to the revolution had been tied to the United States, became entirely reliant on the Soviet Union and Eastern Europe up until the late 1980s. It revolved around an exchange of Cuban sugar (plus nickel and citrus fruits) for Soviet oil (as well as arms and food) that amounted in the 1980s to a massive Soviet subsidy of Cuba by as much as $5 billion a year. One negative consequence of this trade was that, despite sporadic attempts to diversify and industrialize, Cuba's development was hindered by the fact that it was unable to break its dependency on sugar for its prosperity.

Social reforms For the first time in Cuba's history, there was a massive investment in social provision following the revolution—in education, health, and housing. In the early years of the revolution, some

At an early age, children become Young Pioneers and are instilled with revolutionary fervor

250,000 young volunteers were sent into the countryside in order to teach the 1 million illiterate Cubans to read, and schools and universities sprouted up across the country. Educational programs were introduced that combined classroom study and work in the fields. Medical care was improved dramatically, especially in rural areas, with the establishment of new clinics, improving life expectancy and decreasing infant mortality rates enormously. New housing estates were built around the country, often by "micro-brigades" of volunteer workers.

Yet, offsetting these benefits, there was a paucity of consumer goods and, often, food (rationing was introduced in 1962). This balance sheet of pros and cons continues to this day. Moreover, while discrimination against black people was outlawed, the government persecuted homosexuals and Catholics, particularly in the 1960s.

Che Guevara

■ Ernesto "Che" Guevara is idolized in Cuba, with his Christlike features appearing on billboards across the island. Though he was a terrible economist, he was an idealist and guerrilla fighter *par excellence.* Graham Greene descibed him as in "a state of permanent revolt" and Jean-Paul Sartre referred to him as "the most complete human being of our age." ■

Formative years Born in Argentina in 1928, Guevara had a pampered, middle-class upbringing. He went to university in Buenos Aires to study medicine, graduating in 1953, and was disqualified from military service because of chronic asthma, an ailment that afflicted him throughout his life. Something of a wild youth, he was nicknamed *El Chancho,* or the Pig, for his habit of rarely washing. In the early 1950s, his extensive travels in South and Central America, partly on a motorcycle, brought him into close contact with poverty, hunger, and disease, and imbued him with a burning desire to remedy social injustice, first through preventative medicine, then by armed insurrection.

The guerrilla fighter in Cuba Che Guevara joined Castro's group in Mexico in 1955, the only foreigner in the band. It was here that he acquired his sobriquet Che, for his Argentinian habit of saying "*che,*" which translates roughly as "hey pal!"

During his time with the rebels in the Sierra Maestra, Guevara acted as a medic, but more importantly he became inseparable from Castro: Guevara's idealism worked in tandem with Castro's pragmatism. Guevara commanded a rebel column into central Cuba in late 1958; its success proved decisive in Batista's

Che as munificent statesman: a photograph taken in 1963

downfall. As a guerrilla fighter, he developed a reputation for a chilling detachment from violence, and in 1959 he oversaw the execution of some 550 Batistianos.

The economist Guevara spent the first five years of the revolution running the Cuban economy, as President of the National Bank (he signed banknotes just "Che") and Minister of Industry. His Marxist views led to complete state control and central planning. Unconcerned with efficiency or profit and seeking to eliminate the laws of supply and demand, his ideas resulted in half-finished and empty factories and plunged the country into economic crisis. His vision of human nature in the New Man (see page 48) permeated the whole government's philosophy throughout the 1960s.

The internationalist In 1965, Guevara left Cuba to seek, as he put it, "the staccato singing of the machine guns and new battle cries of war and victory." Some historians reckon he fell out with Castro, unhappy with the cozy relationship the president had fostered with the Soviet Union, but most assert he departed simply because he felt no emotional attachment to Cuba and wanted to pursue his belief that imperialism should be fought across the world. Cuba had become a model for revolution for undeveloped countries, and Guevara, with the Cuban government's full backing, wanted to incite other peoples to revolt.

He first went, in secret, to the Congo to train left-wing insurgents, then in late 1966 to Bolivia to incite its peasants to rebel. Both expeditions were disastrous. In October 1967, Guevara was captured by CIA-backed Bolivian troops, then executed and buried in an unmarked grave. His hands were cut off and preserved in a jar of formaldehyde as proof of his death. Days later, the Cuban poet Nicolás Guillén wrote an encomium to the man: "Wait for us. We will go with you. We want to die as you have died, to live as you have lived, Che Comandante, friend." In 1997, the grave was rediscovered

and Guevara's remains (minus the hands) were brought back to Cuba and, after a week of national mourning, placed in his mausoleum in Santa Clara.

❑ To assert itself as a leader in the so-called Third World, Cuba championed politically sympathetic causes worldwide until the late 1980s. The biggest commitment was to Angola, where over 350,000 Cuban troops were sent to support the Marxist government in a civil war against U.S.- and South African-backed forces. In 1988 South Africa was defeated. ❑

This colossal statue stands above Che's mausoleum in Santa Clara

Pigs and missiles

■ **After the revolution, the United States turned against Cuba, partly because of the appropriation of U.S. assets, partly because of the perceived threat of communism so close to shore. Matters came to a head in the two most famous events in Cuba's postrevolutionary history and escalated into one of the most alarming standoffs of the Cold War years.** ■

The demise of Cuban–U.S. relations In 1960, the Cuban government seized American assets, including oil refineries, the telephone exchange, dozens of sugar mills, and hundreds of thousands of acres of land, without providing compensation. Washington estimates the U.S. lost $8 billion of investments. In retaliation, the U.S. canceled its sugar quota, began to impose a trade embargo, and, in January 1961, broke off diplomatic relations. Nearly four decades later, the situation has improved little.

The Bay of Pigs On April 17, 1961, an invasion force of 1,500 Cuban émigrées landed on Cuba's south coast at the Bahía de Cochinos, or Bay of Pigs. They had been trained by the CIA and disembarked from U.S. navy vessels waiting offshore. Within 48 hours the assault had been defeated; 1,180 prisoners were taken, and were ransomed for $53 million's worth of food and medicines. The disaster resulted from the failure, prior to the assault, of U.S. bombers (manned by Cuban exiles) to knock out the tiny Cuban airforce, which harassed the U.S. fleet. Moreover, the exiles expected the U.S. to back them up with military support, but President Kennedy decided against action that he reckoned world opinion would condemn and that might provoke a Soviet response.

Castro played a prominent personal role in the fighting, and his popularity rating soared after "the first defeat of imperialism in Latin America," as he called it. Yet he believed that the Bay of Pigs was a mere prelude to a full-

Top: the wreckage of a US spy plane shot down during the Missile Crisis. Above: Castro leaping from a tank during the Bay of Pigs

scale U.S. invasion; indeed, declassified White House tapes reveal that some U.S. advisers were advocating all-out war. Castro pleaded with Russian premier Nikita Krushchev for military aid as a deterrent, and Moscow jumped at this chance of locating nuclear missiles close to its Cold War foe.

The missile crisis In October 1962, a famous U.S. reconnaissance photo provided evidence of a missile site on Cuba. Intermediate-range nuclear missiles had already been delivered, and more were on the way in a

Russian convoy. Kennedy considered an invasion of Cuba and an air strike on the missile base, but decided to give Krushchev a way of backing down without losing face. He thus announced on October 22 that the U.S. Navy would stop any Russian ships on the way to Cuba that were carrying offensive weapons, that the missiles already in Cuba must be withdrawn, and that the U.S. would not shrink from nuclear war if need be. For six days, the world held its breath as the Soviet ships steamed toward the U.S. fleet. Then the Soviets backed down and the missiles on Cuba were removed in return for a U.S. pledge not to invade the island.

While the Bay of Pigs was arguably Kennedy's greatest failure, the missile crisis was his greatest triumph. Yet many believe his lack of aggressiveness in either situation resulted in his death at the hands of frustrated Cuban exiles.

Counterrevolutionary activities
During the 1960s, tens of thousands of CIA agents operated against Cuba,

attempting assassinations of Castro, sabotaging industrial installations and sugar mills, and even trying to introduce epidemics. Though most anti-Castro Cubans had emigrated, the CIA also supported those left behind. Wholescale counterrevolutionary activity was especially strong in the Escambray Mountains, where thousands died in the fighting, but it was entirely stamped out by 1966. Meanwhile, some 60,000 political prisoners were held in Cuban jails and labor camps, often in terrible conditions.

❏ Wayne Smith, head of U.S. Interests Section in Havana from 1977 to 1982, once famously said: "Cuba has the same effect on American administrations that the full moon used to have on werewolves; they just lose their rationality at the mention of Castro and Cuba." ❏

53

Soviet missiles on the streets of Havana

HAVANA

A to Z

Havana's skyline, seen from Castillo del Morro

HAVANA

Street names
Many street names were changed after the revolution. Maps (including those in this guide) give the new name plus the old name in brackets. In the text, the new name is used, unless the street is still universally referred to by its old name (such as the Prado).

Nighttime Havana
"There was a buzz all around us—that nonstop coffee-and-*samba*, rum-and-*rumba* buzz that made the island feel like an African village dancing to a Spanish guitar...Señoritas in cocktail dresses showed themselves off like treasures in a jewel case...Everyone was dressed up, it seemed, though no one was going anywhere; the whole island was just jiving in place."
Pico Iyer, *Cuba and the Night* (1995)

Havana A combination of communist intrigue, Caribbean sultriness, Latin-American rhythm, and Spanish architectural magnificence, Havana, or more properly, La Habana, is mysterious, decrepit yet ravishingly beautiful. Because of Cuba's economic plight, it is a capital city like no other. Whole districts appear to be on the point of tumbling down and, despite a population of over 2 million, it can be unnervingly quiet and there is little of the commercial bustle that normally pervades a big city. Yet, at the same time, Havana can hardly be called relaxing. It is a place where you are expected to fend for yourself, where every few steps you will be asked whether you want cigars, a taxi, or a girl for the night. But after a few days you may develop an admiration for Habaneros' resilience—more durable than the buildings they have to live in—and may very well fall in love with this most intoxicating of cities.

History Havana was founded in its present position in 1519 because of the protection its deep bay afforded against tropical storms and pirates. In 1553, it became Cuba's capital, with the caravels of Spanish fleets laden with gold, silver, pearls, and cocoa from Mexico and Peru dropping in to stock up with provisions on their return trip to Spain. Often ransacked by pirates, Havana was, by the early 17th century, defended by three fortresses. In 1674 work began on city walls, though they were not completed for over 100 years, and after the English captured the city in 1762 (it was soon given back to Spain in return for Florida) another massive fortress was built.

By this time, Havana was slowly being transformed, on the wealth of the slave and sugar trades, from a violent and putrid port into a sophisticated city. In the 19th century, the city walls came down to allow room for expansion, luxuries poured in from around the Caribbean and South America, "gringos" started coming on vacation from the United States, and evening entertainment ranged from masked balls to grand theater.

Havana spent the first half of the 20th century in the thrall of the United States. Americans started arriving in great numbers during Prohibition; and the city, awash with money, developed a reputation for decadence: "a great open city for a bachelor on the loose," according to Graham Greene. Then, after the revolution, the clubs, casinos, and brothels were all shut down and the city went into physical decline as investment was directed away from Havana to Cuba's provinces. Now, however, with tourism taking off, parts of the city are being given a facelift.

Layout Most of the city's attractions are in Old Havana (La Habana Vieja). It is separated by Havana's grimy, industrial harbor from two impressive castles and, farther east, Playas del Este, the best beaches in the city's vicinity. West of Old Havana lies the new city: first Centro, a poor, untouristy, residential and shopping district, then Vedado, a richer, business-cum-residential area. South of Vedado spreads the Plaza de la Revolución district (often shortened to "Plaza"), around the soulless square of the same name, Cuba's center of government. West of Vedado are upscale neighborhoods such as Miramar, which has a sense of well-being not shared by the rest of the city. See map on inside back cover.

Old Havana

Like a great work of literature, Old Havana elicits sadness and happiness, and like a great meal full of subtle flavors, it needs to be experienced slowly. Stay, if you can, in one of its hotels, amble aimlessly along its streets, and savor it at dusk and at night when the hustlers have called it a day and its thoroughfares are lit only by the neon glow of TV sets. Bounded by the city's harbor, this egg-shaped grid of streets presents two faces. For the most part, it is permeated with decrepitude. Few streets are paved, roofs leak, and walls miss whole chunks. Some houses are so tumbledown they seem to defy gravity, while others would surely collapse were they not propped up by wooden scaffolding. Over 100,000 Habaneros reside here in what might appear to be picturesquely earthy surroundings, whiling away the hours langorously for all to see on the street or on their balconies. But the reality is overcrowded apartments, which often have no running water (buckets being hauled up on a rope to upper stories is an all too common sight).

The other face of Old Havana is one of restoration. More tourists come here than anywhere else in Cuba after the resort of Varadero, so millions of dollars are being spent to turn the finest colonial mansions into museums, art galleries, restaurants, bars, and hotels. The main squares, Plaza de Armas and Plaza de la Catedral, look as handsome as when they were first built, as do both the streets directly south of them and the old harborside fortresses that were built to keep English and Dutch hands off the Spaniards' proudest possession. The restored area is still quite small, but is gradually being extended down towards Plaza Vieja.

Migration
Overcrowding in Havana has worsened since the start of the economic hardships of the Special Period, with a dramatic increase in the influx of people from the provinces to the capital. A new law intended to curb this movement of Palestinos, or Palestines as they have been nicknamed, was introduced in 1997, not only to improve living conditions in Havana but also because the government needs agricultural workers to stay in the countryside.

Market stalls on Plaza de la Catedral

■ **Old Havana is such a wonderful assemblage of colonial buildings that in 1982 UNESCO designated it all a World Heritage Site. Much of it also looks like a bomb site: each year many buildings, rotten to the core, collapse, while others are being salvaged through belated restoration work.** ■

Outstanding colonial buildings

The architectural features described here are best seen in the following buildings: Palacio de los Capitanes Generales (see pages 60–61), Casa de la Obra Pía (see pages 66–67), Museo de Arte Colonial (see page 63), Casa de los Condes de Jaruco (see page 68).

The patio of the Museo de Arte Colonial

History Little remains of Old Havana's oldest buildings as they were constructed of wood rather than stone. Most of the architectural marvels date from the second half of the 18th century and the beginning of the 19th century, in a style that was a synthesis of baroque, Moorish, and Gothic designs—definitely Hispanic but adapted to suit the hot Caribbean climate. During this period Cuba had suddenly found great wealth from its burgeoning sugarcane industry, and these mansions were status symbols for the merchants and the sugar aristocracy who owned them. Floors were made of marble and ceilings of mahogany, walls were painted with murals, hung with tapestries, and decorated with Italianate bands of colored plasterwork called *cenefas*. From around the 1820s, new buildings were neoclassical in style. Some were stern, such as El Templete on Plaza de Armas, others flamboyant, including the mansions along the Prado. Many of the Prado façades also exhibit 20th-century art-nouveau details and arabesque flourishes such as keyhole-shaped windows.

Restoration Tropical humidity and neglect have precipitated the buildings' demise. In the 1960s and 1970s, Cubans were encouraged to live in the countryside or in

new Soviet-style apartment blocks, and the upkeep of Old Havana was not on the government's list of priorities. It was only when tourists started arriving in the 1980s that a massive restoration project was set into motion. The size of the task is overwhelming: there are some 900 buildings of architectural importance within the old city. Some have been completely restored. Elsewhere, the work is superficial and the buildings are still essentially ruinous.

Layout A typical colonial mansion was built on three floors around a central courtyard (patio). The ground floor was given over to shops and storage space, a mid-floor to slaves' quarters and offices, and the top floor to grand, main living rooms. The main door had to be large enough to admit carriages, so peek holes, or *postigos*, were inserted to allow occupants to look out into the street without going to the trouble of opening the door.

Airiness The buildings were designed to make them as airy as possible in the tropical heat. Moorish wooden ceilings called *alfarjes*, often decorated with star patterns, were lofty. Windows were long and glassless, with *persianas*, or slatted shutters, to keep out the rain and sun but let in any breeze, and *rejas*, long wrought-iron or carved window bars to deter unwanted intruders. Rooms were divided by a *mampara*, a swinging door made of wood and frosted glass. Alejo Carpentier, Cuba's famous 20th-century writer, describes the mampara as "a door truncated to the height of a man, the real interior door of the Creole home for hundreds of years, creating a peculiar concept of family relations and communal living."

Soft light The harshness of the tropical sun was filtered and softened with stained glass, creating atmospheric pools of colored light on the mansions' floors. On the squares, covered walkways or *portales* were built to provide shade for vendors and passersby.

Mediopuntos *(see panel below) over-looking El Patio's courtyard, Plaza de la Catedral*

Technical terms
Semicircular fans of colored glass are called *mediopuntos* when separated by wooden struts, and *vitrales* if divided by metal bonds, while rectangular panes of stained glass are termed *lucetas*.

Beyond Havana
To track down other colonial gems beyond Havana, head for Trinidad (see pages 124–128), Remedios (see page 134), Camagüey (see pages 138–141), Santiago (see pages 152–160), Gibara (see page 167), and Baracoa (see pages 174–175).

Room 511
Between 1930 and 1938, Ernest Hemingway often stayed in Room 511 of the Hotel Ambos Mundos (at the corner of Obispo and Mercaderes). He spent much of the last two years working here on *For Whom the Bell Tolls*. The room (*Open* Mon–Sat 10–5), preserved as a shrine to the writer, has a small, rather disappointing collection of Hemingway memorabilia. It includes a few letters forwarded to him at the hotel from Key West.

Fine ceramics decorate Casa de la Obra Pía

Old Havana: around Obispo

Calle Obispo is Old Havana's main street. The pedestrian thoroughfare (where missile heads are used for bollards) is a constant stream of people and bicycles and, being one of the few well-lit streets, is good for an evening stroll. From the famous El Floridita restaurant/bar (see panel, page 88 and page 202) at its western end, it passes down-at-the-heel bookshops, a few touristy crafts shops, and Droguería Johnson at No. 260, a pharmacy that appears to have popped straight out of the 19th century. At its eastern end, Calle Obispo debouches into Plaza de Armas in a row of beautifully restored mansions, including La Mina café/restaurant (see pages 88 and 202–203) and No. 117–119, the oldest house in Havana, dating from 1570. The museums detailed below all stand yards away from here in the most extensively renovated parts of Old Havana after Armas and Catedral squares. They are worth visiting as much for the glorious colonial mansions that house them as for their exhibits.

▶▶ **Casa de África**   59D3

Obrapía No. 157–161
Open: Tue–Sat 10:30–5:30; Sun 9:30–12:30. Admission charge: inexpensive
With space at such a premium in Old Havana, the courtyard of this cavernous mansion often serves as a school classroom. Ground and second floors are given over to costumes, statues, and furnishings donated by African embassies in Cuba or brought back from a trip Castro made to the continent in 1977. Of more interest are the displays on the top floor devoted to Afro-Cuban religions, with dresses, symbols, and beads of the most important *orishas*, or gods, in the Santería pantheon (see page 84), and a *tablero de ifa*, a board used by a *babalawo*, or priest, for making predictions. Note the wrought-iron guards on the sides of the building's main entrance to protect the walls from being knocked by carriages.

▶ **Casa del Árabe**   59D3

Oficios No. 16
Open: daily 9:30–6:30. Admission free
This building and the vaguely Arab restaurant Al Medina next door (see page 202) were once a religious college, and envelop two of the city's loveliest colonial patios. Inside is a mockup of a souk, hung with carpets, robes, and shawls, and a few pieces of Middle Eastern furniture.

▶▶▶ **Casa de la Obra Pía**   59D3

Obrapía No. 158
Open: Tue–Sat 10:30–5:30; Sun 9:30–12:30. Admission charge: inexpensive
This gorgeous mansion is set around a sensational yellow-and-blue courtyard flowing with hibiscus and bougainvillea. Originally it would have been full of shops. Details to look for are tiles depicting Plaza Vieja in the 19th century, and a painted band, or *cenefa*, up the stairs that lead to the living quarters, a series of marble-floored rooms with mahogany furniture, Chinese screens, and fine ceramics. Note the unusual doorless dining room, designed to benefit from the merest breeze. At the

entrance, a little exhibition on Cuban novelist Alejo Carpentier includes the VW Beetle he drove when he lived in France.

The classic colonial yellow-and-blue color scheme ennobles Casa de la Obra Pía

► Casa de Puerto Rico   59D3
Mercaderes No. 120
Open: Tue–Sat 10–6; Sun 9:30–1. Admission free
This tiny museum is devoted to smoking, with cigar box labels, pipes, and lighters, including ones shaped as a pistol, camera, boot, telephone, and piano. Castro donated many of the objects; once an avid cigar smoker, he kicked the habit in 1985.

► Museo de Automóvil   59D3
Oficios No. 13
Open: daily 9–5:30. Admission charge: inexpensive
It is worth browsing around this mediocre collection of vehicles dating from the early 20th century to find Camilo Cienfuegos' 1959 Oldsmobile and the Chevrolet Che cruised around in in the early 1960s.

► Museo Numismático   59D3
Oficios No. 8
Open: Tue–Fri 10–5; Sat 10–4; Sun 10–1. Admission free
Once the residence of Havana's bishop, this building has a small museum dedicated to coins and medals. Look for 16th-century *reals*, and old banknotes the size of books.

► Sala de la Revolución   59D3
Mercaderes No. 109
Open: Tue–Sat 10:30–6; Sun 9–1. Admission free
This one-room museum documents details of the road to revolution in the 1950s, and there is also a little display on Lenin, with holograms of some of his possessions.

Street names
The names of many of Old Havana's streets have historic origins. Lamparilla, meaning small lamp, was the first thoroughfare to have street lighting; Empedrado, meaning cobbled, was the first street to be paved; and the first tiled house was on Calle Tejadillo, or Tiled Street. The city's top ecclesiasts like to stroll along Calle Obispo, or Bishop Street, while Calle Mercaderes takes its name from the many merchants who lived on it, and Calle Inquisidor from a resident member of the Spanish inquisition.

Walk **Southern Old Havana**

See highlighted route on map on pages 58–59.

Few tourists explore this poor, residential area where restoration work has only recently begun. You will be far less hassled than elsewhere in Old Havana, but bag-snatching is a problem and you should not wander around at night. The route concentrates on Havana's ecclesiastical riches. Allow half a day.

Start at **Plaza Vieja**▶▶. Dating from 1584, it was created as a commercial space and meeting place for aristo-cratic Habaneros when the Plaza de Armas was taken over for military drills. A parking lot inserted under the square in the 1950s has recently been uprooted and the plaza is under-going a major facelift. However, its mansions offer a wonderful medley of baroque, neoclassical and art-nouveau styles. While some are homes in a very sorry state of repair, with inhabitants winching pails of water to upper floors, others, such as the **Casa de los Condes de Jaruco**▶▶, have been restored. On the southwest corner, this is one of Havana's colonial masterpieces, with a vast entrance door, coat of arms, and superb *mediopuntos* on its façade. Inside, admire the courtyard and the *cenefas*, or painted borders, running up the broad stairs. The mansion on the square's east side at **Mercaderes No. 307**▶ lays on photo-graphic exhibitions (*Open* Tue–Sat 10–5. *Admission* free).

Take Calle Brasil down to **Iglesia de San Fransisco de Asis**▶▶. Since its beginnings in 1672, this church has twice been brought to its knees by hurricanes and stripped of all its baroque finery. Like its adjacent cloistered quads, where you will find some of the former monastery's treasures, the recently restored church is beautifully austere. Its large square is one of the most recent parts of Old Havana to have been spruced up. Colonial buildings have been converted into art galleries and a multimillion dollar revamp has turned the Lonja del Comercio, or Commodity Exchange, into a snazzy office block for foreign companies.

Walk back west along Calle Brasil to the **Museo Histórico de las Ciencias Carlos J. Finlay**▶▶ (*Open* Mon–Sat 8–5. *Admission charge* inexpensive) at Calle Cuba No. 460. Named after the Cuban who discovered that mosquitoes transmitted yellow fever, this fusty old place was once Havana's science academy. It has a grand library, a room of busts of Cuban scientists, a reproduction 19th-century pharmacy, and a magnif-icent pillared lecture theater (which Einstein visited in 1930).

Head down Calle Cuba to the **Convento de Santa Clara**▶▶, so massive it fills four blocks. Cuba's first convent is now a conservation center: the nuns left in 1919. You can take a guided tour of its three court-yards—the main, cloistered one has a gorgeous garden full of palms and fruit trees and boasts an ancient washhouse (*Open* Mon–Fri 9–3. *Admission charge* inexpensive). If you fall in love with the place, you can stay here (see page 198).

Continue along Cuba to the island's oldest church, **Espíritu Santo**▶ (*Open* daily 8–12, 3–6:30). Dedicated in 1638, it has a fine vaulted roof and catacombs full of bones. Farther down Cuba, **Iglesia de la Merced**▶ is a baroque riot, with every inch of wall and ceiling painted over (*Open* daily 8–12, 3–6). Its Lady of Mercy in the main altar is much venerated by Santería believers (see page 84) as the *orisha* (deity) Obatalá.

Turn west along Calle Leonor Pérez to No. 314, the **Casa Natal de José Martí**▶ (*Open* Tue–Sat 10–5; Sun 9–1. *Admission charge* inexpensive). The Apostle, as he is sometimes called, was born in this cramped house in 1853. It is a good place to appreciate how ardently Martí is venerated: memorabilia include the desk where he wrote articles in New York, the spurs he wore when he fell in battle, and even the woven pony tail he had when he was a child.

You are now close to the train station, outside which stands the largest section of the city's old walls. Directly north of the station is a fun flea market, and at Avenida de Bélgica and Calle Corrales there is the city center's biggest farmers' market.

69

Casa de los Condes de Jaruco, one of Havana's finest mansions

Christ on high
The 66-foot-high marble statue of Christ above the harbor at Casablanca was completed on Christmas Day 1958 after two years' work. It has withstood three bolts of lightning.

Getting there
From a quay opposite Old Havana's Calle Santa Clara, old rustbuckets cross the bottle-shaped, industrialized harbor (rated by the UN as one of the world's 10 most polluted), every 30 minutes to Casablanca, every 10 minutes to Regla. A ferry was hijacked in 1994 for a failed trip to Florida: armed guards are there to stop such an event from recurring. To reach the fortresses, take a cab through the tunnel under the harbor entrance.

Massive walls and a wide moat protect La Cabaña

Old Havana: across Havana Bay

▶▶ **Castillo de los Tres Santos Reyes Magnos del Morro**   *59D5*

Open: daily 9–8. Admission charge: moderate
On a hill over the bay's mouth, El Morro fortress was built between 1589 and 1630; the lighthouse was added in 1845. A chain used to be hung at night between it and the more modest La Punta fortress across the harbor to prevent pirates from gaining access. There is an exhibition on Cuba's early nautical history, but visitors come primarily for the superb panorama of Havana's cityscape.

▶▶ **Fortaleza de San Carlos de la Cabaña**   *59E5*

Open: daily 9 AM–10 PM. Admission charge: moderate
Once the largest fort in the Americas, and dwarfing El Morro, La Cabaña was constructed by the Spanish between 1764 and 1774 to protect El Morro after it had been captured with ease by the English in 1762. A prison up until the 1950s, it was Che Guevara's headquarters during 1959 and then a military academy. Che's office displays possessions and photographs; other rooms outline the history of weapons and castles. In previous centuries, a cannon was fired each evening to announce the dropping of the harbormouth chain and the closing of the city gates—a ceremony reenacted today at 9 PM.

▶ **Regla**   *59E2*

Many slaves settled in this earthy, working-class port, bequeathing it a strong Afro-Cuban religious culture. The waterside church▶ has numerous Catholic/Santería saints/*orishas*, in particular the black Virgen de Regla, Havana's patron saint, who doubles as Yemayá. The Museo Municipal▶ exhibits *orishas'* altars and symbols, as well as divination shells and donations to the deities from bottles of Cinzano to plastic ducks (*Open Mon–Sat 9:30–6; Sun 9–1. Admission charge* inexpensive).

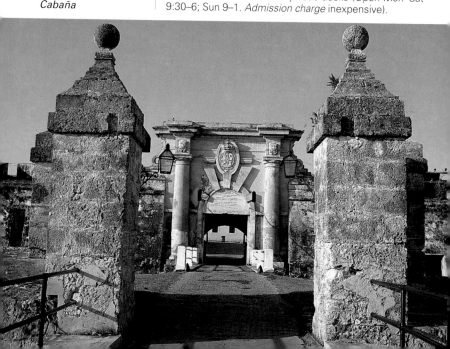

The Hall of Lost Steps takes its name from its acoustics

A serious matter
Just down the street in the Parque Central, you will almost invariably find a cluster of men in a particular spot arguing vehemently about what seems to be some life-and-death matter. If you can speak Spanish, you will discover they are actually discussing baseball.

Old Havana: around the Prado

Just outside the one-time city walls but officially still within Habana Vieja, the three wide avenues that run from the Malecón toward the train station have a completely different character from the rest of the old city. Confusingly, their names were changed after the revolution: Monserrate to Misiones and, to the south, Bélgica; Zululeta to Agramonte; and the Prado to the Paseo de Martí, which is, however, always referred to by its old name. Every visitor to Havana should stroll along the Prado, lined with flamboyant, multicolored buildings. Wander, too, around the Parque Central, and at least take a look at the Capitolio and old presidential palace.

►► Capitolio   58B3

South of Parque Central
Open: Mon–Sat 9–5. Admission charge: moderate
With its dome dominating the city's skyline, the Capitolio needs no address to locate it. This facsimile of Washington, D.C.'s Capitol has been called a monument to the hubris of Machado, the Cuban dictator who built it. From its completion in 1929 until 1959 it was the seat for the House of Representatives and the Senate of the Republic. Behind bronze doors whose panels depict scenes from Cuba's history lies an awesomely large gallery, called the Hall of Lost Steps. It contains a representation of Pallas Athena, claimed to be the world's third tallest indoor statue, and, under the dome, a replica of a 28-carat diamond that marks Havana's center (for measuring distances from the capital). You can wander

Permuta
Cubans are not allowed to buy or sell property, so if they want to move they often swap their houses or flats. The crossroads of the Prado and Calle Colón is a meeting place for swappers, with advertisements marked *permuta* (Spanish for exchange) affixed to the trees.

A typical neo-classical façade on the Prado

Budding Olga Korbuts
One of Havana's hidden wonders is the Gymnastics Academy on the Prado at No. 207 between calles Trocadero and Colón (*Open* Mon–Fri 8–5; Sat 8–12). In magnificent galleries with fluted pillars and stuccoed ceilings, the province's best gymnasts aged from five to 11 perform remarkable feats on the vault and parallel bars before their proud mothers. Discreet visitors are welcome.

around the rest of the building, admiring the handsome semicircular chamber where politicians sat as well as the endless marble corridors and Italian Renaissance ceilings. To have your picture taken by one of the photographers outside the Capitolio, you need to stand still for a number of seconds: their tripod cameras date from the 1920s.

► Museo Nacional de Bellas Artes (National Fine Arts Museum)   59C4

Trocadero between Agramonte and Avenida de las Misiones
This museum is closed for some time for a much-needed overhaul. It houses a sizable array of ancient Greek, Roman, and Egyptian art, and European paintings by artists such as Canaletto, Gainsborough, and Turner (many appropriated from private collections in 1959). Cuban paintings include work from the colonial period, contemporary pieces by Wilfredo Lam, and socialist pop art.

► Museo Nacional de la Música   59C5

Capdevila No. 1 (at the northern end of Avenida de las Misiones)
Open: Mon–Sat 9–4:45. Admission charge: inexpensive
This small but fascinating collection exhibits all sorts of instruments from around the world, from a Russian balalaika to a xylophone from Laos, as well as old phonographs and music boxes. But its most important section has African tribal drums elemental in Afro-Cuban religions.

►►► Museo de la Revolución   59C4

Refugio between Agramonte and Avenida de las Misiones
Open: Tue 10–6; Wed–Sun 10–5. Admission charge: moderate
Everything you wanted to know about revolutionary Cuba, and probably quite a lot more besides, is contained in the former presidential palace: allow a couple of hours to see it all. The building, completed in 1920, is a sight in its own right, with a few rooms retaining their original Tiffany splendor. Most, however, are dedicated to a panegyric on Cuba's road to socialist nirvana. Chronologically arranged, the exposition starts at the top of the building and works down. The island's early history is given short shrift before an exhaustive analysis of the 1950s, with endless maps and battle plans of encounters between Batista's forces and the rebels. Knuckledusters, tongs used on male genitals, and gory photographs of torture victims demonstrate the brutality of the Batista regime, while the revolutionaries are remembered through their keepsakes, weapons, and bloodstained clothes. Look for the guitar that Castro and his fellow prisoners played to entertain themselves on the Isle of Pines, and life-size dummies of Che Guevara and Camilo Cienfuegos in dirt-encrusted fatigues. Downstairs, blown-up pictures of jubilant crowds represent "The Triumph of the Revolution," and postrevolutionary achievements are documented with medals awarded for hard work and the spacesuit of a Cuban astronaut. Don't miss the "Cretins' Gallery," where presidents Reagan and Bush are depicted as cartoon sheriff and Roman emperor, and are thanked for unwittingly helping to strengthen the revolution.

In the square behind the palace, the *Granma*, the cabin cruiser that bore Castro's puny invasion force to Cuba in 1956, is displayed reverentially in a glass house alongside the engine of an American spy plane brought down during the Cuban Missile Crisis.

▶▶ Parque Central   58B3

This large square is one of the city's great hubs. It is virtually impossible to cross it without being accosted by someone on the make; taxis of every description—from Cadillacs to bicycle rickshaws—tout for business, and Havana's articulated buses, called *camellos*, thunder by every few minutes. The Martí statue in the middle was the first of many to be erected in Cuba, in 1905. On the western side next to the Hotel Inglaterra, the **Gran Teatro▶▶**, dripping with caryatids and rising to winged angels on turrets, is neoclassicism and art nouveau run riot. Tours (Tue–Sun 10–6. *Admission charge* inexpensive) often look in on ballet rehearsals (Cuba's national ballet company is based here). A less well-known wonder is the art-deco **Edificio Bacardí▶**, best seen from the rooftop of the Hotel Plaza (see pages 87 and 198).

▶▶▶ The Prado   58B3, B4, 59C5

La Punta fort on the northern waterfront to Parque Central
In the 19th century well-to-do Habaneros would come and promenade here, a tradition maintained to this day, but by all and sundry. On weekdays angelic-looking schoolchildren practice P.E. here. The avenue was constructed in 1772, with a long, thin park down its center. On either side run the most joyous architectural expressions imaginable—grand arcaded and pillared façades in turquoise, lime green, orange, and pink. Havana itself is encapsulated in the image of residents whiling away the hours on their crumbling, balustraded balconies.

An attempted coup
The bullet-pocked van marked "Fast Delivery" in the Museo de la Revolución's park was used in a failed attempt to assassinate Batista. In 1957, 78 rebels, a rival group to Castro's, attacked the presidential palace, but Batista hid on the third floor which, unknown to the rebels, was accessible only by an elevator that Batista had stuck at the top of the shaft.

73

The park down the center of the Prado is flanked with laurels, gas lamps, marble benches, and bronze lions

■ **The famous British novelist Graham Greene originally intended setting his novel about the bunglings of the British secret service in Portugal, but he ended up basing it in Cuba.** *Our Man in Havana*, **which takes place around 1957, captures the Batista years wonderfully. Surprisingly, neither the novel nor the author are commemorated in any way in the capital.** ■

74

Our Man in Havana

Hidden in the Cuban countryside, the English hero, Wormold, a vacuum cleaner salesman, invents weapons to please his Secret Service masters. In 1962, the literary world was, understandably, rocked when real Soviet missiles were discovered on the island. Locations in the novel include Wormold's shop on Old Havana's Calle Lamparilla, Room 501 of the Hotel Sevilla, where he meets his boss, and the Hotel Nacional, where he avoids being poisoned. Castro condoned the book, though he said it did not do justice to the evils of the Batista

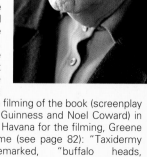

regime, and approved the filming of the book (screenplay by Greene, starring Alec Guinness and Noel Coward) in Havana in 1959. While in Havana for the filming, Greene visited Hemingway's home (see page 82): "Taxidermy everywhere," he remarked, "buffalo heads, antlers...such carnage."

Greene on Castro

After hearing Castro speechify for three hours in 1963, Greene wrote: "In all Castro's speeches there is a sense of a man thinking aloud. He explains his course of action, he admits mistakes, he explains difficulties—one has the sense that he respects the intelligence of his audience..."

Greene on the Tropicana

The description of Havana's top nightclub in *Our Man in Havana* holds good today: "Chorus-girls paraded twenty feet up among the great palm-trees, while pink and mauve searchlights swept the floor...The piano was wheeled away into the undergrowth, and the dancers stepped down like awkward birds from among the branches."

Greene on Cuba Greene visited Cuba in 1957 to research the novel. He enjoyed Havana's decadence, but noted it was "a segregated city" where "every smart bar and restaurant was called a club so that a negro could be legally excluded." He condemned the Batista regime for "the mutilations and torture practiced by leading police officers, the killing of hostages," and deplored the British government for supplying it with arms. During this visit, Greene took a suitcase of warm clothes on the plane from Havana to Santiago to give to the Sierra Maestra rebels. Visiting schools, factories and so forth on trips around Cuba in 1963 and 1966, he was initially optimistic about the revolution, judging the "war against illiteracy as a genuine crusade." However, the forced labor camps to which homosexuals and priests were sent troubled him greatly.

Centro

*Soaking up the rays
on the Malecón's sea
wall*

75

Most tourists pass through this grid of run-down residential and shopping streets on their way between Old Havana and Vedado without stopping. However, city life is at its most arcane and colorful on Havana's two principal shopping streets, Galiano and the pedestrianized eastern end of **San Rafael►**. Dollar shops stocked with the latest electronic goods stand cheek-by-jowl with pawn shops hawking secondhand underpants and cavernous department stores selling little more than plastic flowers and piggy banks. Some 200 descendants of a 150,000-strong 19th-century influx of Chinese slave labor live in Havana's tiny **Barrio Chino►**, around the crossroads of Zanja and Rayo, where there's a bustling farmers' market.

►►► Fábrica de Tabacos Partagás   58B3
Calle Industria No. 520 (directly behind the Capitolio)
Open: tours Mon–Fri 10, 1. Admission charge: expensive
Tours of Cuba's largest cigar factory, founded in 1845, reveal all stages of the process (see pages 104–105: sorting the tobacco leaves, rolling, bundling, labeling, and boxing. There is an excellent cigar shop. In Refugio, the Fábrica de Tabacos La Corona, Agramonte No. 106, also offers tours (*Open Mon–Sat 9 AM. Admission charge* expensive).

►►► Malecón   58B5
Havana's seaside promenade extends from the Prado to the western end of Vedado. On a windy day, 33-foot-high waves break spectacularly over the sea wall. When it's calm, Habaneros come in the evenings to converse and share a bottle of rum, and during the day to sunbathe and fish off the rocks or from inner tubes out in the bay. The Malecón also has its disreputable side, with as many hookers as anywhere in Havana. The most alluring section is Centro's eastern end up to the Prado, lined with barely standing, pastel-colored mansions covered in caryatids and plaster roses. They present an unforgettable melancholic air, especially when softly lit by the early morning or evening sun.

The Tango House
At Calle Neptuno No. 303 (near Galiano), the front room of a house has been turned into the Casa del Tango, a shrine to the Argentinian music and dance form. Walls are coated with record sleeves and magazine covers of famous practitioners, above all one Carlos Gardél. The elderly couple who live here are only too happy to put on an LP, and can recommend places to get dance lessons. There are no specific opening hours.

The Malecón's mansions
After a visit to Havana in 1957, the travel writer Norman Lewis described Malecón's now tumbledown buildings as "millionaires' seaside houses like wedding cakes turned to stone and painted red, blue, or yellow."

Ice cream
Coppelia, at La Rampa and Calle L, is a Havana institution. This vast ice-cream parlor is housed in tentacles of a concrete octopus that spread around an arboreal park house. In better times as many as 30 flavors were offered, but often now there is just vanilla. Nonetheless, Cubans line up for hours for a scoop or two; some slip their servings into saucepans to take home. If you are feeling hard-hearted, as a dollar-paying tourist you can jump ahead in line. Coppelia stays open until the ice cream runs out, sometimes late in the evening.

La Milagrosa is invariably bedecked with floral offerings

Vedado

This district is a strange mix of 1950s high-rises, crumbling neoclassical mansions, and communist slogans written large. From the 1930s to 1950s, its nightclubs, brothels, and casinos contributed in large part to Havana's reputation as an American playground. Meyer Lansky, one of the most powerful Mafia figures, paid Batista millions of dollars a year for a monopoly on the casino business. The legacy of these days still flickers in hotels such as the Nacional and the Riviera (see pages 86 and 199), for a time the world's biggest casino hotel outside Las Vegas, and the Capri (Calle 21 between N and O), built by "Lucky" Luciano and run by U.S. actor George Raft. Havana's mafia last met in the Capri's penthouse suite.

Vedado's heart is **La Rampa▶** (The Ramp), which refers to Calle 23 from Calle L down to the sea. Lined with hideous buildings that house airline and travel agency offices, the press center, and the sugar ministry, Vedado's main artery may lack beauty, but it makes up for it in its dynamic buzz. The grid of leafy streets north and west, occupied by fading, ornate villas, is largely residential.

▶▶▶ Cementerio de Colón
(Columbus Cemetery) 77A1
Main entrance at Zapata and Calle 12
Open: 7–6 daily. Admission charge: inexpensive
In this serene and enormous city of creamy marble, monuments and tombs dating from the 1860s vie for attention in size and elaboration. Ones to look for include the Pantheon of the Revolutionary Armed Forces, the *Granma* memorial carved with a storm-battered boat, and a modernist structure commemorating the 1957 attack on the presidential palace. Mourners arrive on bikes to lay flowers at graves, and your visit might well coincide with a colorful funeral cortège. Many supplicants with illnesses and childbirth problems pray at "La Milagrosa" ("the Miracle Woman"). Under her statue lie a mother and child who died in childbirth in 1901. They were buried side by side, but when the coffin was opened the baby was found in the mother's arms. A map locating well-known tombs is available at the entrance.

▶ Museo Abel Santamaría 77C4
Apartment No. 603 (6th floor) at No. 164 calles O and 25
Open Mon–Fri 10–4; Sat 9–1. Admission charge: inexpensive
This one-bedroom flat in a rundown apartment block is furnished as it was when owned by Abel Santamaría, a revolutionary friend of Castro's in the early 1950s. You can lie on Castro's bed and sit on his toilet.

▶▶ Museo de Artes Decorativas 77A3
Calle 17 No. 502 between calles D and E
Open: Wed–Sun 10–5. Admission charge: moderate
This ostentatious mansion epitomizes individual wealth in prerevolutionary Havana. Completed in 1927, remodeled in the 1930s, and taken over by the state in the 1960s, it contains fabulous set-piece rooms, each furnished in a particular style, from Louis XIV to Asian. The highlight is the camp pink marble, art-deco bathroom. On weekends there are often classical concerts.

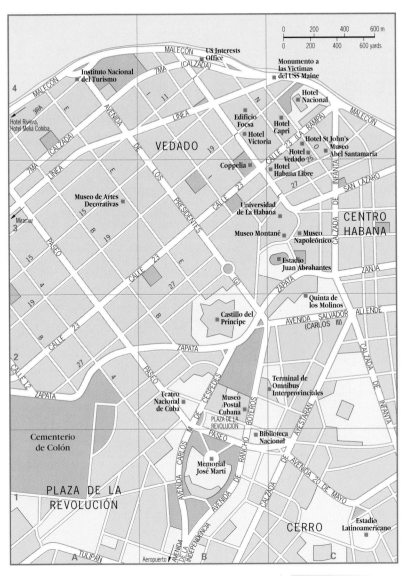

▶▶ Museo Napoleónico   77C3

San Miguel No. 1159 at Ronda
Open: Tue–Sat 10–5:30; Sun 9–12:30. Admission charge:
inexpensive

Built in the late 1920s in the style of a Florentine
Renaissance palace, this mansion, together with its
contents, was appropriated by the state in 1960 when its
owner, a millionaire sugar baron, fled the country.
Included in a treasure trove of French antiques is a fascinating collection of Napoleonic memorabilia: a plethora of
portraits and busts, the emperor's death mask, his trademark felt hat, a tooth, and even a lock of hair. What may
be the largest collection of books on Napoleon anywhere
lines the paneled library.

Views over Vedado
Head for the
restaurant/bar at the
summit of the Edificio
Focsa at calles 17 and M
(many Russians used to
live in this ugly tower block
when Cuba was in the
Soviet Union's pocket), or
the top of the Capri Hotel
or the Habana Libre, a
23-story eyesore that
was Castro's headquarters
in 1959.

U.S. interests
On the Malecón west of the Hotel Nacional stands a monument to the victims of the USS *Maine*. According to a plaque added in 1961, they "were sacrificed by voracious imperialism to gain control of Cuba": the U.S. is suspected of having blown up its own ship in 1898 to provide an excuse to declare war on Spain (see page 43). The only part of Havana now under American control is the U.S. Interests Section, the unmistakable Fort Knox complex a few hundred yards west. Comically combative posters are erected nearby to taunt its occupants (see page 21).

Changing ideals
From the 1920s to 1950s, Havana University was a fulcrum in Cuba's political life. Nowadays, students are more interested in studying English or Western economics: 1996 was the first year for two decades when no degree course in Marxist philosophy was offered.

▶ **Quinta de los Molinos** 77C2

Main entrance off Avenida Salvador Allende
Open: Tue–Sat 9–5; Sun 9–1. Admission charge: inexpensive
This country house, built in the 1830s as the governor's summer residence, later became the home of the hero of the independence wars, General Máximo Gómez. While it displays a few of Gómez's possessions, architecturally it is unremarkable. However, the surrounding gardens, which are used by practicing musicians, are atmospheric.

▶▶ **Plaza de la Revolución** 77B2

This bleak square is the hub of the Cuban government. Big political rallies are held in its vast open space. The 1950s buildings around the edges, with all the aesthetic appeal of giant air-conditioning units, include the Ministry of the Interior (covered by a monumental image of Che) and the Ministry of Communications.

Towering 466-feet high over a statue of José Martí in classic pensive pose is a singularly ugly, star-shaped obelisk. Inside, the **Memorial José Martí**▶▶ (*Open* Mon–Sat 9–5. *Admission charge* moderate) is a sophisticated new exhibition outlining the Cuban hero's life. Note how great efforts are made to promote Castro as the inheritor of Martí's vision. An elevator takes you up for a panorama of Havana and the only chance to peek at Cuba's seat of government and the Communist Party headquarters.

▶ **Universidad de la Habana** 77C3

The country's top university has been located on this hill since 1902. Its neoclassical courtyard, a good place to meet students, holds the Museo de Ciencias Naturales, full of stuffed animals, and the Museo Antropológico Montané (both *Open* Mon–Fri 9–12, 1–4. *Admission charge* inexpensive), given over to pre-Columbian artifacts.

Che's handsome features loom large over the Plaza de la Revolución

Miramar

Before the revolution, wealthy Habaneros used to live in the grand houses that characterize Miramar. It is still an exclusive district, but many of the mansions have been converted into offices for foreign companies and, along the main thoroughfare Avenida 5, embassies. Don't miss the Russian Embassy, a bizarre building of monumental proportions between calles 62 and 64. Although Miramar has only a few sights, it is worth driving through it to appreciate how those who prosper under communist Cuba live.

▶▶   Maqueta de la Habana   IBCB3
Calle 28 between avenidas 1 and 3
Open: Tue–Sat 9:30–5:30. Admission charge: moderate
This enormous model of Havana, at a scale of 1:1000, measures some 258 square feet. However, the project, begun in 1989, is still incomplete. The buildings are colored according to their period: ochre for colonial, yellow for the republic, cream for postrevolution, and white for proposed new projects and national monuments. Financial limitations mean buildings are made of cedar strips from cigar boxes and cardboard, and trees and shrubbery from sponge. The model's neatness stands in stark contrast to the decrepitude of the real city.

▶   Marina Hemingway   IBCA3
Off Avenida 5, about 4 miles west of Miramar
Named after Cuba's adopted writer, the marina has a few restaurants, dollar shops, and hotels, but really the only draw is the deep-sea fishing, sailing, or diving (tel: 241150).

▶   Museo del Ministerio del Interior   IBCB3
Avenida 5 and Calle 14
Open: Tue–Sat 9–5. Admission charge: inexpensive
In a typical old Miramar mansion, this museum honors the work of Cuba's police, firemen and, most interestingly, the much-feared Ministry of the Interior (MININT for short). Considerable space is devoted to all the failed "counterrevolutionary" plots against the island.

Shopping in Miramar
Many Habaneros think of Miramar as the place to go shopping—if you've got dollars, that is. There is no evidence of Cuba's much-heralded social equality in the Centro Comercial at Avenida 5 and Calle 42, where fat cats spend loads of money on everything from sofas to the best olive oil while beggars plead for a few cents change. You used to need a foreign passport to purchase anything at Cuba's best-stocked supermarket, the Diplomercado at Avenida 3 and Calle 70, but now anyone with greenbacks can do so. By Cuban standards a veritable pleasure palace, it is a good place to stock up on provisions if you are spending any time in Cuba.

HIV sanatoriums
Los Cocos, in southern Havana's Santiago de las Vegas, was the first sanatorium created for HIV-positive Cubans, opening in the mid-1980s. Initially Cubans were effectively incarcerated in these sanatoriums (there is now one in every province), with the government justifying such a measure on the grounds that AIDS infection in Cuba is relatively low. Now those who are HIV-positive are not forced into sanatoriums (though they are "encouraged"), are free to visit home when they choose, and can become outpatients. However, many choose to stay because the living conditions in the sanatoria are much better than outside.

The bas-relief of Lenin was erected when old-style communism was in favor

Southern Havana

This clutch of attractions near the airport makes for an alternative half-day's sightseeing. Though busy on weekends with locals, they are deserted on weekdays. To reach them you really need your own transportation (and a good map—the road systems are complicated) or a taxi.

▶ **ExpoCuba** IBCC1
15.5 miles south of the center in Arroyo Naranjo district
Open: Wed–Sun 9–5. Admission charge: inexpensive
This is a communist version of a theme park, with massive pavilions devoted to Cuba's achievements in such fields as energy, construction, and technology. The central hall showcases each of Cuba's regions, with a barrage of statistics on infant mortality rates and patients per doctor. There are also a few fairground attractions.

▶ **Jardín Botánico Nacional** IBCC1
Opposite ExpoCuba (see above)
Open: Wed–Sun 8:30–4:45. Admission charge: moderate
This giant, rather sparse botanical garden is best explored by car. It is divided into three areas: Cuban vegetation, plants from other parts of the world such as Africa and Asia, and special collections such as palms. The most picturesque section, located at the far side of the garden, is the Japanese Garden, with rockeries and tiled pavilions set around a lake.

▶ **Parque Lenin** IBCC2
12 miles south of the center in Arroyo Naranjo
This vast park of rolling meadows opened in 1972, but financial constraints mean many attractions are now rarely open. Most places of interest lie just south of an artificial lake. They include a rodeo (shows once a month), a huge bas-relief of Lenin, and a monument to Celia Sánchez, Castro's longtime companion, in a pretty glade. Nearby, the extraordinary restaurant Las Ruinas (see page 203) is worth a look even if you don't want a drink or a meal. North of the lake, a jolly fairground where you can go horseback riding and drink *guarapo*, or sugarcane juice, served from traditional cane-crushing machines, is up and running most weekends. The nearby serious equestrian center, Club Hípico Iberamericano, rents horses by the hour (tel: 441058).

LENIN FUE DESDE EL PRIMER INSTANTE NO SOLO UN TEORICO DE LA POLITICA, SINO UN HOMBRE DE ACCION UN HOMBRE DE PRACTICA REVOLUCIONARIA CONSTANTE E INCESANTE   FIDEL

Hemingway and Cuba

■ Having written about Cuba and lived on the island for much of his life, the boozing, action man of 20th-century literature is regarded by Cubans as one of their own, often referred to as Ernesto or Papa. There is, however, no evidence to support the government's claim that Hemingway ever endorsed the revolution. ■

His life in Cuba On and off throughout the 1930s, Ernest Hemingway stayed in the Hotel Ambos Mundos in Old Havana. In 1939, aged 40, he moved to Finca La Vigía in Havana's suburbs, where he mostly lived until 1960. Much of his time was spent deep-sea fishing on his yacht, *El Pilar*. This he described as "utterly satisfying as a sport, a living, a spectacle, and a form of exercise." After the revolution, Hemingway returned to the U.S. and, in 1961, he killed himself with a shotgun in Idaho.

The Hemingway Trail
There are half a dozen shrines to the writer in and around Havana:
Room 511 in the Hotel Ambos Mundos (see panel, page 66), El Floridita (see panel, page 88) and La Bodeguita del Medio (see panel, page 89), Museo Hemingway, and Cojímar (see pages 82–83).

81

Novels based in Cuba *The Old Man and the Sea* (1952), a Cuban fisherman's titanic struggle with a big fish, won Hemingway the Nobel Prize for literature in 1954. *To Have and Have Not* (1937), possibly his least successful novel, tells of a sailor who runs drugs and revolutionaries from Cuba to the Florida Keys in the 1930s. *Islands in the Stream*, his last, unfinished and highly autobiographical work, published posthumously in 1970, is set during World War II, partly off the Archipiélago de Camagüey, where Hemingway hunted German U Boats (see panel page 144), and partly in Havana. One long scene is set in his regular haunt, El Floridita (see panel page 88).

Top: a sculpture at Marina Hemingway evoking The Old Man and the Sea
Above: Fidel Castro meeting Hemingway in 1960

His attitude to the revolution Despite photographs showing Hemingway hobnobbing with Castro at the annual marlin fishing tournament in 1960, Hemingway never made any commitment to the new regime. When asked in 1957 what he thought was going to happen to Cuba, he hedged his bets: "My answer to such questions is bound to be that I live here." Leaving Cuba in 1960, he said to a journalist: "We are going to win, we Cubans are going to win. I'm not a Yankee, you know"—words which have been interpreted every which way.

Drive **East of Havana**

See highlighted route on map on inside back cover.

This circular route, roughly 47 miles long, takes in Hemingway's home and Cojímar, the template fishing village in his novel *The Old Man and the Sea*, plus two important centers for Afro-Cuban religion and the best beaches near Havana. Route finding is tricky: get the best map you can.

Leave Old Havana from the western side of the port, then head southeast to San Fransisco de Paula, a suburb 9 miles away, where you will find the **Museo Hemingway**▶▶ (*Open Mon–Sat 9–4; Sun 9–12:30. Admission charge* moderate), housed in the writer's lovely long-term home, Finca La Vigía, built in 1887. After his death in 1961, the house was donated to the state by his second wife, Mary Walsh. Full of Hemingway's possessions— thousands of books, bullfighting posters, stuffed trophies, a Picasso ceramic, his trademark visor placed on his pillow, and a stocked drinks table—it looks as if Papa has just popped into town for a daiquiri. Don't miss his study in the tower where he used to write standing up, and wander through the grounds to see his boat *El Pilar*. Note that you are not allowed to enter the house and may only peer through open windows and doors; if it's raining you can still visit, but the windows and doors are shut.

The pretty village of **Santa María del Rosario**▶, 4 miles southeast, boasts a magnificent church, founded in 1733, on its main square. Ask around and someone will find you the key. In the gloom you can see a host of gilded altars with baroque moldings and delicate paintings, plus a wonderful pulpit and *alfarje* ceiling.

Ancient, sprawling **Guanabacoa▶** is 6 miles north, with picturesque but rundown streets. Once a major slave center, the traditions of Afro-Cuban religions are as strong here as anywhere in Cuba: in 1995, there were even reports of child abduction for voodoo rites. The town has a number of fine colonial churches, where you may see locals praying at statues of Catholic/Santería saints (see pages 84–85). The **Museo Histórico de Guanabacoa▶▶**, two blocks west of the main square at Calle Martí No. 110, normally has a large and fascinating series of displays on Afro-Cuban religions, but for the next few years is likely to be closed. Just farther down Martí at No. 175, the **Bazar de Reproduciones Artisticas▶** *(Open* Mon–Sat 9:30–5:30) has a facsimile of Yemayá's shrine and rooms full of reproductions related to various *orishas*, or gods (many are for sale).

If you've got the Santería bug, hop across to **Regla▶** (see page 70), 2.5

Superb sands at Playas del Este

miles west. Otherwise, drive 4 miles north to **Cojímar▶**. The outskirts of the fishing village, from where thousands of Cubans set sail for Florida in 1994, have been heavily developed, but the waterfront is still attractive. A bust of Hemingway stands next to a cute 17th-century fort used as a coast guard post. Cojímar's most famous spot is **La Terraza▶** (see page 203), a waterside restaurant once frequented by Hemingway and now covered in pictures of him. Hemingway's boatman Gregorio Fuentes (see photo below), who reached 100 in 1997 and was the probable inspiration for the Old Man in *The Old Man and the Sea*, lunches here daily. For a few dollars, he will spout prorevolutionary dogma and let you take his photograph. After lunch, consider heading 9 mi east to the **Playas del Este▶**. While ghastly 1960s and '70s hotel complexes spoil the Eastern Beaches, an afternoon on the 6 mi of superb palm-fringed sands is enjoyable. The best, most peaceful beach is at Santa María del Mar. The town of Guanabo, just east, is much livelier, especially on weekends when lots of Habaneros come to party, but the beach is poorer here.

The return 12 mi journey to Havana passes Alamar, a community of endless tower blocks built by microbrigades of volunteers in the 1970s, and then the rotting sports stadiums erected for the 1991 Pan American Games. Before going through the tunnel under the harbor back to the city, you could stop off at Havana's **fortresses▶▶** (see page 70).

Hemingway's boatman, inspiration for **The Old Man and the Sea**

Religion in Cuba

■ **Around 85 percent of Cubans admit to some sort of adherence to African deities, most to the gods of Santería, a hybrid religion that mixes Roman Catholicism with African beliefs. Until recently, the state frowned on any form of worship in Cuba, but that is changing, and the Afro-Cuban culture is now promoted through museums, literature and organized trips.** ■

Principal *orishas*
• Ochún, goddess of love and rivers. Catholic equivalent: Virgen de la Caridad del Cobre (Cuba's patron saint). Color: yellow. Symbols: rocks, oars, rivers, fans.
• Yemayá, goddess of the sea. Catholic equivalent: Virgen de Regla (Havana's patron saint). Color: blue. Symbols: boats, the sun and moon.
• Changó, god of thunder, lightning, and fire. Catholic equivalent: Santa Bárbara. Colors: red and white. Symbols: double-headed axe, sword, cup, castle. Other orishas include: Obatalá (equivalent Our Lady of Mercy), goddess of peace and purity; Elegguá (or St. Anthony), god of good and evil; Babalú Ayé (or St. Lazarus), god of illness.

Orisha *dolls in their traditional colors*

Roman Catholicism The Catholic faith was never as strong in Cuba as in other Latin-American countries, mainly because the church was perceived to be an expression of the unwanted colonial government. Figures vary enormously, but about 5–10 percent of Cubans are practicing Catholics. Soon after the revolution, Castro accused the church of campaigning against the state. Places of worship were locked up, worshipers were sent to prison, priests were expelled from the island or left voluntarily, and religious holidays were banned.

Since the 1980s, greater tolerance has been shown. In 1991, for the first time, Catholics could be members of the Communist Party, and in 1992 Cuba changed its constitution to call itself a lay rather than atheist state. In 1997, Christmas was declared a public holiday for the first time since the 1960s, in anticipation of the first papal visit to communist Cuba, by Pope John Paul II, in January 1998. At masses attended by tens of thousands, the pope called for Catholic schools to be allowed again and attacked Cuba's record on abortion and human rights, but also, to Castro's relief, lambasted the U.S. embargo against the island.

Afro-Cuban religions When slaves from Africa came to Cuba, they naturally brought with them their beliefs, which were fostered in *cabildos*, or mutual aid societies. As the island was one of the last to abolish slavery and as the missionary movement here was weak, their religions—namely Palo Monte, Abakuá, and, above all, Santería, have

held stronger sway here than anywhere else in the Caribbean. Their rituals have had a fundamental influence on Cuban music, notably the rumba and conga.

The communist regime has begun to show more respect to the Afro-Cuban religions it once tried to undermine, and since the late 1980s there has been an especially large increase in popularity in Santería. Faced with severe material hardships, people have been looking for spiritual help. In the absence of basic medicines, they have also sought comfort from faith healers. Meanwhile, the state has started to promote the religions as a tourist attraction, opening up exhibitions once closed to foreigners and selling faux religious dolls in gift shops.

Santería By far the most widely practiced Afro-Cuban religion, Santería, also known as the Regla de Ocha, is a fusion of Yorubá beliefs from Nigeria and Roman Catholicism. Slaves intermingled their religion with Catholicism so they would go unhindered by the Spanish. The blending is so complete that it is often very difficult to establish where Catholicism ends and Santería begins.

Santería means "the cult of the saints": there are some 400 gods, called *orishas*, in its pantheon. Each orisha has a Catholic saint as its counterpart and has its own color, number, and symbols. *Babalawos*, high priests and spokesmen for the orishas, offer advice, using divination by means of pieces of coconut, shells, pebbles, and animal bones, and try to make people better. Propitiatory offerings are made at orishas' altars. Believers, called *santeros/santeras*, have to undergo rather gruesome initiation ceremonies. Orishas, or saints' days, are celebrated with fascinating fiestas, during which gods may possess santeros, who writhe about in a trance.

The Virgen de Regla being paraded on her saint's day (September 8)

Voodoo
Palo Monte, imported by Bantus from the Congo River basin, is the closest Cuban religion to witchcraft and voodoo. If someone wants to affect the destiny of another person, they obtain a piece of their clothing, or a nail clipping, hair, or skin, and stuff it in a doll in the victim's image. Two dolls are placed back to back to split up a couple. Abakuá, a secret all-male sect from Nigeria and Cameroon, is the most feared Afro-Cuban religion. A hundred years ago, an initiate, or *ñáñigo*, would have to kill the first passerby he met: half the murders in Havana in the 1960s were said to be associated with this group.

Accommodations

Resrvations

Book as far in advance as possible for accommodations in Old Havana, particularly in the winter months (high season). Elsewhere, you should always be able to find a room on short notice. Book accommodations from abroad for at least the first night or two: immigration officials at Havana's José Martí airport often harangue travelers who have not done so, forcing them to pay for accommodations before leaving the airport.

Cubans and hotels

Cubans are not allowed on their own into most of the hotels that tourists use—blatant apartheid some visitors find disquieting. If you treat locals to a drink or meal in a hotel, be aware that they may feel concerned that they are being overheard or watched by the authorities. On no account are Cubans allowed to visit foreigners' bedrooms.

Superb tilework in the Inglaterra

Havana is not a relaxing place. Choosing an appealing hotel where you can escape from the hubbub and wind down is the most important decision you will make when planning your visit to the city. See pages 198–199 for hotel phone numbers and addresses. You might also consider staying in a private home: see page 198.

Choosing your district Try to stay in Old Havana. In the last few years a half dozen historic hotels, all characterful enough to be sights in their own right, have been entirely revamped. Most places of interest lie within walking distance of these hotels, allowing you to go out for an hour or two, then come back for a bite to eat or a siesta.

As public transportation is virtually unusable, if you stay elsewhere in the city you will probably end up spending a small fortune on taxis. Visiting businesspeople tend to stay in Vedado, where the hotels, with a couple of notable exceptions, are lackluster places built in the 1950s. Nonetheless, after Old Havana, this is the next best district for vacationers to stay, as it is just a couple of miles from Old Havana and has plenty of vibrant street life right outside the door. Farther west along the coast, in Miramar, lies a clutch of large and often tawdry hotels, a long way from any action and only worth considering if you intend to spend a lot of time by the swimming pool. The Playas del Este, half an hour's drive east of downtown Havana, have fine sands but terrible accommodations: if you want time on the beach, visit for the day rather than stay here.

Big spenders The Meliá Cohiba, opened in 1995, is the city's only slick modern hotel that reaches international standards, but it is soulless. Most tourists are happier in the Nacional; built in 1930 in ocean liner proportions and ostentatiousness, it is worth a visit just to see its excessive chandeliered and tiled public rooms. For intimate luxury and personal service, choose the Santa Isabel; this, Old Havana's recent hotel conversion, is the former palace of the Count of Santovenia, with a magical courtyard and balconied bedrooms overlooking Plaza de Armas.

On a budget The cheapest way to stay in Havana is in a private room: for advice, see page 198. Really cheap hotels are pretty awful and few and far between. Most hard-up travelers head for the rather seedy Caribbean and Lido, close to Old Havana. Marginally more comfortable but twice the price are the Lincoln in Centro, and the St. John's and Vedado, both 1950s high-rises off La Rampa in Vedado. Given the scarcity of palatable budget lodgings, consider stretching your finances to pay for somewhere like the Deauville, where you will be unlucky not to bag a big sea-facing room. Considerably better, though hard to secure a booking, is the Convento de Santa Clara or Hostal Valencia. So magnificent is this latter colonial specimen that tour groups come every day simply to gawk at it.

Mid-priced hotels The choicest mid-range hotels are four Old Havana establishments. The only one not to have been recently restored, and therefore the cheapest and most colorful (if also the least comfortable and serving the worst food), is the oldest hotel in Cuba. Called the Inglaterra, it is at its best in its wonderful Spanish-tiled interior and three bars. Next up in price comes the Plaza, with far more appealing bedrooms. The Ambos Mundos, with similar rates and recently thoroughly and imaginatively overhauled, was built in 1918 and has Hemingway connections. More expensive and stylish is the Sevilla, where your extra dollars will secure you a better bedroom, a grand rooftop restaurant, and access to Old Havana's only swimming pool. Ask also about the Central Park, a reconstruction of a colonial building on the Parque Central due to open in 1998.

Havana hotel bests
• Best value: Hostal Valencia.
• Best pool: Sevilla.
• Best food: Meliá Cohiba.
• Best bedrooms: Santa Isabel.
• Best for magnificence: Nacional.
• Best for immersing in Havana's atmosphere: Inglaterra.

The Santa Isabel's palatial courtyard

Havana's most famous bar—la cuna, or cradle, of the daiquiri

El Floridita
This fancy tourist trap is *the* place to drink a daiquiri (150,000 are made here each year), even if it costs twice as much here as anywhere else in the city. Choose between the original—invented, it is claimed, by a barman called Constante in 1914—or Hemingway's own macho version (double rum, grapefruit juice, no sugar). An El Floridita regular, Papa features with friends (and Fidel) in photographs on the walls and as a bust (erected after he won his Nobel prize). His bar stool is roped off in the corner. In the formal restaurant behind the bar you can gorge yourself on seafood with El Gran Plato Hemingway.

Havana's eating and drinking scene has improved dramatically in recent years. At the beginning of the 1990s, aside from hotels there were only a handful of restaurants and bars worth visiting. Thanks to the massive growth in tourism and the legalization of private restaurants, or *paladares* (see page 34), all that has changed. For restaurant addresses, see pages 202–203.

Restaurants For a romantic dinner, head to Old Havana. The food may not be memorable in restaurants such as El Patio, D'Giovanni, Al Medina, and La Mina, but the setting certainly is, for each occupies a glorious colonial court-yard. For a splurge, take a taxi to Miramar for the city's priciest restaurants, such as La Cecilia, La Ferminia, and Tocororo. These sophisticated establishments (dress smartly) cater as much to embassy staff and business-people as to tourists.

Hotel dining The Meliá Cohiba's evening buffet (mountains of fruit and cheeses, lobster and roast beef) is the island's priciest and most lavish. Dishes such as *foie gras* appear in the Nacional's stunning chandeliered dining room; in the basement you will find good buffet dinners and a fast-food cafeteria. In Old Havana, the Sevilla provides decent buffets downstairs and a pricy à la carte menu in the dazzling Roof Garden Restaurant. The candlelit restaurant in the Santa Isabel is as elegant as any in the city. Less intimidating is the cozy, classy rooftop aerie at the Ambos Mundos.

Paladares Be sure to eat at least once in a *paladar*, or private restaurant, a unique Cuban experience. The invari-ably cheap food usually comprises tasty Creole fare. There are some paladares in Old Havana, but more (and generally better and less touristy ones) lie in the new city, where space for a dining room is at less of a premium. The most rewarding hunting ground is in Vedado around La Rampa and in the grid of streets to its west, where many paladares occupy the verandas of decaying neocolonial homes. You will be besieged with offers to lead you to any particular one you choose.

Cafés and bars In Old Havana, new drinking spots open virtually daily. But it is the well-established haunts that are worth rooting out. The following places all stay open 24 hours. The most popular tourist drinking holes, thanks to their prime locations and frequent live music, are El Patio's terrace bar on Plaza de la Catedral and the terraced cafés that make up La Mina, on the corner of Obispo and Plaza de Armas. For a greater mix of locals, head for the buzzing Café Paris (at San Ignacio and Obispo), which has live music as well as good cheap snacks, or sleepier Café O'Reilly, around the corner at O'Reilly No. 203, with a second-floor balcony to snoop from. Bar Monserrate (at Avenida de Bélgica and Obrapía) attracts a steamy young crowd, while Bar Dos Hermanos, by the port across the road from the ferry to Regla, is appealingly unfancy. In Vedado, for a drink in a historic waterside spot, visit the miniature 17th-century fort next to the tunnel to Miramar.

Hotel bars The Plaza, Sevilla, and Ambos Mundos all have atmospheric lobby or courtyard bars. They are, however, no match for the Inglaterra's rooftop bar, which is a lively nightspot with close-up views of the Gran Teatro, and its terrace bar facing the Parque Central, an ideal people-watching spot where a jazz orchestra sometimes plays. A more secluded Old Havana haunt is the Hostal Valencia's Bar Nostalgia, which also often features live jazz. In Vedado, stop by at the Meliá Cohiba for a smoke in its clublike cigar bar, and at the Nacional's bar for a bit of history: it is covered in photographs of former visitors, from John Wayne and Winston Churchill to mafia luminaries Meyer Lansky and Santos Trafficante.

La Bodeguita del Medio
La B del M translates as "the grocery store in the middle of the block"—which is all it was when it opened in 1942. In the 1950s, business from a nearby printing house turned it into a hangout for writers such as Nicolás Guillén, and international celebrities followed, from Nat King Cole to Brigitte Bardot. Many left their mark on the graffiti-ridden walls; Salvador Allende's reads "Cuba is free, Chile waits." Hemingway's sign above the cramped bar—"My mojito in La Bodeguita, my daiquiri in El Floridita"—is reckoned to be fake, erected to increase trade. Nonetheless, the *mojitos* are good, as is the Creole cuisine, if overpriced. Droves of tourists now replace the intellectuals.

89

La Bodeguita del Medio is more salubrious than its graffiti-covered walls might suggest

Trademark chandelier headdresses at the Tropicana

A few years ago, Havana had just a handful of appealing places to go after dark. It is still a long way from regaining its 1950s status as one of the world's most decadent capitals, but the city is gradually getting hotter, with more nightspots opening each year. Pinning down what's going on where and when can be difficult: word of mouth is your best bet, along with the *Cartelera* listings magazine. For low-key live music in an atmospheric bar, see recommendations on page 89. On weekend evenings consider doing what young Habaneros do and head for the Malecón with a bottle of rum.

Tropicana practicalities
The Tropicana (tel: 240110) is at Calle 72 No. 4504 at Calle 43 in the district of Marianao, about 2 miles south of Miramar. The show itself runs Tuesday to Sunday from 10 PM to 11:30 PM and then, after a 45-minute interval with dancing, there is a 20-minute finale, ending about 12:30. You can make arrangements through a travel agent from any hotel. When the cost of a taxi there and back has been taken into account, prices work out about the same as visiting independently. Rates vary depending on the view (the cheapest seats are by the bar), and there is a hefty surcharge for using a camera or video. The complex includes an expensive restaurant for dining before the show, and a disco that opens afterward.

The Tropicana Founded in 1939, this became possibly the world's most famous nightclub when Carmen Miranda, Nat King Cole, and Beny Moré performed here in the 1940s and 1950s. It is still one of the most spectacular cabarets imaginable. Set in a shady, open-air auditorium, the show, with over 200 dancers and a big band, manages to be both magical and the height of kitsch. Mulatta dancers wearing next to nothing or sequined costumes and giant plumed headdresses parade and perform to the whole gamut of Latin-American music. Afro-Cuban legends are reenacted, and even acrobatic acts are thrown in for good measure. Although it is by far the most expensive night out in Cuba, it is arguably worth it (see panel for practical details).

Other cabarets On a far smaller scale but cheaper, more centrally located than the Tropicana and still gaudily fun are the Cabaret Parisien at the Hotel Nacional in Vedado (performances at 10:30 and 12:15 nightly), and, just up the road, the tackier Salón Rojo at the Hotel Capri (Calle 21 between N and O).

Live bands If you want to hear (and dance to) the best contemporary Cuban music, skip the cabarets. Recently, a number of atmospheric venues have opened where you may well catch Cuba's top bands and singers, such as Los Van Van, Isaac Delgado, and El Médico de la Salsa. The most famous and liveliest spot is the Palacio de la Salsa at the Hotel Riviera (Paseo and Malecón, Vedado), where groups perform from midnight onward except on Fridays. Expect a heady atmosphere, with plenty of Cubans drinking and dancing in the aisles. Smaller and by comparison slightly sterile is the Casa de La Música, a former American social club at Avenida 35 and Calle 20 in Miramar; again, bands perform from around midnight. Also worth checking out are the Café Cantante in the Teatro Nacional at Plaza de la Revolución, and La Cecilia, set in a pretty garden in Miramar (see Restaurants, page 203). Irakere, Cuba's most famous jazz band, seems to have made the Bar Turquino, at the top of the Hotel Habana Libre (La Rampa and L, Vedado), its home on weekend evenings; on weekdays this venue has cabaret shows.

Discos Havana's discos play a mix of *salsa* and Western pop music and liven up only after midnight. Currently the chicest and most popular is Aché in the Hotel Melía Cohiba (Paseo and Malecón, Vedado). Next most sophisticated are Havana Club at the Hotel Comodoro (Calle 84 and Avenida 1, Miramar) and Ipanema at the Hotel Copacabana (Avenida 1 between calles 44 and 46, Miramar). The closest mainstream disco to Old Havana is in the Hotel Deauville (Galiano and Malecón, Centro), and is cheap, sweaty, and very crowded.

High culture The most prestigious performance venue, especially for ballet, is the Gran Teatro (see page 73), with six performance salons; apart from ballet, it also has classical concerts, opera, and theater—the week's events are posted by the main entrance. Running a close second is the modern Teatro Nacional at Paseo and Calle 39, Plaza de la Revolución. If you understand Spanish, it is worth finding out what's on at the city's half-dozen well-established theatrical venues. Classical concerts are held most Friday evenings in the Iglesia de San Fransisco de Asis (see page 68).

La Maison
Every evening at 10PM a fashion show is held in the garden of Havana's only fashion house. Hunks and belles show off everything from swimming costumes to *haute couture,* and although it's hard to take the whole thing seriously, it's good for a laugh.
La Maison occupies a fine Miramar mansion (at Calle 16 and Avenida 7) that was owned by a sugar baron before the revolution. Inside, amid marble and antiques, are half a dozen boutiques selling designer clothes and jewelry.

91

Irakere, Cuba's most famous jazz group

A tourist supermarket
The best place for a one-stop souvenir shop is the Palacio de la Artesanía (daily 9–7) in Old Havana at calles Tacón and Cuba. A giant mansion built by the mayor of Havana in 1780, it stocks a good selection of CDs and tapes, rum, cigars, coffee, and T-shirts.

Farmers' markets
The fruit, vegetable, and meat markets in the Barrio Chino (see page 75) and near the train station (see page 69) are fascinating places, worth visiting even if you don't want to purchase anything.

There is more worth buying in Havana now than a few years ago, and more for sale here than elsewhere in Cuba, but shopping remains a better spectator sport than active pastime. Getting to grips with which shops sell in dollars, pesos, or only on ration cards can be absorbing. Hotel stores stock basic essentials and also great black-and-white postcards of Cuba's revolutionary heroes.

Arts and crafts The large crafts market on Plaza de la Catedral (see page 62) sells junk and countless portraits of Che Guevara, but also decent paintings, maracas, and palm-frond hats. Another big touristy market (Tue–Sun 8–6) is on the Malecón at Calle D, Vedado. Private hole-in-the-wall arts and crafts stalls are cropping up all over Old Havana, a number along Calle Obispo. La Travesía (daily 8–8), on Calle O'Reilly opposite La Floridita, specializes in Santería objects. The Hotel Meliá Cohiba (see page 199) sells charming miniature copies of Old Havana mansions.

Rum and cigars La Casa del Ron (daily 10–7) above El Floridita on Calle Obispo in Old Havana, and La Taberna del Galeón off the southeast corner of Plaza de Armas, both sell a vast selection of rums, and have tasting bars. The Partagás cigar factory (see page 75) has the best cigar selection, along with the Hotel Meliá Cobiha.

Books, music, and maps Most foreign language books sold in Cuba are political tracts. For a cultural selection, try the Palacio del Segundo Cabo or stallholders in Plaza de Armas, and ARTEX at La Rampa and Calle L, Vedado. This store also stocks a good collection of CDs and tapes of Cuban music, as does Miramar's Casa de la Música (see page 91). Some department stores along San Rafael in Centro sell old LPs. Cuba's best map shop is El Navegante, at Calle Mercaderes No. 115 in Old Havana.

Palm-frond hats— souvenirs made before your eyes in the crafts market in Plaza de la Catedral

Information sources Havana has no proper tourist offices. Tourist desks in hotels are affiliated to Cuban travel agencies, so treat their information skeptically: their purpose is to sell you tours. Often hotel reception desks and local people are more help for such matters as independent travel or nightlife. Remember, however, that many Habaneros are on the make; for example, anyone who leads you to private rooms or restaurants is probably hoping for a commission. The free weekly listings magazine *Cartelera*, and the weekly business-oriented *Opciones*, are useful. Go to La Rampa in Vedado for airline and travel agency offices and major banks.

Transportation Havana is huge: Old Havana is the only area compact enough to get around on foot. City buses, many converted from articulated trucks and called *camellos*, or camels, because of their two humps, are normally horrifically overcrowded, so tourists almost invariably travel by taxi. Official, metered, dollar taxis wait outside hotels and other establishments. Panataxi's rates are the lowest (tel: 813113, 813257, 813265). Peso taxis and private cars (frequently Cadillacs) are often breaking the law by offering lifts to tourists, but their drivers still pester passersby for business: agree a rate before setting off. If you are not met by a tour bus at José Martí airport, the only sensible way to travel the 15.5 miles to the city center is by taxi.

It is best not to have a rental car in Havana, as security is a real headache. Few hotels have private parking, and the likelihood of having the car vandalized and/or its contents stolen, especially at night, is very high. Presently, the only way to rent a bike is from a local: if you do (or if you bring your own bike from abroad) use the ubiquitous *parqueos*, or garages, to keep it safe. Hundreds of *bicitaxis*, or bicycle rickshaws, roam Old Havana offering lifts for a dollar.

A hump-backed city bus, called a camello

City tours
Half-day tours whizz around Vedado, along the Malecón, and to the Plaza de La Revolución by minibus, as well as visiting Old Havana on foot, focusing on Plaza de la Catedral and Plaza de Armas. Book at any hotel's tourist desk.

Crime
Security is a greater problem in Havana than anywhere else in Cuba, and it is getting worse. Crimes are rarely violent, but *carteristas* (pickpockets and bag snatchers) are common. Be careful, especially after dark, anywhere in Old Havana, particularly south of Obispo, and also in Centro immediately west of the Prado, and on the Malecón. The best police station for tourist problems is at Dragones and Agramonte, near the Capitolio. In any emergency, contact Asistur (see page 188).

WESTERN CUBA

REGION HIGHLIGHTS ◄ ◄ ◄ ◄ ◄

The beautiful and mesmerizing Valle de Viñales

WESTERN CUBA

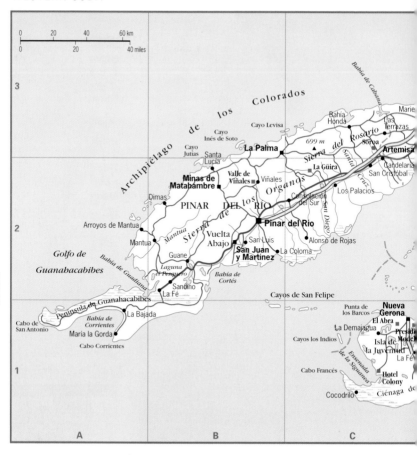

Itineraries
Viñales—west from Havana—is worth a couple of nights' stay. Allow half a day for Pinar del Río city, and if possible an extra day or two for venturing farther afield. You could return to Havana via the slow but scenic coastal route. East from Havana, Matanzas deserves half a day, Cárdenas a couple of hours, and the only obvious base is Varadero. All sights on the Península de Zapata to the south can be visited in a day; bird watchers should stay longer. Unless you are a diver, the Isla de la Juventud warrants two days maximum, or makes for an offbeat day-trip on a flight from Havana.

Western Cuba Ranging from the unforgettable tobacco-rich landscape of Viñales to the brash colossus of a resort of Varadero and the swamplands of the Zapata, western Cuba is the most varied part of the island. The change of pace as you leave Havana is abrupt. Like most of Cuba, the western provinces are thoroughly rural and unmodernized: vultures wheel over *bohíos*, or thatched peasant dwellings, and settlements are typically sleepy, dilapidated agricultural centers. Save for horses, bikes, and open trucks laden with workers, there is little traffic: even the six-lane autopista, compared to an electric wire running through the island in the early 1960s, is eerily empty, as though someone has switched the current off.

Thanks to the autopista, western Cuba is very accessible. It can whisk you westward from Havana down to Pinar del Río or eastward down to the Zapata in little over two hours. Likewise, you can speed along the north coast's dual carriageway from Havana to Matanzas in an hour, and on to Varadero in 90 minutes. You can therefore visit almost everywhere covered in this chapter on day trips from Havana (though the day may be a very long one in some cases). But to explore more thoroughly, you should tour the region at a gentle pace, allowing at least a week to do so.

A cigar and wide-brimmed hat are necessary accoutrements in western Cuba

Time on the beach
For creature comforts, choose either the huge resort of Varadero, where sophisticated hotel complexes line the country's longest, most highly touted beach, or the vacation island of Cayo Largo, which is at its best in Playa Sirena, a magical strip of sand reached by boat. If you are looking for a few-frills Robinson Crusoe experience, consider tiny Cayo Levisa. The Zapata's beaches, Playa Larga and Playa Girón, are not in the same league as any of the above, but are decent enough for a day's sunning and swimming.

Biological warfare
In 1997, the Cuban government accused the United States at the United Nations of carrying out a "biological attack" against the island. It claimed a U.S. crop duster flying over Matanzas Province released a plague of tiny, juice-sucking bugs that have adversely affected vegetable crops. The U.S. denied the allegation, and some commentators suggest it was merely an attempt by Cuba to justify food shortages. Over the last three decades, Cuba has also accused the U.S. of spreading other crop and animal diseases, such as swine fever and blue mold, and of introducing an outbreak of dengue fever to the island.

Pinar del Río Province The big draw in the crooked finger of land pointing west of Havana is the scenery, some of the most beguiling in Cuba. Whereas the greater part of the island is covered in sugarcane fields, here the prime crop is tobacco. It is generally grown in small holdings using preindustrial farming methods such as oxen and plowshares. The prime destination for visitors is the Valle de Viñales, an extraordinarily beautiful landscape of limestone knolls slumbering amid tobacco fields. A wonderfully serene place that needs appreciating slowly, it is ideal for recuperating after the hassle of Havana.

The *autopista* from Havana down to Pinar del Río, the province's colorful capital, runs through dull plains but alongside two lush mountain ranges, the Sierra de los Organos and Sierra del Rosario (designated a UNESCO Biosphere Reserve), which offer a number of alluring stop-offs in its foothills. First is Moka, an imaginative new hotel and ecotourism center (see page 199) by modern Las Terrazas, with picturesque ruins of a 19th-century coffee plantation nearby. Soon after comes Soroa, with its famous orchid garden, and farther west La Güira, an atmospheric but run-down estate dating from colonial times that is now termed a national park.

Few tourists except cigar aficionados and divers venture west of Pinar del Río. Those who do are treated to the absorbing Vuelta Abajo countryside west of the provincial capital, where the world's best tobacco grows, en route to Cuba's westernmost tip, the wild and forested Península de Guanahacabibes. Likewise, few except those heading for the beach at Cayo Levisa make it north of Viñales, which is a pity, because the rolling countryside of tobacco fields and *bohíos* drenched in bougainvillea is delightful.

Archipiélago de los Canarreos A group of 350 islands lies off western Cuba's southern shores. The two largest islands are very different from each other, and are both something of an acquired taste. The Isla de la Juventud, or Isle of Youth, sounds like a place from William Golding's *Lord of the Flies*, but turns out to have taken its name from Castro's costly efforts to contribute to Third World education. The diving here is Cuba's best, but otherwise the island, with uninteresting scenery and few accessible good beaches, is disappointing. Nonetheless, it is a refreshingly unhassled backwater. By contrast Cayo Largo, thanks to its gorgeous beaches, is firmly on the tourist map. However, apart from some exotic wildlife, it is a sterile place with little else of interest.

Matanzas Province In the mid-19th century this part of Cuba produced over half the country's sugar, and the flat, monotonous plains across the province's center are still covered in vast sugarcane fields, as well as giant citrus fruit plantations. Interest is concentrated along the coasts. Sprawled along the Península de Hicacos (the northernmost point in Cuba), Varadero is insulated from Cuba's economic woes and is thus unlike anywhere else on the island. Indeed, much of this huge resort is so characterless it could be transplanted elsewhere in the world without looking particularly out of place. Although you will learn more about Cuba by reading a good book than by

staying in Varadero's mushrooming rash of all-inclusive hotels, there is no disputing the quality of its endless beach.

Just down the road from Varadero but remarkably untouched by tourism, Matanzas and Cárdenas deliver sharp doses of everyday Cuban reality, namely lines, little food, and evocatively decrepit old buildings. If you are based in Varadero and go on no other excursion, at least spend an hour or two wandering the streets of these towns, or you will end up with a totally warped impression of Cuba. Cárdenas has more atmosphere, Matanzas more sights.

Two hours' drive south from Varadero, the Península de Zapata is shaped like a shoe, hence its name. It is a vast *ciénaga*, or swamp, some 99 miles across. Much is a limited-access national park, preserving 170 species of migratory birds and other wildlife. Most visitors come on day trips, unless they are staying at Playa Larga and Playa Girón, for although the area is interesting, there is little to keep you longer.

Time has stood still in Matanzas's Museo Farmaceutico

Pinar del Río Province

►►► Valle de Viñales 96B2

Viñales Valley is like nowhere else in the world. Giant limestone outcrops coated in thick vegetation, called *mogotes*, rise sheer above a valley floor of russet-colored earth and a patchwork of small *vegas*, or tobacco plantations. The scenery looks at its best between January and March, when tobacco leaves grow to the size of dinner plates before being picked and hung in A-shaped barns, covered in shaggy dried palm fronds. This is virtually a preindustrial society, where cigar-chewing *campesinos* in wide-brimmed hats plow with oxen and frequently get around on homemade and horse-pulled wooden sledges.

Day excursions leave from Havana and Varadero, but do try to stay a night or longer at one of the very appealing and inexpensive hotels detailed on page 199; both have mesmerizing valley views and alluring swimming pools (Los Jazmines wins on both fronts). Only thus can you appreciate the scenery at its loveliest—in the early morning, when a light trail of mist often lies over the vegas and winds around the mogotes, and in the soft evening twilight. Staying over also gives you time to wander through the fields and meet the overwhelmingly friendly

A karst region
The mogotes are all that remain of a limestone plateau which, owing to the dissolving effect of underground rivers, collapsed in the Jurassic period 160 million years ago (effectively the mogotes acted as columns supporting the plateau roof). The erosion-formed valley is called a karst region, named after a similar area along Croatia's Dalmatian coast. Comparable formations exist in a few other parts of the world, the Guangxi region of southern China being the best known.

Farmers still till their precious land with oxen

locals, who are only too happy to have their photograph taken and may well ply you with fruit, coffee, and cigars (for which you should offer some gift in return).

Viñales town►► This serene rural community, hardly larger than a village, has a spruce arcaded, pine-lined main street and a little square with a fetching church. Down dusty side streets, goats and pigs are tethered to thatched, clapboard bungalows. Come evening, owners sit in His and Hers rocking chairs on immaculate verandas watching the sun disappear as the sky turns to a deep violet.

Mural de la Prehistoria►► (*Admission charge* inexpensive). This bizarre, monumental mural, 393 feet high by 590 feet wide, covers one of a number of mogotes that form a beautiful amphitheater 2.5 miles west of Viñales town. Commissioned by Castro in 1961 and created by a student of Mexican artist Diego Rivera, with the help of numerous painters who dangled on ropes to carry out the task, it depicts evolution's progress from ammonite to *homo sapiens*.

Cueva del Indio► (*Open* daily 9–5. *Admission charge* moderate). The mogotes are riddled with caves and subterranean river systems, one of which, 3 miles north of Viñales town, can be explored on a short and rather anti-climactic boat trip. The cave was once an Indian refuge and cemetery; more recently, the boat was stolen by locals trying to flee to Florida. Another nearby cave has somewhat irreverently been turned into a disco.

►► Cayo Levisa 96B3

Just 2.5 miles long and a few hundred feet wide, this key amounts to no more than a strip of dreamy white sand and mangrove thickets. The accommodations (see page 199) are overpriced and far from luxurious but are adequately comfortable. Aside from the beach, entertainment is limited to floating around in a boat. Most visitors are Italians on package trips, but you can book independently; transfers are available from Havana. From Viñales, which is the nearest place of interest, it is a very pleasant hour-long, 31-miles drive to the departure point for the island, a marina 13 miles northeast of La Palma. A boat makes the 30-minute crossing (*Charge* expensive) daily at 11 AM, returning at 5 PM. You need your passport.

► Península de Guanahacabibes 96A1

This flat forest, the last refuge for Indians escaping the Spanish conquest, has been designated a UNESCO Biosphere Reserve: you must pay to enter (*Admission charge* expensive). There are superb beaches on Bahía de Corrientes, where you will also find the simple Hotel María La Gorda (see page 199). The hotel's name translates as Fat Mary: legend has it that pirates arrived here from Venezuela with an amply proportioned woman; they left her here, trading her body for water. Most people now come for the diving: the underwater world is said to be nearly as exciting as that off the Isla de la Juventud, but far fewer divers explore its 50 sites, some of them just a couple of minutes by boat from the shore.

The Mural de la Prehistoria is one of the island's stranger sights

101

La Casa del Veguero
One tobacco smallholding just south of Viñales town has recently been turned into a tourist attraction. It is run by a wizened *veguero*, or tobacco planter, whom everyone calls El Niño (the Kid). Between tobacco barn and bungalow, the state has erected a restaurant and gift shop, selling T-shirts emblazoned with El Niño's handsome features. While he finds this amusing and admits to making plenty of dollars posing for photographs, he reminisces wistfully about his former, simpler life, not least because now that so much time is taken up entertaining visitors he has to cultivate his tobacco very early and very late in the day.

Guava rum

The local tipple is a concoction of rum, spices, and guayabita, a wild type of guava that grows in the region. It is made in the Fábrica Casa Garay (*Open* Mon–Fri 8–4:30), four blocks south of Pinar del Río's main street on Isabel Rubio. The factory has a shop where you can taste and purchase the two versions produced, the sweet Guayabita Liqueur and dry Guayabita Seca. In truth, both taste better in Cuba than back home.

▶ **Pinar del Río** 96B2

With a population of 125,000, western Cuba's regional capital is the only big town west of Havana. As such it is a bustling agricultural center, its streets sometimes virtually jammed with horse-and-carts laden with country produce. Most tourists, understandably, press on to Viñales rather than dawdling long, but if you like provincial town life Pinar del Río, being reasonably well served with hotels and restaurants, is worth considering as a base for exploring the area. All that mars the atmosphere are the persistent kids on bikes who pester any tourist traffic.

The *autopista* becomes the main street, José Martí, lined with a wonderful array of neoclassical buildings with fluted pillars and elaborate cornicing and capitals. Though most are badly decayed, many are gaily painted shocking pink or livid green; gaudy carts touting iced drinks and cakes complete the picture.

The most riotous building, at the eastern end of José Martí at No. 202, is the early 20th-century **Palacio Guasch▶**. Coated with excessive decorative devices, it houses the **Museo de Ciencias Naturales** (*Open* Tue–Sat 9–4:30; Sun 8–11:30. *Admission charge* inexpensive). It is full of stuffed examples of Cuban species such as a *jutía* (a large rat regarded locally as a culinary delicacy), plus *polymitas* (colored snail shells) and butterflies.

A five-minute stroll along the main street brings you to the **Museo Provincial** (*Open* Mon, Wed–Sat 8–4; Sun 9–1. *Admission charge* inexpensive) at No. 58. On show is the first motorized vehicle used in town (a fire engine made in Britain in 1894) and the guitar of locally born Enrique Jorrín, inventor of the *chachachá*. Next door, the Teatro Milanés is under restoration but is a late-colonial gem, made entirely of wood.

Just south of the main street's western end, at Maceo No. 157, is a **cigar factory▶▶** (*Open* Mon–Fri 7:30–4:30; Sat 7:30–11:30. *Admission charge* moderate). It is tiny, but one of Cuba's most attractive. Here they make just *vegueros*, or coarse cigars, which are not exported. Buy them, plus the top brands, in the sophisticated cigar shop.

Cotton-candy contours on Pinar del Río's main street

Soroa's waterfall—an ideal place to cool off

► **Soroa** 96C3

In the foothills of the lush Sierra del Rosario 4 miles north of the autopista and about 43 miles southwest of Havana, this little resort is worth an hour's break on the journey between the capital and Pinar del Río. The hotel complex is lackluster, but a 547-yard path through the jungle leads to a lovely 66-foot-high waterfall cascading into a pool deep enough for bathing. The main attraction, however, is the orchid garden (*Open* daily 8–11:30, 1–3:30; guided tours every half hour. *Admission charge* moderate). Founded in 1943 by a lawyer from the Canary Islands, it is said to contain 700 types of orchid, as well as epiphytes (non-parasitic species that grow on other plants), begonias, and mango and lychee trees.

►► **Vuelta Abajo** 96B2

Tobacco is grown across Pinar del Río Province, near Havana, and in pockets of Oriente and Villa Clara, but the finest in the world comes from the Vuelta Abajo. This is thanks to the district's ideal reddish sandy loam and perfect climate, which has a good rainfall annually but, crucially, very little in the growing season. The heart of the district is the Meca del Tabaco around San Juan y Martínez, 14 miles southwest of Pinar del Río. In this fascinating agricultural landscape, sheets of cheesecloth called *tapados* cover many of the fields to protect from direct sunlight the prime tobacco leaves that are used to wrap cigars. Alongside stand handsome wooden barns that look like Swiss chalets or turretless churches, where the leaves are hung to cure. Just wander in to any of the farms and ask to be shown around.

A multilayered object
A cigar is made up of a wrapper leaf (*capa*), a binder leaf (*capote*), and layers of filler leaves. Capas are the best quality leaves; the plants that produce them are different from those that produce capotes and filler leaves. A cigar's flavor is primarily determined by the composition of filler leaves. Those from the top of the plant (called *ligero*) are very strong, those halfway down (*seco*) are lighter, while those at the bottom (*volado*) taste of little but have good burning qualities. The cigar's filler leaves need to be the right density to let smoke pass through: too tight and it is "plugged," too loose and it will burn too fast.

■ How ironic that, thanks to its ideal soil and climate, communist Cuba produces the world's finest cigar—the ultimate symbol of capitalism. Cigars are the country's fifth most important hard-currency earner, with nearly a third of the 350 million cigars made each year destined for the all-important export market. ■

Smoking and preservation Cut the cigar near the closed end with a special "guillotine" or a sharp knife. To light a cigar, use a match rather than a lighter (the gas affects the flavor); char the end before drawing. Do not inhale as you smoke. A good cigar should develop a long ash, which you shouldn't tap off regularly, as you would a cigarette's. Keep cigars in a cool place in an airtight box: the boxes in which they are sold are fine, but aficionados transfer them to a humidor. Some brands keep better than others, and if well looked after are good for up to 10 years.

104

A dexterous cigar roller in Pinar del Río

Growing and preparation Tobacco seeds are grown in a nursery before being transplanted to the fields in late October. The resultant plants are harvested by hand around 120 days later. The leaves are strung up, using needle and thread, on poles in a tobacco barn, where they are left to cure from 45 to 60 days. They are then taken to a sorting house, or *escogida*, where the leaves ferment for one to three months before being graded, then normally fermented again. Fermentation means cigar tobacco has less tar and nicotine than cigarette tobacco. Finally, the leaves are sent to the cigar factories where they are left to mature, sometimes for up to two years.

The tobacco factory Until the revolution, the women's role in the factory was limited to sorting tobacco leaves and all rollers, or *torcedores*, were men. Torcedores train for nine months, earn well (by Cuban standards), and are paid piece rate: experienced rollers make around 100 cigars a day. Many puff away as they toil at what look like old-fashioned school desks; a free perk is being allowed to smoke as many cigars as they want while working. Each day a lector reads out extracts from newspapers and books over a microphone, a tradition dating from the last century. The Montecristo brand apparently took its name from the fact that rollers particularly enjoyed Dumas' *The*

Cigars

Count of Monte Cristo. Elsewhere in the factory, cigars are tested by professional smokers, sorted by color, banded with the brand name, and put into cedar boxes (cedar helps keep cigars from drying out).

You can observe the production process in cigar factories in various towns across Cuba. However, the best ones to visit are Partagás and La Corona, two of the country's top five factories in Havana, where all export cigars are made (the others being H Upmann, Romeo y Julieta, and El Laguito). See page 75 for details.

Types of cigar Each of the 10 or so export brands offers a bewildering range of cigars, with varying lengths (from 4 to over 9 inches), widths (called ring gauges), and shapes (in addition to classic cylindrical cigars you can buy those shaped like torpedoes, for example). Fatter cigars are usually better made, fuller flavored, and smoke more smoothly and slowly. Darker cigars tend to be stronger and sweeter, and age better.

Taking its name from the Taíno Indian word for tobacco, the world's top brand is Cohiba. Its cigars are made by the best rollers using the best leaves, uniquely fermented three times. Invented after the revolution, Cohibas were first put into production just for foreign dignitaries, after Castro took a liking to certain homemade cigars smoked by one of his bodyguards.

Many say Montecristo is the number two brand, known for a tangy flavor; the 9¼ inch Montecristo A is the world's most expensive cigar. Other famous brands include Partagás, producing full-bodied cigars; H Upmann, mild-to medium-flavored and a good beginners' choice; and Romeo y Julieta, famous for its Churchills in aluminum tubes.

Buying cigars First check the box. It should be stamped "*hecho en Cuba*" ("made in Cuba") and "*totalmente a mano*" ("entirely made by hand"), and there should be a two- or three-letter code signifying the Havana factory where the cigars were made. Open the box and check that the cigars have a fairly uniform color. Take out a couple: they shouldn't crackle when you roll them between your fingers and should be springy if you press them. Note that there is a blanket ban on importing Cuban cigars into the U.S.

The black market
Some 30 percent of tobacco disappears between the countryside and the end of the production line in state-run factories; clandestine factories are regularly busted in raids. Hustlers pester you to purchase cigars, but unless you are an expert it is virtually impossible to tell whether they are the real thing. For example, the boxes may be authentic but the cigars themselves may well have been constructed from inferior tobacco so always buy cigars from an official shop; the best are in tobacco factories. Prices at these stores are much higher than on the black market.

105

Top: tobacco drying
Below: a cigar box label dated 1890

LA FREQUENSA

Diving
The Isle of Youth offers diving that is not just the best in Cuba, but ranks high in world league tables. Divers are based at the Hotel Colony, and are taken by boat to an area off Cabo Francés, the island's southwestern tip; nondivers can pass the day at the cape's fine beach. Such is the quality of the 50 or more sites, which include a vertical coral wall, caves, and wrecks, that international underwater photographic competitions are held here. Courses, night dives, and a compression chamber are on offer. However, you should note that there is nothing else to do at the Colony except dive.

Archipiélago de los Canarreos

Isla de la Juventud (Isle of Youth)   97D1

Cuba's biggest offshore island, roughly circular and 31 miles in diameter, sounds deceptively interesting, but turns out to be largely flat, scrubby, and uneventful. It has a couple of peculiar sights, but unless you have come for the exceptional diving, it is not a place to stay longer than a day or two.

History The island was discovered in 1494 by Christopher Columbus on his second trip. It served as a pirates' lair in the next three centuries, being close to the shipping lanes used by Spanish fleets. Any buccaneer worthy of the name (John Hawkins and Francis Drake are but two) seems to have holed up here at some time, and it is supposed to have been the model for Robert Louis Stevenson's *Treasure Island*.

The Spanish turned the island into a place of exile in the 19th century, a kind of tropical Siberia. In the early 20th century, the United States had vague hopes of making the island another American state and a few U.S. settlers emigrated here, but this never materialized. By the 1940s, when it was known as the Isla de Pinos, the Mafia was considering purchasing it with the intention of turning it into a vast gambling center.

After the revolution, the island's character changed radically, with a significant investment into the production of citrus fruits and an increase in population from around 7,000 to 60,000. In 1978, it was renamed the Isla de la Juventud, or Isle of Youth, after the thousands of foreign students, mainly from politically sympathetic African countries, who came here to combine academic work with labor in the orchards. However, since the Special Period the number of students has dropped dramatically, from a peak of 22,000 to under 3,000 at the last count; most of the dozens of boarding schools dotting the countryside are now decaying concrete blocks.

Layout The island has three main areas. In the north lies Nueva Gerona, the only sizable settlement and the only place apart from the two tourist hotels where you can get a meal, taxi, or gasoline. Around the town lie enormous fields of vegetables and low hills from which marble is quarried (the island also holds Cuba's largest-known gold and silver deposits; mining may start soon). Monotonous scrubland and orchards growing mainly grapefruits cover the center, while a little-inhabited swamp, the Ciénaga de Lanier, occupies the southern third; you may visit only with a guide. Most tourists hole up in the diving ghetto of the Hotel Colony, which has a decent beach but is in an isolated location on the west coast; you may not come across another vacationer anywhere else on the island. The only other appealing beaches lie on the hard-to-reach southern coast.

Nueva Gerona▶ The island's capital is a cheerful, fresh-looking but soporific place. Its main street, Calle 39, is a long arcade of bulbous, multicolored pillars and striped awnings where horse-and-buggies are parked outside shops and sunflowers are sold from bicycle paniers. This

Rush hour in Nueva Gerona

is as lively as the island gets. If you have an hour to spare, wander down to the river near the ferry terminal to see *El Pinero*, the boat on which Castro left the island after imprisonment in 1955, and stop in at the **Museo de la Lucha Clandestina▶** (*Open* Tue–Sat 9–5; Sun 8–12. *Admission charge* inexpensive) at calles 45 and 24. It has a small but interesting collection of exhibits related to the local 26 July Movement, including a letter concealed in a fake cigar.

El Abra▶ (2 miles southwest of Nueva Gerona. *Open* Tue–Sun 9–12, 1–5. *Admission charge* inexpensive). Prior to being deported to Spain in 1870, José Martí stayed for nine weeks under guard in this lovely little *finca*, which stands near a marble quarry at the end of a long, oak-lined drive. Descendants of the same family who had asked the authorities to let him come to El Abra still live here. On show in the stable block is Martí's simple room, with his bed and a few possessions.

Getting there
The easiest way to get to the Isle of Youth is on one of the three flights a day from Havana. The journey takes 40 minutes; the airport is 4 miles south of Nueva Gerona. There are also two hydrofoils (called *kometas*) a day to Nueva Gerona and one ferry a day from Surgidero de Batabanó on the mainland. The hydrofoil crossing takes two hours, the ferry five and a half hours.

The beach at Hotel El Colony

107

The chilling residential blocks of the Presidio Modelo

Presidio Modelo (Model Prison)▶▶▶ (2.5 miles east of Nueva Gerona. *Open* prison buildings accessible all hours; museum Mon–Sat 8–4; Sun 8–1. *Admission charge* inexpensive). The prison was built between 1926 and 1931 by the dictator Machado as a copy of an infamous American penitentiary in Illinois; since 1967 it has been a museum. Five thousand prisoners lived in barbaric conditions, in tiers of miniscule, doorless cells in four colossal circular buildings, constantly overseen by guards from sinister watchtowers at the buildings' center. A fifth block, the refectory hall, where prisoners were not allowed to speak, was called El Comedor del Tres Mil Silencios (the Dining Room of 3,000 Silences). During World War II, Japanese and German POWs were kept here, and from October 1953 to May 1955 Castro and 26 of his rebels were sent here after storming the Moncada Barracks. Being high-profile prisoners, they were treated much better than most and were housed in the prison hospital. For much of the time, however, Castro was kept in solitary confinement or with his brother Raúl. While incarcerated, he penned from memory his famous trial speech, *"La Historia Me Absolverá"* ("History Will Absolve Me"), and spent his time reading voraciously. "By the time I left prison my education was complete," he has said.

You can wander freely around the prison blocks, and the hospital has been turned into an excellent museum with reconstructions of Castro's (rather spacious) cell and the ward where his colleagues slept.

Ciénaga de Lanier▶. A visit to the island's swampland is costly and time-consuming. Ask for a guide at the Colony or Villa Gaviota hotels (see page 199); you need to provide the transportation. Possible destinations are a crocodile breeding farm, Cocodrilo (see panel, left,) and **Punta del Este**▶. Here there are seven caves with paintings created by Ciboney Indians 3,000 years ago. The enigmatic circles and phallic symbols are amazingly clear, but be warned that the caves are plagued by mosquitoes and bees. There is a long stretch of virgin sand nearby.

English speakers
During the 19th century, emigrants from the British colony of the Cayman Islands settled on the Isle of Youth. There are still a few inhabitants here who speak English as a first language, especially around Cocodrilo on the south coast.

▶ **Cayo Largo** *97E1*

This get-away-from-it-all vacation island excels in prime sandy beaches and seductive aquamarine waters. About 14 miles long and varying from a half mile to 4 miles wide, it is largely featureless but for one continuous beach all along one shore. Most of the island is undeveloped, with the six side-by-side hotel complexes (see page 199)—catering mainly to Canadian and Italian vacationers—along the beach near the western end. For a hassle-free beach vacation (topless and even bottomless sunbathing is tolerated), Cayo Largo may fit the bill. However, if you want somewhere stimulating and are interested in learning about Cuba, don't bother coming here. It is a sanitized place, where the only Cubans you will meet work in tourism. While the hotels offer round-the-clock activities, for lively nightlife you should look elsewhere, too.

Exploring The hotels offer car and motorbike rental, but there is really nowhere to go except a virgin stretch of sand—perhaps Playa Tortuga near the island's eastern end, where green turtles lay their eggs. Most people spend their days at **Playa Sirena▶▶**, a superb 2 miles spit of the finest white sand on the island's western side. Though it is rather commercialized, with a restaurant, café, and watersports, it is big enough not to be crowded. A 10-minute-long ferry ride (free; outbound in the morning, return in the evening) plies between the beach and Combinado, where there are a couple of restaurants and a marina (yacht charters possible). A bus service links Combinado to the hotels, about 4 miles away.

Boat trips from Playa Sirena offer fishing, snorkeling, and diving at the nearby reef, and a visit to other unspoiled nearby keys, including **Cayo Iguana▶▶**, home to thousands of scaly, scampering reptiles.

There are day-long excursions to the mainland, but of course they are all by air and therefore expensive.

Getting there
Most Cayo Largo visitors fly directly from abroad. There are also 40-minute-long charter flights from Havana and Varadero. You can either book a package including accommodations, or come on a day trip. The latter includes a visit to Cayo Iguana, snorkeling at the offshore reef, and about four hours on Playa Sirena, with lunch included in the price.

109

An iguana being fed for the entertainment of tourists

Matanzas Province

The closest equivalent to tourist offices are travel agencies, which sell tours: they have offices along Avenida 1 and desks in hotels. Hotels change money, but commission rates are lower in banks. The Clínica Internacional at Avenida 1 and Calle 61 has a pharmacy open 24 hours. There is no public transportation, but taxis (i.e., horse-and-buggies or metered vehicles) are plentiful. Alhough it is against the law, locals can easily be persuaded to drive you around in a Cadillac for a day: just ask around downtown. Demand often outstrips supply for rental cars, so book well in advance. There are also plenty of places to rent bicycles and mopeds; note that helmets are never provided.

►   **Varadero**   *97E3*

With over 50 hotels strung out along mile after mile of fantastic beach, this is far and away Cuba's largest, fastest developing resort. Few visitors respond impassively to its charms. Apologists praise its soft white sands, which are so extensive that they are never crowded; the shallow, clean, aquamarine waters; and accommodations and food that at their best match standards in resorts across the world. Yet detractors see Varadero as a tourist ghetto from which most Cubans are effectively barred. They argue it bears no relation to or parodies the real Cuba, and that one end is a building site and the other is affected by fumes from visible oil wells. Until recently, Varadero also had a fair reputation for being the Bangkok of the Caribbean. However, in 1996, literally thousands of prostitutes were sent back to their home towns, and a new police force was installed (the old one being corrupt to the core). The resort is now heavily policed and considerably more peaceful, and safer.

History Varadero was inhabited by Indians until the Spanish invasion of Cuba. Its modern history began around the turn of the 20th century, when a few boarding houses were erected for summer vacationers from Cárdenas. Development only really took off, however, in 1926, when American industrialist Irenée du Pont, who had made his fortune during World War I selling dynamite, bought 1,265 acres of the peninsula for four cents a hectare. He ended up owning the whole of the peninsula east of the Hotel Internacional. Built in 1950, this is the

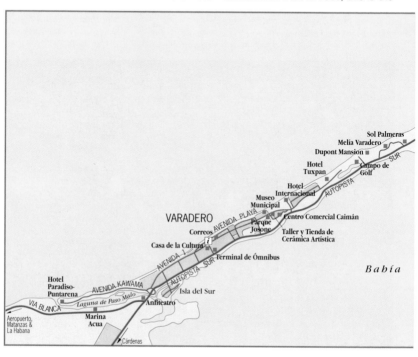

only big prerevolutionary hotel left in Varadero; photographs off the lobby capture the heady days just before the revolution, when Varadero was a playground for rich Americans. The scale of Varadero's latest hotel building boom, which began in 1990 when Cuba started its tourism drive and which is financed largely by foreign companies, has eclipsed any previous development and threatens to turn the resort into a concrete jungle.

Sand, sea, and water-sports: three of Varadero's main attractions

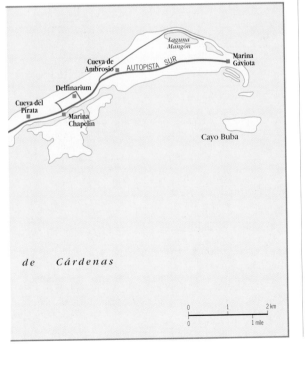

Where to eat
Most tourists eat in their hotels, the majority of which provide gargantuan buffets for breakfast and dinner. Except in all-inclusive hotels, the buffets are available to nonresidents, and are good value if you have a big appetite. Away from hotels, restaurants (see pages 203–204) serve more authentic Cuban food, but are little frequented. *Paladares*, or restaurants in private houses, are not allowed in Varadero because of the competition they would make for hotels and restaurants. However, in downtown Varadero you will be swamped with offers for cheap, clandestine dinners.

Layout Varadero is a 12-mile-long, pencil-thin island connected to the mainland by a short bridge. The beach runs virtually all along the northern shore without a break, while the southern side of the island is marshland. The resort has three main parts. The western end is a peaceful, pretty area of prerevolution villas turned into hotel complexes. The resort's center, from calles 3 to 64, doubles as the town where the locals live in dilapidated American-style wooden homes with handsome verandas, going about their daily lives tinkering with their Cadillacs and shopping with ration cards. Downtown's tourist heart, with the biggest concentration of shops and restaurants, runs from calles 53 to 64 around Parque Josone (also called Retiro Josone). This is a manicured park with a little lake, plastic flamingos, real ducks, and cafés and restaurants (see pages 203–204). From east of Calle 64 to near the peninsula's eastern end, some 20 massive hotel complexes have recently been built, or are still under construction, along a 5-mile stretch of beach.

Where to stay (See also pages 198 and 199–200.) Avoid the hotels at the peninsula's western end, which are plagued by sulfurous fumes from the oil wells and face the worst section of beach. If being in walking distance of restaurants, shops, and so forth is important, stay in downtown Varadero, where all the modest hotels are located. While travelers on a tight budget may consider renting private rooms elsewhere in Cuba, be aware that although letting private accommodations on the island was legalized in 1997, it is not tolerated in Varadero (or any beach resort, for that matter). One of the fancy, big new hotel complexes on the peninsula's eastern half (most of which are all-inclusive) may suit you if you do not really intend to leave the beach or hotel. However, those nearest the center are likely to stand amid a building site for years to come, and those farthest away are very isolated.

Parrots can be seen in Parque Josone

Sightseeing The **Museo Municipal▶** (*Open* Tue–Sat 9–6; Sun 9–12. *Admission charge* inexpensive), by the beach on Calle 57, is Varadero's prettiest house, built entirely of wood as a private residence in 1921. Inside, as well as a few Dupont possessions, are atmospheric photographs of early Varadero and of Che and Fidel being welcomed at the Hotel Internacional after the revolution.

Farther east, the **Dupont Mansion▶** (*Open* daily 10–10. *Admission charge* inexpensive; free if you are eating or drinking) was built by the industrialist in 1929 at a cost of $400,000 and was originally called Xanadu. The Samuel Taylor Coleridge poem that begins "In Xanadu did Kubla Khan/A stately pleasure-dome decree" is written large on a wall. You can wander around admiring the paneled walls and antique furniture, or eat in the grand restaurant (see page 203). Plans are afoot to convert the house into a golf club, but it should still be open to the general public.

Continuing east, the **Delfinarium▶** has 30-minute shows (*Open* daily at 11, 2:.30, and 4. *Admission charge* moderate) of acrobatic dolphins in a natural lake; you can swim briefly with them for an extra fee. Farther east lies the **Cueva de Ambrosio▶** (*Open* Mon–Sat 10–12, 2–4. *Admission charge* inexpensive), a bat-infested cave

thought to have been used by Indians for religious ceremonies. You can see some 70 geometric drawings spanning about 3,000 years prior to the Spanish arrival in Cuba.

Activities The big hotels have their own watersports. In all-inclusive complexes there is no charge for non-motorized sports. Boat outings (book from your hotel rather than just show up) leave from three marinas: Marina Acua, just over the bridge off the peninsula's western end; Marina Chapelín, toward the peninsula's eastern end, and Marina Gaviota, at the eastern tip. You can play at being Hemingway on a deep-sea fishing trip, or take a more leisurely cruise on a "seafari," which normally includes lunch, a free bar, snorkeling on the offshore coral reef, and a visit to a virgin key. The marinas also offer the pricier option of chartering a whole motorboat or yacht. The most popular nautical excursion, however, is a 90-minute (and rather overpriced) trip on *Varasub*, which has an underwater viewing area; it leaves regularly from the Hotel Paradiso-Puntarena at the peninsula's western tip. Diving is extremely popular. The Barracuda Diving Center Avenida at Avenida 1 and Calle 58 offers everything from weeklong courses for all levels of ability to cave- and night diving.

Land-based sports include golf (the island's only 18-hole course has just been completed) and skydiving. Aircraft drop you from 9,842 feet in tandem with an instructor to land, if the winds allow, on the beach outside your hotel. Planes leave from Varadero's old airport, just off the peninsula; reserve by calling 667256.

Nightlife In contrast to its prerevolution heyday, Varadero is quiet after dark. Few tourists leave their hotel compounds in the evening, as big hotels offer plenty of entertainment in the form of cabarets, fashion parades, and *salsa* bands every night. The best show is the Cabaret

The finest of downtown Varadero's old beach villas is now a museum

Excursions
Day-long bus trips leave for Havana, Trinidad, and Guamá, and half-day trips visit Matanzas. There is so much to see in Havana it's worth an overnight excursion; these offer an evening at Havana's Tropicana show. Day-long excursions by plane visit Cayo Largo (where you simply substitute one beach for another), Viñales, and Trinidad again (the flight option gives you much more time there). A little-known local outing is a boat trip on the Río Canímar just east of Matanzas, stopping off upstream for fishing, horseback riding, and swimming.

Varadero nightlife at its most sophisticated—at La Bamba disco

Continental at the Hotel Internacional (Mon–Sat from 10 PM), a wonderfully kitsch extravaganza in garish 1950s surroundings. Other cabaret venues worth considering include: the Cueva del Pirata, a pirate-themed show in a cave toward the peninsula's eastern end; the outdoor anfiteatro off the peninsula right by the bridge; and Parque Josone. Famous Cuban bands sometimes perform at the anfiteatro and Parque Josone: ask around for details. The resort's top disco, mixing Western and Latin-American sounds, is slick La Bamba in the Hotel Tuxpan. Second best is the Havana Club, at Avenida 2 and Calle 62. To mix with the locals, try the Mediterráneo, a spit-and-sawdust bar and small cabaret venue at Avenida 1 and Calle 54, or La Patana, a seedy bar on a barge by the anfiteatro. More civilized is the Casa de la Cultura at Avenida 1 and Calle 34, which has cultural events on some evenings.

▶ Cárdenas   97E3

Unaffected by the opulence of Varadero just 9 miles north, this poverty-stricken town is as good a place as any to witness real-life Cuba. Boasting many (now tumble-down) neoclassical buildings, it was an important port during the 19th century, though its significance waned as its waters were not deep enough to accommodate large vessels. Now motorized traffic is virtually nonexistent, replaced by a teeming flow of bicycles and horse-and-buggies clip-clopping past old-fashioned barbers and radio repair shops.

The main street bisects Parque Colón—where stands the oldest statue of Columbus in the Americas (erected 1862)—on its way to the waterfront, where a flagpole recalls the first raising of the Cuban flag. It happened in 1850, when a force of 600 Mississippians and Kentuckians led by a Venezuelan landed here intending (and failing) to incite the Cubans to revolt against the Spanish. On Calle 12, three blocks east of the main street, the fun **Museo Oscar María de Rojas▶** (*Open* Tue–Sat 9–5; Sun 8–12. *Admission charge* inexpensive) holds lovely insect and *polymitas* displays, as well as a lavish funeral coach and two fleas dressed to get married. Close by, the **Museo Casa Natal de José Antonio Echeverría** (*Open* Tue–Sat 8–4; Sun 8–12. *Admission charge* inexpensive), the grand former home of a student leader killed in 1957, houses the town's historical collections. Don't leave Cárdenas without seeing its most surprising building on Calle 12, two blocks west of the main street. Called **Plaza Malokoff▶**, it is a dazzlingly restored market hall with a silver dome.

▶ Matanzas   97E3

A sizable, rather grimy city with industrial outskirts set around a big bay that holds Cuba's deepest port, on paper Matanzas doesn't sound very promising. Yet it boasts a number of fine buildings from the 19th century, when the city was a prestigious sugar and slave port.

The city center, wedged between two rivers, focuses on two squares. Though it suffers from all the traffic traveling between Havana and Varadero funneling through it, Plaza de la Vigía, immediately behind the bay, is surrounded by stately buildings. The Palacio Junco, the

The Hershey Line
Cuba's only electric train line was constructed in the 1920s by Milton S. Hershey, owner of the American Hershey Chocolate Corporation, to carry sugar from a plantation near Santa Cruz del Norte to Matanzas. It was soon extended as a passenger service to Casablanca, on the eastern side of Havana's harbor. The original electric locomotives and passenger cars still run the 62 miles between Casablanca and Matanzas, ending up winding through the scenic Valle de Yumurí. The trip costs just a few pesos, but if you are in a hurry choose another form of transportation—the journey takes four hours.

mansion of a plantation owner, now serves as the earnest **Museo Provincial▶** (*Open* Tue–Sat 10–12, 1–5; Sun 8:30–12:30. *Admission charge* inexpensive), devoted to recording Matanzas's history and displaying antiques. Across the square the exquisite **Teatro Sauto▶▶** (*Open* Tue–Sat 9–12; 1–3. *Admission charge* inexpensive) has tiers of boxes, supported by bronze posts, and murals of the muses on the ceiling; ask about performances. The theater captures well Matanzas's reputation for being a booming cultural center, nicknamed the Athens of Cuba, in the 19th century. Facing the theater stand a crafts shop, art gallery, and Ediciones Vigía, which sells handmade books, and nearby a *casa de la trova* where Cuba's top *rumba* band, Muñequitos de Matanzas, is based.

Head west up Calle 83 past Matanzas's **cathedral▶** (*Open* Mon–Sat 9–5; Sun 9–12), whose moldy frescoes are in dire need of attention, to the city's second and much more peaceful square, Plaza de la Libertad, which is enveloped in neoclassical buildings. Its **Museo Farmaceutico▶▶▶** (*Open* Mon–Sat 10–5; Sun 10–2. *Admission charge* inexpensive) is an extraordinary time capsule. A pharmacy founded by a Frenchman in 1882 and closed only in 1964, it has rows of elaborately -decorated porcelain pots and glass medicine bottles labeled with the names of obscure remedies. The dispensary still has its original rolling pin, pestels, and mortar for making medicines, as well as its old reference books. A drink next door at the **Hotel Louvre▶** (see page 200), a superb yet very crumbly mansion encompassing two ferny courtyards, keeps you firmly in the 19th century.

Excursions from Matanzas

The most touristy spot in the city's vicinity is **Las Cuevas de Bellamar▶** (*Open* daily 8–5. *Admission charge* moderate), 4 miles southeast. This is a 2-mile underground cave system, much of which is explored on the 45-minute tour. As an alternative to the caves, you could venture into the little-explored **Valle de Yumuri▶**, a valley of fertile hills, palm-dotted farmsteads, and a lazy river valley north of the city—or you can just view it from the shell of the Iglesia de Monserrate on a hill on Matanzas's northwestern outskirts.

Slaughter city
Matanzas means slaughter in Spanish. One explanation for this odd name is that, as Cuba's chief colonial port for the export of pork and beef to Spain, it saw the butchering of a vast number of pigs and cattle. Another theory suggests the name stems from an incident when a ship carrying 30 Spaniards foundered here in the early days of the island's conquest, and local Indians, pretending to come to their assistance in canoes, killed all but four of them.

The flower-bedecked courtyard of the Hotel Louvre, Matanzas

A magnificent turn-of-the-century locomotive at Australia

Crab season
Land crabs live in the swamp but reproduce in the sea. From around May to August, a moving red mass of thousands of creatures often coats the road along the Bahía de Cochinos. Many don't make it across but are crushed under the wheels of passing vehicles, while the sheer density of crabs at certain times makes the road impassable.

Memorials
Look for the gray concrete slabs that appear irregularly by the roadside between La Boca and Playa Girón. They commemorate some of the 161 Cubans who lost their lives in the fighting in 1961.

▶ **Península de Zapata** 97E2

This vast swampland is the largest wetlands area in the Caribbean. Though scenically dull—it is as flat as a pancake—it is home to much of the island's wildlife, from manatees (sea cows) to 18 of the 22 bird species found only in Cuba and dozens of migratory species that come here from North America for the winter. Its other claim to fame is as the disembarkation area for the ill-conceived Bay of Pigs invasion in 1961 (see page 52). One reason the peninsula was chosen for the landing was that it was unpopulated but for a few charcoal burners, and was hardly accessible. Since then, however, three modest resorts have been built, along with a tarmac road.

Australia▶ Castro's headquarters during the 1961 invasion has been turned into a simple museum (*Open* Tue–Fri 8–4; Sat and Sun 8–12. *Admission charge* inexpensive). More diverting is the vast sugar mill it stands alongside, a gigantic corrugated cathedral to which cane is brought by rail in ancient trains.

La Boca The main attraction of this ghastly tourist trap is the *criadero de crocodrilos* (*Open* daily 9–5. *Admission charge* moderate). From disconcerting rickety viewing platforms at this large crocodile nursery you can watch the reptiles lie like floating logs with just their back, nose, and eyes visible. You can also pose with a (muzzled) baby crocodile. There are two large Indian-style restaurants where you can have a crocodile steak, plus half a dozen souvenir shops, including a ceramics workshop. The only good reason for visiting La Boca is to get to Guamá.

Guamá▶▶ In the very heart of the swamp, this little resort spreads across 12 islets at the eastern end of the

vast Laguna del Tesoro. Treasure Lake is so called because Indians were said to have thrown their valuables in its waters rather than allow them to be seized by the conquistadors. Picturesque wooden bridges connect the islets, where thatched huts offer accommodations (see page 200), a restaurant, and souvenir shops. One islet is given over to statues of Indians in striking poses, created by the Cuban sculptor Rita Longa. Four cruise boats make the 5-mile trip daily from La Boca (*Charge* expensive); alternatively, hire a motor boat for a couple of dollars extra.

Playa Girón The focus of this dreary modern settlement is a sprawling low-rise hotel (see page 200) with a diving school, alongside a beach aesthetically ruined by a giant concrete breakwater. Dive sites line the coast to the northwest: the coral wall is so close to the shore there is no need to take a boat out. The **Museo Playa Girón**►► (*Open* daily 8–12, 1–5. *Admission charge* inexpensive), one of Cuba's most engrossing, tells the story of the 1961 invasion clearly (if, naturally, one-sidedly), even for non-Spanish speakers, by using evocative period photos. They show the build-up to the invasion with the bombing of Cuba's airstrips, the battle itself with women and children killed by "mercenaries" and Castro jumping from a tank, and classic images of victory and defeat. One wall is devoted to those who died defending the revolution.

Playa Larga At the top of the deep inlet of the Bahía de Cochinos (Bay of Pigs), this one-horse resort amounts to a decent sandy beach, single hotel, and diving school. It is the starting point for excursions into the virtually uninhabited western half of the Zapata (see panel). A checkpoint allows traffic through only with a guide (*Charge* expensive) from Villa Playa Larga hotel (see page 200).

Bird-watching
The Zapata's abundant birdlife is best observed at two nature reserves, reached by car via rutted tracks. Ideally visit from January to April, when migratory birds are abundant, there are fewer mosquitoes, and the tracks are not water-logged. At Las Salinas, 15.5 miles from Playa Larga, pink flamingos stud brackish waters, and other migratory species such as herons, spoonbills, and wood storks can also be seen. Expert ornithologists head for Santo Tomás, 22 miles from Playa Larga, to study species endemic to Cuba, such as the bee hummingbird, or *zunzuncito*, at 2 inches long the world's smallest bird, and the Zapata wren, sparrow, and rail, found only in these marshes.

117

Guamá, a mock Indian settlement built in the 1960s

CENTRAL CUBA

REGION HIGHLIGHTS ◀ ◀ ◀ ◀ ◀

*Trinidad's
bewitching jumble of
old roofs and streets*

CENTRAL CUBA

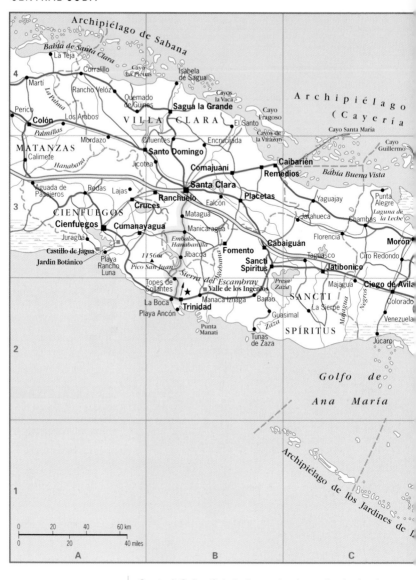

In Trinidad's main square—Cuba's prettiest

Central Cuba Cuba's long, slender waist is the least scenically rewarding part of the country. The six provinces in the middle of the island constitute its agricultural heartland. For the most part they amount to unremittingly flat plains covered in a vast ocean of livid green sugarcane and, especially in the east, cattle-grazing pastures. Many visitors pass quickly through on Cuba's arterial highway—first the *autopista*, then, after Sancti Spíritus, the island's most traffic-ridden country road, clogged with trucks laden with cut cane. Others bother only with central Cuba's single unmissable destination, the time-warped colonial town of Trinidad. Consequently, the regional centers dotted across the plains are refreshingly untouristy and ripe for off-the-beaten-track exploring.

see drive page 129

de
del Camagüey
Norte)

Cayo Coco

Bahía de Perros

Laguna
La Redonda

Cayo Romano

Cayo
Cruz

Bolivia

CIEGO
Primero
de Enero

DE AVILA

Gaspar

Esmeralda

Jiquí

Cayo
Guajaba

Cubitas

Sola

Cayo
Sabinal

Piedrecitas

Carlos Manuel
de Céspedes

Florida

CAMAGÜEY

Máximo

Lugareño

Minas

La Boca

Playa Los Cocos

Playa Santa Lucía

Nuevitas

San
Antonio

Las Yueras

Camagüey

Camalote

Manatí

Vertientes

Jimaguayú

Sibanicú

Las Cabreras

Hatuey

Puerto
Padre

Jesús
Menéndez

Vázquez

San Pedro

Martí

Maniabón

Velasco

Najasa

Colombia

Guáimaro

LAS TUNAS

Najasa

Yaguimo

Serilla

Jobabo

Las Tunas

Calixto

Holguín

Buenaventura

Cándido
González

Haití

Amancio

Guayabal

Jobabo

Dormitorio

Mir

Antonio
Maceo

HOLGUÍN

Cacocum

Reina

Santa Cruz
del Sur

Golfo de Guacanayabo

GRANMA

Río Cauto

Cauto

Cauto
Cristo

D   E   F

Some, such as Ciego de Avila and Las Tunas, are admittedly dull backwaters, but others, such as Santa Clara and Camagüey, are vibrant cities with a rich historical and architectural heritage.

Tourists, however, will soon be flooding to central Cuba. The virtually uninhabited islands off the north coast, the Cayería del Norte, have been earmarked for massive development and Cayo Santa María has been connected to the mainland by a 30-mile causeway. There are four large hotel complexes on Cayo Coco and Cayo Guillermo; three more have just been completed, and Cayo Coco will end up with 5,000 hotel rooms if all goes according to plan. So, if you like your beaches empty and your towns unspoiled, come to central Cuba sooner rather than later.

CENTRAL CUBA

The countryside in the Escambray foothills is stunning

Itineraries
Western central Cuba is more rewarding for touring than the eastern part, with better scenery and more places of interest. A leisurely week's tour might be: Cienfuegos (allow one to two days), Trinidad (two to three days), across the Escambray Mountains to Santa Clara (½ day), Remedios (½ day), Sancti Spíritus (½ day). Most tourists in eastern central Cuba are on package beach holidays in all-inclusive complexes on the north coast. The only place of significant interest inland is Camagüey, which needs two days to get to know well: you could fly here from Havana, and combine the city with a sojourn at Playa Santa Lucía.

Western central Cuba The modern provinces of Cienfuegos, Villa Clara, and Sancti Spíritus, equating with the defunct old province of Las Villas, share central Cuba's loveliest scenery in its only mountain range, the little-visited Sierra del Escambray. It was the strongest area of resistance to Castro's revolution in the early 1960s; locals were evacuated to stop them from providing food to rebels. Few visitors make it farther than the Escambray's health resort of Topes de Collantes and Embalse Hanabanilla, a large reservoir in a memorable position, both of which are good walking bases.

Set against a backdrop of the sea and the sierra's foothills, Trinidad is Cuba's most complete and least altered colonial town, and as such a UNESCO World Heritage Site. Though partially marred by being a honeypot tourist destination (the only one in central Cuba), it is still the single place in the region you would be foolish to miss. The main road east through the lovely Sugar Mills Valley, whence Trinidad's riches came, brings you in an hour to Sancti Spíritus, a town with as ancient a pedigree as Trinidad's but with far less to show for it.

The 45-mile highway west of Trinidad reaches Cienfuegos via an undulating, pretty landscape. Founded by French emigrants from Bordeaux in 1819, it soon eclipsed Trinidad and since the revolution has been developed into one of Cuba's busiest ports, from where much of the island's sugar is exported. Though its city center and the surrounding countryside are not without their attractions, Cienfuegos receives more visitors than it deserves because of its proximity to Trinidad.

Sitting in the plains north of the Escambray, Santa Clara, capital of Villa Clara Province and the second biggest city in central Cuba, milks its links with Che Guevara (see panel, page 136). While, by Cuban standards, it has prospered, Remedios, 45 minutes down the road, has stagnated. This unspoiled little colonial throwback is inexplicably ignored by the official tourist literature and most coach tours. Come before it is spoiled by the hordes who will descend upon the town from the hotels that are being built on Cayo Santa María, at the end of the causeway east of the sleepy port of Caibarién.

Eastern central Cuba Ciego de Avila Province is Cuba at its flattest. It is known for having the island's largest fruit orchards: its eponymous capital is nicknamed Pineapple Town, and orange groves line the road to more interesting Morón. North of Morón is prime wildfowl hunting and fishing territory in and around Laguna La Redonda and Laguna de la Leche, the country's largest and milky-colored lake: enquire at the Hotel Morón (see page 201) if you are interested. Offshore lie prime sandy beaches on Cayo Coco and Cayo Guillermo, where luxury hotels offer everything from aerobics to nightly cabarets and a full range of watersports. The hotels are geared to package-tour vacationers and are prohibitively expensive for independent travelers.

Camagüey is Cuba's largest but most thinly populated province. It is also relentlessly flat, with its vast plains punctuated only by the occasional rusty windmill. This is cattle country: lean-looking *vaqueros*, or cowboys, with stetsuns and lassos, herd their livestock on horseback.

Camagüey city, which grew from the profits of ranching and sugar plantations, cannot compete with Havana or Santiago in appeal, lacking their dramatic seaside locations and upbeat tempos. However, it is enjoyably undiscovered, with a host of stately buildings worth ferreting out. Most tourists to the province stay 68 miles northeast in the resort of Playa Santa Lucía. To its west, beyond the best-avoided industrial port of Nuevitas, stretch the undeveloped islands of the Archipiélago de Camagüey. Off the province's inaccessible, swampy south coast lies the 93-mile-long necklace of virgin islets, called by Columbus the Archipiélago de los Jardines de la Reina (the Queen's Gardens) after the Spanish monarch Isabella. The only way to reach them is on airborne excursions from the north coast resorts.

Central Cuba ends with a whimper in Las Tunas Province, where endless, arrow-straight roads cut across monotonous sugarcane plains. If you are heading east it is difficult not to pass through thoroughly agricultural Las Tunas town. Bizarre modern statuary—a giant rifle, crown, and fish—and a small museum commemorating the 54 Cubans (including the national fencing team) who died in a plane blown up by terrorists over Barbados in 1976 might break your journey.

Time on the beach
Fantastic white-sand beaches line the Cayería del Norte, the string of islands off the northcoast. To date, only Cayo Coco and Cayo Guillermo have hotels, though this will soon change. Presently, the most fully-fledged resort is Playa Santa Lucía. Near by is Playa Los Cocos, which fulfills most expectations of the dream Caribbean beach. On Cuba's south coast, Playa Rancho Luna near Cienfuegos, and better Playa Ancón near Trinidad, are good for a days' outing, but the hotels are poor.

Independence hero Ignacio Agramonte in Camagüey

123

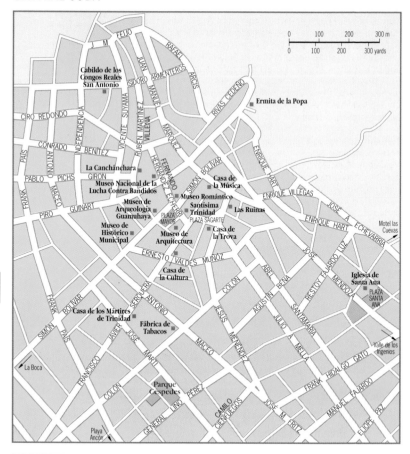

Cockfighting

La riña de gallos is a long-established, passionate pastime for Cubans, but after the revolution it was practiced only in secret. However, it has been legalized again—at least around Trinidad. Every Sunday morning from around 7 AM, dozens of locals gather at the Finca Dolores, 1 mile west of Trinidad; if you go, you will probably be the only tourist there. Prize specimens are shown off, plenty of beer is drunk, and hundreds of pesos change hands in bets before the fights start at around 8:30. There's such a throng around the ring it's hard to see anything; young lads shimmy up trees to get a view.

Western central Cuba

▶▶▶ Trinidad   120B2

In 1514, Trinidad became the third settlement to be founded on Cuba by Diego Velázquez, as a base for exploiting the surrounding mountains for gold. But its heyday came in the first half of the 19th century, when it was one of Cuba's most important centers for the slave trade and sugarcane industry. Yet decline, brought about by the abolition of slavery, the destruction of plantations in the independence wars, and the emergence of big new estates elsewhere on the island, followed swiftly.

Consequently, aside from a recent restoration program in its center, Trinidad has hardly changed for more than a hundred years. Single-story, primary-colored houses, topped by curvaceous clay-tiled roofs and enclosing palm- and bougainvillea-rich courtyards, line higgledy-piggledy streets cobbled with stones used as ballast in trading ships. The pace of life is wonderfully lethargic: residents snooze in rocking chairs in the shade behind the grilles that cover the houses' long windows. With no motorized traffic to speak of, the only sounds are of mules' hooves on the cobbles and crowing cocks.

All that upsets such serenity is what happens wherever

droves of tourists descend on any poor population. The begging here is as persistent as anywhere in Cuba, and you may end up being a pied piper to a column of barefoot kids as you wander around. You will be hassled far less after the tour buses leave in the late afternoon, and not at all at night, when the streets, partly pitch black, partly bathed in a soft yellow glow from the occasional street-lamp, feel even further removed from the late 20th century than in daylight.

The center The hub of the old town is Plaza Mayor▶▶▶. This gorgeous ensemble of gaily painted colonial mansions, once owned by sugar barons and now converted into museums, encloses playful railings, urns, and grayhound statues. The most stunning mansion, the Palacio Brunet, dates from 1740, with the first floor added in 1808. Now the **Museo Romántico**▶▶ (*Open* Tue–Sun 9–5. *Admission charge* inexpensive), it has a dozen set-piece rooms equipped with exquisite furniture used by the local aristocracy. The **Museo de Arqueología Guamuhaya** (*Open* Sun–Fri 9–5. *Admission charge* inexpensive) is a far more modest 18th-century house that exhibits a few stuffed animals, Indian bones, and slave shackles. From the same period, the **Museo de Arquitectura**▶ (*Open* Sat–Wed 9–5; Thu 9–10. *Admission charge* inexpensive) is more interesting, with an assortment of old tiles, doors, wrought iron, and stained glass culled from around the town, and a lovely courtyard full of roses. Lastly, the square's **Santísima Trinidad Church**, rebuilt in 1892, has limited hours (*Open* daily 11:30–1) and is, in any case, disappointingly plain inside.

La Canchánchara
This bar, on Calle RM Villena two blocks north of Plaza Mayor, is a tourist trap, but a very pleasant one at that. Arranged around a leafy courtyard, it takes its name from its signature cocktail, a concoction of *aguardiente*, honey, and lime juice that was allegedly first created for *mambises* (independence fighters) in the 19th century. It is open daily 9–5, with spirited live music from about 10 AM until 3 PM.

125

The main salon in Trinidad's Museo Histórico Municipal (see overleaf)

There are two more first-rate attractions a few steps from the square. The dull-sounding **Museo Histórico Municipal**▶▶ (*Open* Sun–Fri 9–5. *Admission charge* inexpensive), a block south on Simón Bolivar, was formerly the Palacio Cantero. A thoroughly grand affair, its contents are eclipsed by the superb murals of classical scenes, scrolls, shells, drapes, and pediments that have been painted over doorways and windows. Pass through the arcaded courtyard and up a steep staircase to the roof of a watchtower for a mesmerizingly beautiful view of the town. The panorama is even better from the top of the yellow bell tower of the former 18th-century convent, now the **Museo Nacional de la Lucha Contra Bandidos (National Museum of the Struggle against the Bandits)**▶▶. Below it, the museum looks at the fight against the U.S.-backed counterrevolutionaries in the 1960s, when they controlled much of the Escambray Mountains. Intriguing exhibits include a CIA radio transmitter, Che Guevara's hammock, and, in the courtyard, a boat used by the *bandidos* and a chunk of a U.S. spy plane (*Open* Tue–Sun 9–5. *Admission charge* inexpensive).

Beyond the center Its museums are fine, but Trinidad's real charm lies in the atmosphere of its gently decaying back streets. Here are a few suggested destinations to give your wanderings a focus.

North from Plaza Mayor and just before the streets peter out into dirt tracks is the **Cabildo de los Congos Reales San Antonio**, at Calle Isidro Armenteros No. 168. This modest hall, which began as a kind of religious/social club for slaves, is a center for Santería worship: the Catholic saint San Antonio pairs up with the Santería *orisha*, or god, Hogún. Ask about evening musical events.

Northeast from the center, it is a steep 10-minute climb up to **Ermita de la Popa**▶, Trinidad's oldest church, built in 1715 (and now disused); kids are often flying homemade kites from this hilltop spot. A 10-minute stroll southeast is **Plaza Santa Ana**▶, on the edge of the old part of town. Here a prison has been sensitively converted into a tourist complex, with crafts shops, a restaurant, and cool bar around a lovely orange-painted courtyard.

About four blocks south of Plaza Mayor at Maceo No. 403 at the corner of Colón there is a friendly one-room **cigar factory** (*Open* Mon–Sat 7–12, 1–4. *Admission charge* inexpensive); you will smell it long before you see it. Keep going south and you leave the old town and soon come to **Parque Central**, the new town's pleasant main square, refreshingly free of Trinidad's many hustlers.

Shopping Trinidad has many street stalls and shops, often in lovely colonial buildings, selling decent arts and crafts. The best selection of paintings of Trinidad can be found in the mansion (once the local governor's house) facing the church across Plaza Mayor. Other nearby galleries sell fun ceramic representations of old Trinidadian buildings. There is a sizable crafts market on Plaza Sagarte, one block east of Plaza Mayor, every day 8–5, and more stalls selling lace one block south of Sagarte. Many items are homemade and not perhaps of the highest quality, but you may be happier to give a few dollars direct to a local than into the state's coffers.

Music in Trinidad
The Casa de la Trova, a fine 18th-century building one block east of Plaza Mayor at Echerri No. 29, and Las Ruinas, a stylish courtyard bar just north on Calle Jésus Menéndez, offer live entertainment during the day and most evenings. The Casa de la Cultura, a fine mansion one block south of Plaza Mayor on Calle FJ Serquera, puts on events on Saturday evenings. The Santa Ana complex holds *rumba* dances most lunchtimes and evenings. The two big nighttime venues are the Casa de la Música, above Plaza Mayor's church, which often has a live *salsa* band, and Las Cuevas disco, located in impressive caves a few hundred yards from the Motel Las Cuevas above the town.

The view from Trinidad's bell tower has appeared in scores of brochures

Taking the train
You can visit the Valley of the Sugar Mills by rail. Some of the trains that run frequently from Trinidad to Manaca Iznaga (40 minutes away) and beyond turn out to be buses adapted to run on railway tracks: only in Cuba! Make enquiries, too, about tourist excursions on a steam train: normally it runs only if the whole train has been chartered.

Manaca Iznaga Tower (below) and (opposite) the panorama from the top of it

Excursions from Trinidad

▶   **Playa Ancón**   120B2

This 2-mile-long beach, on a marshy peninsula 9 miles south from Trinidad, makes a fair claim to be the best on mainland Cuba's south coast. However, while the quality of its sand is indisputable and the offshore diving is excellent, the mosquitoes can be a nuisance and it is blighted by the eyesore Hotel Ancón, which, along with the nearby Hotel Costasur, is geared to package tourists. Interestingly, Playa Ancón was considered as an alternative landing point to the Bahía de Cochinos for the Cuban exiles in 1961. La Boca, 4 miles west of Trinidad, is the locals' beach, a fun though rather scruffy place in a river-mouth setting.

▶▶   **Valle de los Ingenios**   120B2

The road east from Trinidad to Sancti Spíritus passes through what translates as the Valley of the Sugar Mills. The valley was the source of Trinidad's prosperity, and in the early 1800s there were more than 50 small sugar mills here worked by over 11,000 slaves. Hidden remains of old haciendas and mills pepper the countryside: the whole area has been designated a World Heritage Site by UNESCO.

A **mirador**▶, which has a bar, about 3 miles east of Trinidad, offers a magnificent overview of the valley's lime-green cane fields set against a bank of dark green mountains. **Manaca Iznaga**▶▶, 6 miles farther on, is the valley's top attraction (*Open* daily 8–5. *Admission* free). A beautifully restored early 19th-century hacienda with windows and doors placed to make the most of the merest breeze, it doubles as a little information center and restaurant. Its grandeur still contrasts as sharply with the poverty of the homesteads in the surrounding village as it must always have done. The rocket-like 148-foot-high tower in its grounds (you can climb to the top) allowed the sugar baron to keep an eye on his slaves working in the fields below, where rebellions and runaways were common.

Casa Guachinango, 2.5 miles north deep into the valley, is a smaller, far less frequented hacienda: even when it is closed, it is worth visiting for its serene setting.

Drive The Sierra del Escambray

See highlighted route on map on pages 120–121.

This 87-mile-long, little-traversed route from Trinidad to Santa Clara crosses the wooded Escambray Mountains, the wildest and most scenic area in central Cuba. You can drive it in about three hours, but ideally allow a day.

About 2.5 miles west of Trinidad turn right and make a steep and windy 9-mile climb through pine and eucalyptus woods to **Topes de Collantes▶**. This normally deserted health resort is dominated by the sinister-looking Kurhotel Escambray, a sanatorium that is trying to woo foreign patients with such treatments as hydrotherapy and cosmetic surgery. There are lovely walks in the surrounding woods. One leads to a waterfall 1.5 miles away called El Salto del Caburní: ask for directions or hire a guide from the Gaviota tourist office 656 feet below the sanatorium.

The road north (unmarked on some maps and initially potholed) takes in panoramic views of the Escambray's peaks and passes waterfalls on its 15 miles way to Jibacoa. This is the main settlement in an idyllic **valley▶▶**, where ramshackle, primary-colored wooden huts sit surrounded by blooming gardens and banana and coffee plantations. The only traffic will be open trucks full of *campesinos*, local country people. The valley continues most of the next 9 miles to the town of Manicaragua, where you turn left toward Cumanayagua. This is tobacco country, but the quality of the leaves drying in the ubiquitous shaggy Y-framed barns is nowhere near as good as in Pinar del Río. After 14 miles you reach **Embalse Hanabanilla▶▶**, a picturesque reservoir enclosed by a ridge of palm-dotted hills. You could stay at the Hotel Hanabanilla (see page 200), go on a bass fishing trip, or rent a boat. Otherwise, return to Manicaragua, and continue 20.5 miles to **Santa Clara▶** (see pages 136–137).

Teatro Tomás Terry, where Sarah Bernhardt and Enrico Caruso performed

Juraguá nuclear power plant
The *Wall Street Journal* recently called this plant a "Chernobyl-sized time bomb waiting to explode", citing defective cooling systems and containment domes. Blighting the view west of the Castillo de Jagua, it was begun as long ago as 1980, but lack of money means it is still unfinished. Russia has promised to provide the necessary investment to start up one of the two reactors, in return for being able to retain a signals intelligence facility in western Cuba. But if Russia does invest, the United States has in turn threatened to cut the aid it supplies its former adversary.

► **Cienfuegos**   120A3

The brochures call Cienfuegos the "the pearl of the south," but they overstate its charms. Admittedly it enjoys a great position, spread over fingers of land that protrude into a vast glassy bay, and it has some grand buildings from the late 19th and early 20th centuries, when it was one of Cuba's most prosperous sugar-producing centers. However, its port is heavily industrialized, making the bay's waters some of the most polluted around the island and marring the view with oil tankers and chimneys belching fumes.

Around the center Cienfuegos' most stately architecture surrounds a pretty bandstand and a triumphal arch that marks the founding of the republic on large, palmy **Parque José Martí►►**. On the north side, **Teatro Tomás Terry►►** (*Open* daily 9–6. *Admission charge* inexpensive), perhaps the most exquisite of Cuba's many colonial theaters, was built in 1890 and named after a rich sugar plantation owner. Delicate pillars divide tiers of boxes below a ceiling covered in cavorting naked ladies and a clock showing four o'clock, the time when the painter finished his work. It is still used for opera, ballet, and contemporary dance, with performances most weekend evenings. The nearby 19th-century **cathedral►** (*Open* daily 7–12) boasts fine stained-glass windows and a gold-painted interior. The ornate blue and white mansion on the square's west side was built as the private Palacio Ferrer in the early 20th century, but is now the **Casa de la Cultura**; you can climb its turreted folly (*Open* daily 8–5. *Admission charge* inexpensive). The square's south flank is lined with a monumental government building, a good art gallery, a mellow touristy bar called El Palatino, and the opulent old Spanish casino (or social club), which, when restored, will house the local history museum.

Pedestrianized **Avenida 54►**, east from Parque José Martí, is Cienfuegos's main shopping street. There is little of interest to buy, but it is a good showcase of Cuba's arcane shopping system, with pawn shops, empty department stores, and well-stocked dollar emporiums. The street ends up at **Paseo del Prado►**. This is Cienfuegos's main thoroughfare, whose rows of neoclassical, balustraded, and arcaded buildings are painted every color of the rainbow. It is alive with a constant stream of horse-drawn taxis and bicycles, and on weekend evenings the whole town seems to turn out here for a gossip and a stroll.

Beyond the center The Prado descends south along the bay to **Punta Gorda►**, a spit of land with lovely turreted and clapboard villas built as vacation homes in the early 20th century. The most extraordinary is **Palacio Valle►►**, completed in 1917 in extravagant Gothic/Arabian style for the Valle family (see Restaurants, page 204). Its interior is a riot of tracery and toothed arches, and there are magnificent views over the bay from its rooftop bar.

Cementerio Tomás Acea►, 1 mile east of the center, is no match for the cemeteries in Havana, Camagüey, or Santiago, but it has a monumental marble pavilion with 64 massive columns (a replica of the Parthenon in Athens, Greece) at its entrance.

Excursions from Cienfuegos

►► Castillo de Jagua   120A3

Open: daily 8–4. Admission charge: inexpensive.
Guarding the narrow harbormouth entrance of Cienfuegos' bay, this small fort was completed in 1745 to keep pirates away. Though the castle itself is disappointing (there is nothing inside except a restaurant), the photogenic village of Perché below it has battered old houses on stilts over the water and stalls selling fried fish. A nearby giant mural announces "Bienvenidos Cuba Socialista" to passing ships. See also panel.

Playa Rancho Luna   120A3

This mediocre, coarse sandy beach 4 miles south of the entrance to Cienfuegos's bay is the best in the area. It is busy with Canadian package tourists, who stay at its eponymous, third-rate hotel (which offers diving).

►► Jardín Botánico   120A3

Open: daily 8–4. Admission charge: moderate.
Lying about 12 miles east of Cienfuegos near Pepito Tey, this is a vast botanical garden, founded in 1901 by Harvard University. Though very run down, with few paths and no labeling, it has an enormous variety of cacti, bamboo, and palms (some in spectacular avenues). Guides are available from the bar in its center.

Getting to Castillo de Jagua
If you have a car, the easiest way to get to Castillo de Jagua is to drive 17 miles to the eastern side of the bay's mouth beneath the Hotel Pasacaballo, and take the three-minute crossing on a little ferry. Alternatively, from a dock at Avenida 46 at Calle 25 in downtown Cienfuegos, half a dozen ferries leave daily for a 45-minute trip. Marina Puertosol on Punta Gorda offers pricy boat charters for groups of tourists.

131

One of many neo-classical buildings on Cienfuegos's Paseo del Prado

■ Cuba has been called "the greatest living American car museum in the world." The streets are full of classic 1940s and 1950s automobiles, imported before the revolution. Most somehow still function, thanks to the Cubans' legendary ingenuity. Flamboyant icons of capitalism and consumer wealth, they should look out of place in a communist country. ■

Ladas for Cadillacs
A state company called Cubalse scours the country for vintage American cars, offering their owners a brand-new Lada in exchange. The idea is that the owner benefits from having a car that actually works, while Cubalse sells the Cadillacs for thousands of dollars to foreigners. Any vehicle with the number plate "Expo-Transporte" (including most of those on show in museums) should be up for sale. Many cars are given a special provenance to increase their value: if all the claims are true, both Frank Sinatra's and Batista's wives must have had an entire fleet of vehicles each.

132

Old crocks Cubans fondly call these expressions of individuality in a sea of government uniformity *cacharros* ("old crocks"). Packards, Oldsmobiles, Buicks, De Sotos, Studebakers, Chevys, and of course, Cadillacs (the name is often used generically for all these classic cars)—every make imaginable is on show. Many are wheezing mechanical dinosaurs, but a few are in prime condition, sporting flared fins, hood ornaments such as streamlined birds, and banquette leather seats.

Keeping the cars on the road These vehicles were designed as frivolous fashion accessories, to be discarded after a couple of years. Yet, since the revolution most Cubans have not been able to afford a new car, and many anyway will not countenance the idea of driving a "tin can on wheels" Lada—which, until recently, was the only make available. So, by fair means or foul, owners have to be resourceful to keep their prized possessions running. Mechanics mix neat alcohol, brown sugar, and shampoo for brake fluid, and rejuvenate flat batteries from overhead power lines. There is an enormous black market in spare parts: most old vehicles actually run on Lada engines. Leave a car unguarded overnight and

chances are its wing mirrors and windshield wipers will have entered the resale trade by morning. Gasoline is strictly rationed, so fuel is often siphoned from garages and sold in back streets from plastic containers. Cubans love just taking their cars out for a short spin—"*un paseito*"—but, understandably, many owners use them (usually illegally) as dollar-earning machines by driving tourists around. Reports have even surfaced of vehicles in quasi sumo wrestling events—nose to nose, trying to push each other over a painted line across the road.

Opposite: Cubans refuse to allow their old cars (and bikes) to die
Above: turquoise waters...and a turquoise Cadillac

Pretty in pink: Remedios's bandstand

Las Parrandas
On the last Saturday before Christmas every year, Remedios holds one of Cuba's largest festivals. Its origins lie in the noise townsfolk used to make on Christmas Eve to summon people to midnight Mass. The town's two districts, or *barrios*, El Carmen and San Salvador, spend months preparing floats, fireworks, and a multistoried edifice called a *trabajo de plaza*, each hoping to outdo the other. The pyrotechnics got so out of hand in 1996 that some houses were set on fire. The excellent Parrandas museum has models of amazingly elaborate *trabajos de plaza* used in previous years, including ones designed as a sunflower, art-deco radio, and windmill.

►► **Remedios** *120B3*

This somnolent colonial backwater is one of the most seductive places in Cuba. Though there has been a settlement here since the mid-16th century, its buildings date mainly from the early 19th century, when the small town was rebuilt after a fire. Little has changed since, and with horse-and-buggies the sole form of transportation, the only motorized vehicle you are likely to see is your own. Tourism has not reached Remedios: you're likely to be the only visitor in town, there is nowhere decent to stay or eat, and the locals have not yet learned how to badger foreigners to distraction.

Everything of significance lies on or near **Parque Martí**►►►, Remedios's achingly beautiful main square, which is so perfectly colonial it could be a fake film set. It centers on a fanciful pink bandstand, but what makes it particularly distinctive is the fact that it holds two churches. The smaller has a plain interior, but the larger, the **Parroquial de San Juan Bautista**►►, is special (*Open* Sun–Fri 9–5; Sat 9–12; knock on the office door at the rear if shut). Extensively restored after an earthquake in 1939 with a $1 million donation from a local Cuban, it includes among its highlights a floor-to-ceiling baroque altarpiece encrusted with gold leaf, a mahogany ceiling, and an unusual statue of a pregnant Mary. Closer inspection of the square reveals a couple of earthy bars, a *casa de la cultura* (in the old Spanish casino), and the **Museo de Musica Alejandro García Caturla**► (*Open* Tue–Sat 8–12, 1–5; Sun 9–1. *Admission charge* inexpensive). It honors a musical lawyer who married a black woman and was assassinated for his incorruptibility; his life story is more interesting than the museum. Across the square is the Hotel Mascotte (see page 200), where General Máximo Gómez and President McKinley met in February 1899 to discuss the discharge of Cuban troops who had fought in the Spanish–American War. A block and a half down Calle Máximo Gómez lies the **Museo de las Parrandas Remedianas**►► (*Open* Tue–Sat 9–12, 1–5; Sunday 9–1. *Admission charge* inexpensive); see panel.

▶ **Sancti Spíritus** *120B3*

In 1895, the future British statesman Winston Churchill, while serving with the Spanish forces in Cuba, described Sancti Spíritus as "second-rate" and "most unhealthy." Many visitors still find this mid-size town disappointing. It has its appealing corners, but you expect more from a place that was one of Cuba's original seven townships and has been on its present riverside site since 1522.

The Parroquial Mayor, Sancti Spíritus

Herbal remedies

Since the advent of the Special Period, many pharmacists all over Cuba have been forced to start prescribing their customers alternatives to conventional medicines. One such place in Sancti Spíritus is the Farmacia de Medicinas Verdes at the southern end of Máximo Gómez, across from the Parroquial Mayor. Despite the fact that, like many Cuban pharmacies, it looks like a museum, with lovely old ceramic jars lining its shelves and photos on the wall of plants such as eucalyptus, rue, and lime used in preparations, make no mistake—this place is fully operational.

Santa Clara entertainment

A brass band usually plays in the bandstand on Parque Vidal on weekend afternoons, and Santa Clara's top contemporary band, Los Fakires, can normally be heard on Sunday afternoons at the *casa de la trova* next to the Hotel Santa Clara Libre. El Mejunje, two blocks west of Parque Vidal at Marta Abreu No. 107, is something of a bohemian hangout, with theatrical performances and live music on weekend evenings.

Che and Santa Clara

In summer 1958, Che Guevara was dispatched from the Sierra Maestra to spread the guerrilla campaign into central Cuba and effectively cut the island in two. His efforts culminated in the decisive battle for Santa Clara in December 1958: Batista fled the country days after the city fell.

Parque Serafín Sánchez, the main square, is traffic-ridden by Cuban standards, but matters improve if you head south down Máximo Gómez. Stop halfway at No. 26 at the welcoming *Casa de la Trova* to see if anything is going on. The orange bell tower of the **Parroquial Mayor►** *(Open* Mon–Fri 9–11, 2–4; Sat 8–12) beckons you on to the end of the street. Standing on the site of a wooden edifice that was built in 1522 but destroyed in a pirate raid, this stone church is supposed to have the oldest origins in Cuba. What you see dates from 1680; apart from a fine carved roof, it is rather plain inside. The same cannot be said for the **Museo de Arte Colonial►►**, a block south *(Open* Tue–Sat 8.30–5; Sun 8–12. *Admission charge* inexpensive). This former palace of the Valle-Iznaga family (see page 128) has a dozen lavishly furnished rooms, with, for example, grand cedar beds in the bedrooms and an old harp in the music room. All are bathed in a soft yellow light refracted through stained-glass windows. The street down from the museum leads to a hump-backed, early 19th-century bridge; turn left immediately before it to reach a winding cobbled lane called Calle Llano, the prettiest in town.

►   **Santa Clara**   *120B3*

Too bustling and sprawling to be charming, Santa Clara is nonetheless worth visiting for its classic main square and its monuments related to Che Guevara, who captured the city from Batista's forces in late 1958.

Around Parque Vidal► Grand, mainly neo-classical public buildings enclose the city's main square, around an elegant bandstand and an oval track where children are taken for goat-and-trap rides on weekends. The only eyesore is the Hotel Santa Clara Libre, a 1950s tower block; there is, however, a good view over the city from its rooftop bar. The hotel was the last holdout of Batista's troops; bullet holes riddle its facade. On the square's north side stands the Teatro Caridad, built in 1885, and an earlier colonial mansion, now the **Museo de Artes Decorativas►** *(Open* Mon 1–6; Wed–Thu 9–6; Fri–Sat 1–10; Sun 6–10. *Admission charge* inexpensive). Recreated living rooms display an impressive collection of antiques that were used by the local nobility, from a brass four-poster bed to French tapestries and a set of beautiful fans.

If you have time to spare, browse along Independencia, a pedestrian shopping street a block north of Parque Vidal that is a classic Cuban combination of empty, cavernous department stores and heavily guarded dollar shops.

On the Che trail Follow Independencia east to the Armored Train, or **Tren Blindado►** *(Open* Tue–Sun 8–12, 2–6. *Admission charge* inexpensive). On December 29, 1958, Che Guevara derailed a troop train bringing reinforcements to Batista's forces in the city. The bulldozer used in the ambush and three of the 30 wagons are on display; simple exhibitions inside tell the story.

The **Plaza de la Revolución►►**, a massive open space where political rallies are held 1 mile west of Parque Vidal, may be the highlight of a visit to Cuba for Che lovers.

A mausoleum has been built to house the revolutionary icon's bones, recovered from Bolivia in 1997. The words of the letter Fidel gave Che on his departure for Bolivia (which are sometimes broadcast through loudspeakers) and a giant bas-relief of significant events in the 1950s flank Che's towering statue.

Beneath the memorial, the **Museo Comandante Ernesto Che Guevara**►► (*Open* Mon–Sat 9–5; Sun 9–12. *Admission charge* inexpensive) is full of great photos of the revolutionary icon in many guises: as baby, rebel youth, guerrilla fighter, cane cutter, public speaker. There is also a large number of his possessions, from a trend setting beret to a saddle used in Bolivia and binoculars and pipe from the Congo.

The arcade of one of Santa Clara's grand public buildings

Pirates or devils?
Santa Clara was founded in 1689 by inhabitants from Remedios. Some claim they had fled the constant attentions of pirates, others devils who, according to a local priest, had taken over their town.

Eastern central Cuba

▶▶ **Camagüey** *121D2*

Cuba's third largest city, with a population of nearly 300,000, was originally founded, in 1514, on the north coast near present-day Nuevitas. Called Santa María del Puerto Príncipe, the settlement was forced by pirate attacks to move inland, and it ended up in its present site in 1528. Still pestered by pirates (including the infamous Henry Morgan, who went on the rampage in 1668), the city was redesigned on a labyrinthine layout in order to disorientate unwelcome visitors and enable the inhabitants to ambush them. In contrast with most other Cuban communities, which are arranged in a grid around a main

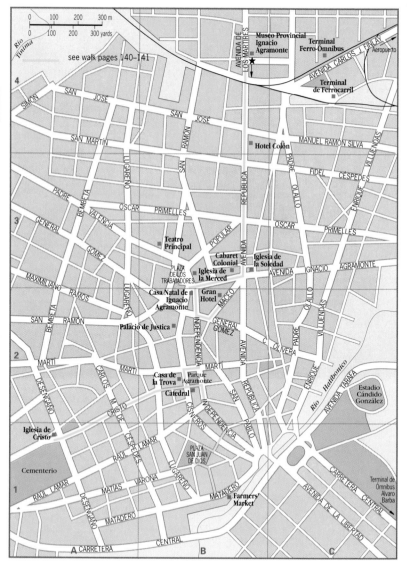

see walk pages 140–141

A fine doorway on Plaza San Juan de Dios

Entertainment
The *casa de la trova* on Parque Agramonte is one of Cuba's prettiest and liveliest (if also rather touristy), with a bar and a lovely big courtyard. A troubadour group strikes up to greet visitors throughout the day and around 9 PM on weekday evenings (a dance band is more common at weekends). The Cabaret Colonial, a locals' dive at Agramonte No. 406 (near the corner of República), operates 8:30 PM until late daily except Wednesday. For high culture, enquire at the grand Teatro Principal near Plaza de los Trabajadores, where Camagüey's often-praised ballet company sometimes performs.

square, Camagüey is still a maze of narrow streets, interlinking with a number of small squares. Most streets are one-way—drive around at your peril. The best way to explore is on foot, or by *bicitaxi*, the Cuban equivalent of a rickshaw.

The city lends itself to gentle wandering. With the exception of its perfect colonial square, Plaza San Juan de Dios, it has no outstanding individual sights and, unlike other Cuban cities, Camagüey is largely devoid of architectural flourishes. Its buildings are restrained and even somber, though behind their wooden doors and shuttered full-length windows you can often spy a living room with a fluted pillar or perhaps a gorgeous secluded patio. The city's most ostentatious decoration is in its colonial churches, which are among the country's finest. There are 25 religious buildings in all in Camagüey, of which eight are still functioning.

Most tourists come to the city on day-long bus tours from Playa Santa Lucía. Stay the night if you can. There are a number of dirt-cheap, hugely atmospheric hotels right in the center, and after dark the poorly lit streets take on a Dickensian feel, particularly when a horse-and-buggy plods by with a little fire burning at the rear for a lamp.

Water shortages
Camagüey is not blessed with good water supplies and has little rainfall for much of the year. So early Camagüeyanos came up with the idea of capturing and storing the rain that fell in the summer's short heavy showers in massive earthenware jars, similar in design to those once used in Spain to transport wine and oil. Called *tinajones*, they were positioned under gutters and, to keep their contents cool, were placed under the shade of a tree or were half buried in the ground. They have become the symbol of the city, and can still be seen in many courtyards.

Walk Camagüey's highlights

See highlighted route on map on page 138.

The only way to explore the city's network of meandering streets is on foot. This tour links up the best museums, finest churches, main squares, and shopping streets. Allow the best part of a day.

Start just north of the train station at the **Museo Provincial Ignacio Agramonte►** (*Open* Tue–Sat 9–5; Sun 8–12. *Admission charge* inexpensive). The old Spanish barracks now house everything from stuffed Cuban birds and mammals to fine art and opulent antiques. The highlight, however, is the lovely courtyard garden, where *tinajones* (see panel page 139) rest beneath exotic trees, including some whose fruits make the *güiro* musical instrument.

Head south down Avenida República, a bustling commercial thoroughfare that serves as a fascinating microcosm of Cuban life. The nationwide austerity is revealed in shop windows that display only shuttlecocks and plastic flowers and by the fact that every other store is offering to repair something (from hats to sewing machines).

After about 660 yards you come to the decrepit-looking **Iglesia de la Soledad►** (*Open* Mon–Sat 7–11, 4–6; Sun 6–12). Its interior, however, is impressive, with baroque frescoes covering its arches. Turn right and walk down to inelegant Plaza de los Trabajadores. On one corner, see **Casa Natal de Ignacio Agramonte►**, the birthplace of the

Soledad church has one of the best restored interiors

pugilistic general who fought many battles in the Ten Years' War (*Open* Tue–Wed 10–5; Thu–Fri 12–10; Sat 10–6; Sun 8–12. *Admission charge* inexpensive). This grand but dour mansion exhibits Agramonte's matrimonial bed, revolver, and even pencil, along with the tattered Cuban flag from a battle at nearby Jimaguayú, where he died in 1873. The slaves would have lived on the lower floor, the family upstairs. Across the street is the **Iglesia de la Merced**▶ (*Open* Mon–Sat 8–5:30), part of a convent built in 1748 and still functioning. Its beautiful courtyard and the church's art-nouveau murals have benefited from a lengthy restoration project. Ask to see the relics in its little crypt.

Take Independencia southward, detouring for a stroll along Maceo, Camagüey's garish pedestrianized main shopping street, with a fun mix of art-deco and neoclassical architecture. There's always a line at the giant Coppelia ice cream parlor.

Return to Independencia and continue to **Parque Agramonte**▶, a restful square that served as the military parade ground in colonial times. It is ennobled by a statue of a dashing Agramonte on his steed and a palm in each corner commemorating patriots executed in 1851. On the south side stands the city's forlorn cathedral, which has been supported by a forest of wooden scaffolding for many years, and on the west side the super **Casa de la Trova**▶▶ (see page 139).

From here, it is a five-minute stroll down to Camagüey's **cemetery**▶▶. A place of great melancholy beauty, it comprises a large grid of marble tombs decked out with crosses and plastic flowers.

Retrace your footsteps to Parque Agramonte, and press on to serene and cobbled **Plaza San Juan de Dios**▶▶, far and away Camagüey's loveliest square. Three of its sides are enclosed by harmonious, single-story red-tiled buildings, all from the 18th century and painted in blues and russets and sporting long *rejas*, or wooden bars, over their windows. The fourth is taken up by a church, built in 1728 (*Open* Mon–Sat 7–12), which has a photogenic yellow bell

Camagüey's farmers' market is one of the island's most colorful

tower and an intimate interior with a mahogany *alfarje* ceiling. Alongside, the arcaded **courtyard**▶ (*Open* Mon–Fri 8–5; Sat 8–12. *Admission charge* inexpensive) of what was once its convent and later became a hospital, has requisite *tinajones* and a plaque marking the spot where Agramonte's body lay for a day before being buried.

If you're weary, have a drink or a meal in the square's Campana de Toledo (see page 204). Otherwise, for a change of tone and pace, head south to the **farmers' market**▶▶. *Campesinos* in wide-brimmed stetsons preside over stalls selling everything from strings of garlic to whole pigs that arrive on the back of bikes and horse-drawn carts. The produce may be bounteous, but for most Cubans prices are astronomical.

■ **All creative expression in Cuba is permissible—as long as it doesn't speak out too strongly against the regime. At the same time, the communist government has made culture more available to all Cubans. Virtually every town now has a library, museum, art gallery, theater, and *casa de la cultura*, or culture house.** ■

Film

Film production only really took off in any significant way after the revolution, with the creation of the Cuban Institute of Cinematographic Art and Industry (ICAIC). The institute has worked away creating glowing propagandist images of Cuba in political documentaries, but also, despite financial constraints, has made some quality feature films. A groundbreaking movie was Tomás Gutiérrez Alea's Fresa y Chocolate (Strawberry and Chocolate), nominated for an Oscar in 1995 for Best Foreign Film. It deals with a relationship between a gay artist and a repressed young communist in a country where homosexuality is largely a taboo subject.

Statue in Havana tourist office

Freedom of expression "*Dentro de la revolución, todo; contra la revolución, nada*" ("within the revolution, everything; against the revolution, nothing"). Castro's pronouncement in a 1961 speech on the arts still largely holds sway today. What is "against the revolution" is an elastic concept defined by the Communist Party that changes according to how confident the government is feeling. In the early 1960s, the government set up the National Union of Cuban Writers and Artists (UNEAC), declaring that "all writers and artists…should take part in the great work of defending and consolidating the revolution." Since then, all creative outpourings in Cuba—film, art, literature—have effectively fallen under state control in order to produce politically positive work. As a consequence, many top writers and artists have emigrated.

Painting and sculpture In the early 1960s, the Soviets pressed Castro to follow their lead and ban nonrepresentational art altogether, but Castro replied: "Our enemies are capitalism and socialism, not abstract painting." Cuba's most renowned artist is Wilfredo Lam (1902–1982), a surrealist who made much use of jungle and folkloric scenes in his work. Other leading 20th-century painters include René Portocarrero and pop artist Raúl Martínez, whose creations include lauded poster-style portraits of Cuba's revolutionary leaders. Havana's Museo Nacional de Bellas Artes (see page 72) has examples of these three painters' works. Many contemporary artists are employed to produce the striking political billboards that enliven the towns and countryside. Meanwhile, since the introduction of legalized private enterprise, artists have also started selling their works to tourists in markets and in their front rooms. Cuba's best-known sculptress is Rita Longa: see her sculptures in Guamá, Las Tunas, and Morón (see pages 117, 123, 144).

Literature After all-round Cuban hero José Martí (see page 42), who was deported for his anticolonial writings, Cuba's most revered writer is Alejo Carpentier (1904–1980). A leader of the Latin-American style of writing called "magical realism," he was exiled under Batista's regime, but returned to Cuba after the revolution. Long-time president of UNEAC and the revolution's foremost poet is Nicolás Guillén (1902–1989). His poetry is outspoken about the exploitation of blacks and shows marked Afro-Cuban rhythms. Cuba's greatest living author, Guillermo Cabrera Infante, a very outspoken critic of Castro and his regime, has lived in exile in London since

1965. His *oeuvre*, along with those of other dissidents, is banned in Cuba. Indeed, most bookshops in Cuba are stocked with little more than dusty tomes of Marxist economics and speeches by Castro and Che Guevara.

Dance In the performing arts field, Cuba excels in dance. The Ballet Nacional de Cuba, founded by prima ballerina Alicia Alonso in 1948 and based at Havana's Gran Teatro (see page 73), has an outstanding reputation for modern and classical work, as has Camagüey's ballet company.

Carnivals Cuba's carnivals originated in colonial times as a period for slaves to celebrate at the end of the sugar harvest. A mix of Spanish and African religious customs, carnivals have at their heart processions called *comparsas*, formed by neighborhood religious societies, that dance, make music, and wear costumes traditional to African folklore. Today, they are also an excuse for holding a huge street party. By far the most famous is Santiago's carnival (see page 159). Havana's (also large) is now being held over four weekends in February. Varadero's, a more touristy affair, takes place on four weekends starting mid-January.

Festivals
Every November, Havana holds the prestigious Havana International Ballet Festival, and every December there is the New Latin American Film Festival—a good opportunity to see Cuban films and arguably the most important event of its kind in the Spanish-speaking world. Havana also holds an outstanding jazz festival biennially (next in 1999), featuring the best Cuban musicians and top international artists (ask for details).

A difficult to decipher, untitled work by Wilfredo Lam, painted in 1944

143

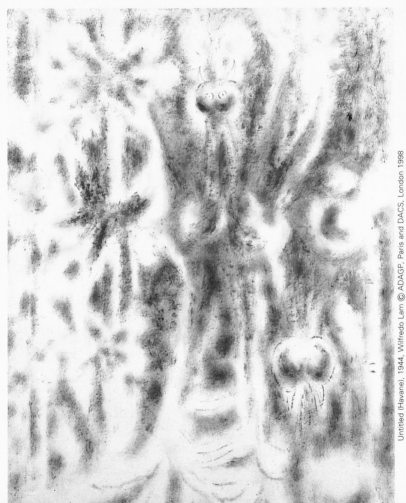

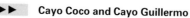

War on the keys
For two years from mid-1942, Ernest Hemingway patrolled the shores of the Cayería del Norte looking for Germans in his armed yacht, *El Pilar*. He describes his adventures in *Islands in the Stream*. In May 1995, another gunboat reappeared on Cayo Coco's shores, this time operated by members of the Miami-based paramilitary group Alpha 66. Apparently, they strafed the Hotel Tryp Cayo Coco, but no one was injured.

Cuba's beaches don't come any better than Playa Los Cocos

►► **Cayo Coco and Cayo Guillermo**   *121D3*

If all you are looking for from your Cuban holiday are pristine sands and azure seas, these offshore keys fit the bill perfectly. However, they are fantasy vacation islands that bear absolutely no relation to the real Cuba: no Cubans live here and the only locals allowed even to visit are authorized workers.

Cayo Coco From the mainland you reach Cayo Coco via a tollbooth and the Pedralpen, a 17-mile-long causeway that seems to be taking you straight out into the ocean. Cuba's fourth-largest island, roughly 6 miles wide and 25 miles long, was recently used for rearing cattle and charcoal burning, but now is almost completely covered by dense, wild woodland. Its allure rests with its 14 miles of dazzling white sands running along the north shore. In 1997 two large hotel complexes, including the Spanish-run Tryp Cayo Coco (see page 201), superbly designed in colonial style and opened by Castro himself in 1993, were finished. Work is underway for more complexes. The Tryp Cayo Coco sits on a peach of a palm-fringed beach, where a diving center takes the adventurous out to a 6-mile-long coral reef offshore.

Cayo Guillermo Connected to the western end of Cayo Coco by a 1-mile causeway, Guillermo is a mere 5 square miles, and much of that is marshland. At its southern end are two (soon to be more) hotel complexes, an enticing beach with sandbars, shallow waters, and a marina. A vehicle track leads to Playa Pilar, an unspoiled pine-backed strand.

Excursions Isolation is the major drawback of vacationing on these keys. However, there are "seafaris," deep-sea fishing trips, and, from Cayo Coco's own little airport, expensive charter flights to places such as Havana, Trinidad, and the Bahamas. On land, head for likable **Morón►**, on the mainland 37 miles from Cayo Coco. (Look for a bizarre settlement of Dutch-styled houses en route called Celia Sánchez, named after and dreamt up by Castro's secretary). Morón offers a refreshing dose of Cuban normality in a long, whimsically colored pillared main street, horse-and-buggy taxis, and wonderful old steam engines in the train station. Just south from the center, a giant metal rooster crows every day at 6 AM and 6 PM.

► ▓▓▓ **Playa Santa Lucía** *121E3*

This isolated, rather soulless resort comprises little more than five adjacent hotels along a fine section of a 12-mile-long sandy beach, on a peninsula separated from the mainland by salt flats and mosquito-ridden marshland. The hotels are pitched at convivial package tourists, offering cocktail lessons and Mr. Tarzan contests. Where Santa Lucía excels is in its diving: the brochures claim the coral reef (on which you can see the waves breaking from the beach) is the world's second largest (but this is disputed by Belize). A sophisticated diving center by the Hotel Quatro Vientos offers 35 diving sites, including ones with wrecks and black coral, and courses for all abilities. Another plus for Santa Lucía is that, unlike some other resorts, it does not exclude local Cubans.

Excursions Playa Los Cocos►►►, 4 miles along a dirt track and served by a daily bus from Santa Lucía, is one of Cuba's most fetching beaches, a palm-fringed curve of sand around protected milky-blue waters. But for a few cafés serving fresh fish, it is entirely undeveloped. An even better place for a seafood blowout is one of the homespun restaurants in next-door La Boca, a ramshackle community of brightly painted shacks. Across the mouth of the bay lie virgin beaches on Cayo Sabinal►, which can be reached on boat trips from Santa Lucía or by road. There is little else of interest in the vicinity, but there are excursions by air to most corners of the island and by land to Camagüey►► (see pages 138–141), the nearest big town, 90 minutes away. On the way you pass Rancho King►, until recently a retreat for Castro and his cronies and now a tourist center with a rustic restaurant, horseback riding, and rodeos.

Ecology and the keys
Completed in 1988, the Pedralpen (the causeway to Cayo Coco) is an environmental disaster, creating a brackish lagoon and disturbing the area's ecosystem. There are belated plans to put arches in the causeway to let the sea flow freely. The concern is for the abundant birdlife: the keys and surrounding mudflats are popular destinations for birds migrating from the north in winter. You may be lucky enough to spot flocks of flamingos around the Pedralpen, especially early or late in the day, as well as herons, pelicans, and ibises perched statuesquely in the shallows. Cayo Coco, in fact, translates as Key Ibis, not Key Coconut as you might suppose.

145

There are plenty of watersports options from Playa Santa Lucía

EASTERN CUBA

147

Peasant dwellings in a remote corner of the Sierra Maestra

EASTERN CUBA

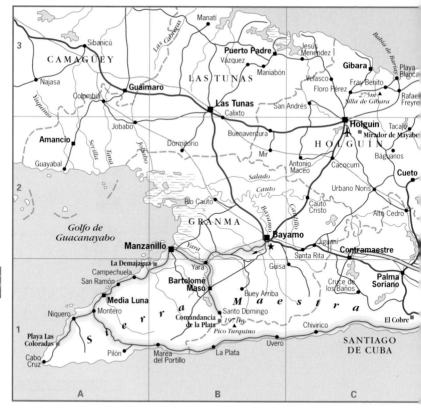

Time on the beach
Eastern Cuba's best destination for a stay-put beach vacation is Guardalavaca or nearby Playa Esmeralda; both have long golden sands, good watersports facilities, and comfortable hotels. Added to which, there is plenty to see in the area should the weather be poor. Next best are the Hotel Sierra Mar at Chivirico or Parque Baconao—but the dark-sand beaches are not as good as at Guardalavaca and the hotels, though close to Santiago, are rather isolated. There are some gorgeous, unspoiled beaches around Baracoa, including a contender for the best beach in Cuba at Maguana.

One of Holguín's placid squares

Eastern Cuba Scenically, Oriente (the East)—which pre-1976 was a single region and is now made up of four provinces—is Cuba at its grandest and wildest. Though the monotonous plains of central Cuba continue into Oriente, they soon give way to a series of mountain ranges, the largest of which, the Sierra Maestra, extends along much of the southern coast. The changing country-side means that the region is Cuba's most agriculturally diverse, with fields of cane covering its plains, and coffee, banana, and cocoa plantations coating the lush mountain foothills.

Eastern Cuba's tourism potential is only just starting to be tapped. There is one full-scale resort in Guardalavaca and a small scattering of other package beach hotel complexes. Elsewhere, apart from in the region's main city, Santiago, and in its loveliest town, Baracoa, there is a good chance you will be the only tourist for miles around.

The east–west divide Culturally, the East is the most African-feeling part of Cuba, with a predominantly black population and the island's strongest musical heritage. Soon after Spanish colonization, Cuba's commerce gravitated westward to Havana, leaving Oriente the poorest province, a frontierland for freed slaves, fugitives, and small-time *criollo* plantation owners. In the 19th century it was the most anti-Spanish part of the island, and, owing to its distance from the capital, the least encumbered by

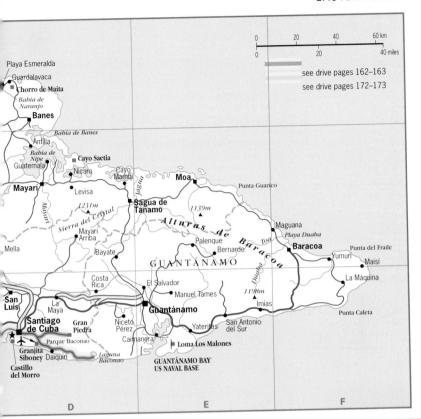

0	20	40	60 km
0	20		40 miles

see drive pages 162–163
see drive pages 172–173

Playa Esmeralda
Guardalavaca
Chorro de Maíta
Bahía de Naranjo
Banes
Bahía de Banes
Antilla
Bahía de Nipe
Guatemala
Nicaro
Cayo Saetia
Cayo Mambí
Moa
Punta Guarico
Mayarí
Levisa
1231m
Sierra del Cristal
Mayarí Arriba
Sagua de Tánamo
1139m
Alturas de
Maguana
Playa Duaba
Baracoa
Mella
Bayate
Palenque
Bernardo
Toa
Baracoa
Punta del Fraile
Yumurí
Maisí
GUANTÁNAMO
Duaba
La Máquina
Costa Rica
El Salvador
Manuel Tames
1198m
San Luis
La Maya
Niceto Pérez
Guantánamo
Imías
Punta Caleta
Santiago de Cuba
Gran Piedra
Parque Baconao
Yateritas
San Antonio del Sur
Caimanera
Loma Los Malones
Granjita Siboney
Daiquirí
Laguna Baconao
GUANTÁNAMO BAY US NAVAL BASE
Castillo del Morro

Mayarí
Jiguaní

149

D E F

colonial rule. It is no accident that the independence movement took off in the 1860s in Oriente, nor that the ensuing wars were largely fought here. Likewise, in the 1950s, when the East still had the lowest living standards and highest level of discontent in Cuba, it was not by chance that Castro chose to land here with his rebels, or that he created his guerrilla base and soon afterward a liberated zone in the lawless Sierra Maestra mountains. While much of eastern Cuba is still impoverished, it could be argued that this is the region that has benefited the most from Castro's revolution. Roads now reach the most remote corners, and the *campesinos'* quality of life has improved dramatically with the introduction of free social services.

Holguín Province Columbus understandably waxed lyrical about the lush, hilly scenery of the province's north coast that made up his first impressions of Cuba. A couple of its prime sandy beaches, at and around Guardalavaca, have been sensitively developed for tourism. Spitting distance away await sleepy towns, visually hardly altered

EASTERN CUBA

since colonial times, and aboriginal sights—this area was one of the most heavily populated prior to the Spanish arrival. Holguín city, though pleasantly open and green, pales by comparison. The eastern end of the province has three little-visited mountain ranges, and, to their north, a good road to Moa, which is an industrial center for nearby nickel mines. After Moa, the road deteriorates as it makes its way to Baracoa, a full day's journey away from Holguín city.

Granma Province The only province on the island not named after its capital, Granma has two distinct parts. Sugarcane fields and rice paddies cover the boring plains around the Río Cauto (Cuba's longest river) in the north and behind the west-facing coast. The most appealing spot is Granma's plucky little capital, Bayamo, which played a pivotal role in Cuba's 19th-century independence wars. Few visitors make it to Manzanillo, even fewer to Playa Las Coloradas along the coast, where Castro's motorlaunch, *Granma*, landed in 1956 (and hence the province's name). But it is the brooding Sierra Maestra in the south of the province, whose peaks loom large above the plains, that dominates Granma's topography. The mountains have virtually no tourist infrastructure but offer great rewards for the adventurous. The only fellow travelers you are likely to encounter are Canadians vacationing at Marea del Portillo, a pair of beach hotels on the south coast that have suddenly become marginally less remote with the completion of a dramatic and fast new coastal road east to Santiago.

Santiago de Cuba Province Much of the Sierra Maestra actually lies within this province, but here the focus is urban rather than rural. The island's second-largest city, Santiago de Cuba (which everyone calls simply Santiago), is big enough to be enervating, and it takes a few days before you feel at home, but it offers the best music venues and museums outside Havana, and its old quarters have an infectiously languorous air. Outside the city, the province's most explored area is Parque Baconao, which is not so much a park as a set of often quirky attractions, mediocre beaches, and package hotels along a 31-mile coastal strip.

Guantánamo Province Cuba's far east varies from the ridiculous to the sublime. The Guantánamo Bay Naval Base is a post-Cold War anomaly. Most visitors don't bother going to Guantánamo city unless they are going to the lookout over the base, which must rate as Cuba's most peculiar tourist attraction. According to local hearsay, the highway westward toward Santiago is said to double as a runway in case of an American attack. Eastward, it is a long drive, first along a barren, cactus-ridden coast, then on a tortuously windy route over the mountains called La Farola (the Beacon) to Baracoa. This isolated colonial town, ensconced in idyllic countryside, is a true Shangri-La. Separated from the rest of the island by mountains where, it is said, descendants of Taíno Indians still live, Baracoa has an otherworldly quality. Before La Farola was built in the 1960s, the town was accessible only by sea.

Itineraries
If you have only a few days to spare in eastern Cuba, visit either Santiago (served by frequent daily flights from Havana) or Baracoa (there are just a couple of flights a week from Havana, so book well in advance). With a week to play with, you could spend four days in and around Santiago, then either make a beeline for Baracoa, or, if you want beachside comforts, consider heading up to Guardalavaca. In two weeks, if you kept on the move, you could explore just about everything described in this chapter.

Castro the numerologist
July 26 is the date on which Castro attacked the Moncada Barracks in Santiago and also the name given to the underground rebels' movement that formed soon after. In an interview in 1987, Castro noted other significances to the number 26, saying: "I was born in 1926...I was 26 when I began the armed struggle, and I was born on the thirteenth, which is half of 26. Batista staged his coup in '52, which is twice 26. Now that I think of it, there is something mystical about the number 26."

The roof of eastern Cuba, from Parque Baconao's Gran Piedra

Santiago de Cuba

The allure of hilly, hot, sticky Santiago de Cuba, to give the city its full name, rests with its atmosphere rather than any specific sights. The sounds of jazz and *rumba*, *son*, and *salsa* waft from hidden sources; provocative sidelong glances are thrown at passersby from balconies and through long, wrought-iron window grilles; the clickety-clack of dominos emanates from the shadow of a doorway. Cuba's number two city may be less dazzling and tumbledown than Havana, but it is almost as captivating. Its geographical position, facing Jamaica and Haiti rather than Florida, meant it was never Americanized in the way Havana was, and instead it has a more laid-back Caribbean flavor. Its population of 400,000 is said to be the most ethnically diverse on the island.

152

The elements have felled Santiago's cathedral three times

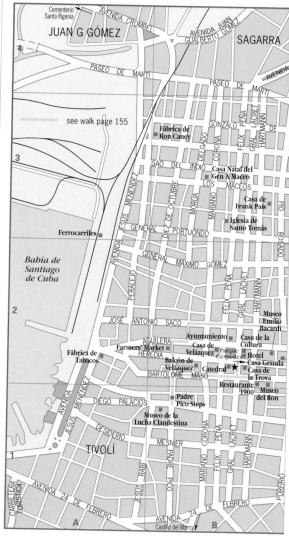

see walk page 155

SANTIAGO DE CUBA

You can find live music in the Casa de la Trova morning, noon, and night

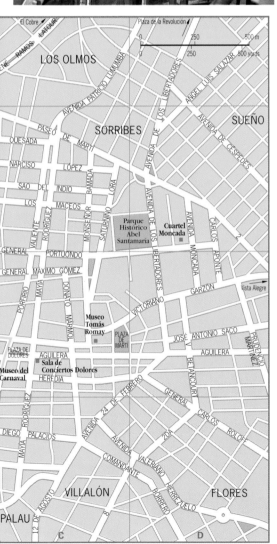

Where to stay

Santiago has a dearth of city center accommodations, the fabulous Casa Granda being the only comfortable exception. Most tourist hotels are located in the Vista Alegre district. The nearest to the center (1.8 miles away) are the ostentatious Santiago de Cuba and the shabby, noisy Las Américas, opposite. Other Vista Alegre choices, such as the Villa Gaviota and San Juan, are considerably more peaceful but another mile away. Many package tourists stay an hour from the city at Chivirico (see page 170) and Parque Baconao (see pages 162–163), while independent travelers often lodge in private rooms: just ask around if you are interested in this option.

EASTERN CUBA

History Founded in 1514, Santiago was the island's capital until 1553, when the title passed to Havana because of its more convenient position on the trading route between the New World and Europe. Subjected to frequent pirate attacks and often shaken by earthquakes, the city only really took off in the 1790s with the arrival of some 30,000 French settlers fleeing slave risings in neighboring Hispaniola. Since then, Santiago has played a seminal part in Cuba's road to independence, earning it the sobriquet Hero City. Many of the island's most important 19th-century patriots were buried in the city's cemetery, and in 1898 the Spanish forces were defeated on the outskirts of the city at San Juan Hill (Loma de San Juan). Half a century later, Santiago became the urban center of the rebel movement, beginning with the attack on the Moncada Barracks in 1953 that kicked off the armed struggle, and culminating in Castro declaring the "triumph of the Revolution" from a balcony overlooking the city's main square on January 1, 1959.

Layout Santiago is clasped within a horseshoe of the Sierra Maestra foothills, making the south-facing city airless and stiflingly hot in the height of summer. Fortunately, it largely turns its back on its deep bay, which is dominated by a power plant, oil refinery, and cement factory. Instead the old center, a large grid of streets just east of the bay's head that comprises the city's cultural and commercial heart, focuses in on itself, around Parque Céspedes (the main square) and José A Saco (the main street). This area is where you will want to spend most time, not least to immerse yourself in the languid ambience of the residential, colonial back streets. A number of sights are scattered around the city's surrounding modern districts, of which the most salubrious is Vista Alegre, with broad tree-lined avenues and grand mansions. Once the homes of the well-to-do, these are now mainly converted into cultural centers and schools.

The bronze Titan on Plaza de la Revolución

Walk **Old Santiago highlights**

*See highlighted route on map on
pages 152–153.*

Covering the most atmospheric
streets in the city center, this walk
could take an hour or a day, depending on whether you stop off at the
sights it passes and how friendly you
are to the many characters you will
encounter on the way. It is best tack-
led early or late in the day to avoid
the heat.

Start at **Parque Céspedes**▶▶ (see
pages 156–157), Santiago's bustling
outdoor living-room. Head down **Calle
Heredia**▶▶ (see page 156), the city's
cultural center and most touristy
street, for three blocks. Turn left onto
Porfirio Valiente, and pass Plaza de
Dolores, a square full of hustlers,
cafés, and restaurants. Bear left onto
José A Saco▶. Santiago's main
shopping thoroughfare has wonderful
1950s shop signs hanging across the
street that vie for attention with
Moorish, baroque, art-deco, and
Italianate architecture. If you are
thirsty, try a *granizado*, or flavored
water ice, which you can buy from

streetside carts. Six blocks down,
turn left again onto Padre Pico, pass
the farmers' market, and follow the
street down to Padre Pico steps. You
have reached a very picturesque residential neighborhood called **Tivolí**▶
(see page 158). Climb the stairs up to
the **Museo de la Lucha
Clandestina**▶▶ (see page 158) for
one of the best views over the old
center, then retrace your steps down
Padre Pico, and turn right onto
cobbled Bartolomé Masó, arguably
the city's most characterful colonial
street. Drop in at Restaurante 1900
(see page 204) at No. 354, the
grand former Bacardí home. The
neoclassical mansion just along the
street at No. 358 has recently been
turned into the **Museo del Ron**▶
(*Open* Mon–Fri 9–5, Sat 9–1.
Admission free); its exhibitions on rum
processing are dull, but it displays
some colorful prerevolutionary postcards promoting Cuban Bacardí rum.

Head back to Parque Céspedes just
two blocks away and resuscitate
yourself with a tall drink at one of the
bars in the **Hotel Casa Granda**▶ (see
page 157).

Santiago de Cuba: old Santiago

▶▶ **Calle Heredia** 153C2

Lined with photogenic, single-story colonial buildings, Calle Heredia is Santiago's most famous street. Some buildings have been turned into art galleries, while others serve as cultural centers, such as the Casa del Estudiante across from the Casa Granda, where *rumba* groups perform some evenings, and the **Casa de la Trova▶▶▶** (see page 159). The street is named after the poet José María Heredia, born in 1803 in the pretty house at No. 260 (*Open* daily 9–9. *Admission charge* inexpensive). One block farther on, at No. 303, the **Museo del Carnaval▶** (*Open* Tue–Sun 9–5. *Admission charge* inexpensive) is crying out for an overhaul, but has evocative photographs of the Santiago carnival (see page 159) in its heyday, and some colorful costumes worn by groups from the various *barrios*. Ask about the folklore dances that take place in its courtyard.

One block north is the much more fulfilling **Museo Emilio Bacardí▶▶** (*Open* Mon 3–6; Tue–Sat 9–8; Sun 9–1. *Admission charge* inexpensive), recently reopened after years of restoration. The neoclassical building was erected in the 1920s to house the expansive collection of the son of the original rum magnate; when the Bacardí family fled in 1959, the works passed to the state. Highlights include Bacardí memorabilia and a good European and Cuban art collection, in which the most eye-catching piece is a rugged sculpture of Che Guevara by Alberto Lescay, who also created the Maceo statue in Plaza de la Revolución (see page 160). Egyptian crocodile and ibis mummies number among the archeological exhibits in a room reached by a side entrance on Aguilera.

▶▶ **Parque Céspedes** 152B2

Though surrounded by striking buildings, this is not one of Cuba's most beautiful squares. It is, however, the place to feel Santiago's pulse. Effectively it is a social club for Santiagüeros (especially on weekend evenings), and its shaded benches are occupied day and night. Unfortunately, though, persistent tourist hustlers work flat out here, too.

The Museo Emilio Bacardí houses one of Cuba's best art collections

Casa de Velázquez▶▶ (*Open* Mon–Sat 9–5; Sun 9–1. *Admission charge* inexpensive). The somber-looking building on the square's west side, built between 1516 and 1530 as a commercial and gold-smelting center (downstairs) and Diego Velásquez's private quarters (upstairs), is said to be the oldest house in the Americas. Its most interesting feature is the screen enclosing its balcony, which allowed the governor to peek at his citizens unseen. Also admire the wonderful *alfarje* ceiling and antiques such as four-poster beds. When the house became a museum in the 1970s, it was joined to a fine 19th-century mansion at its rear, which

has a second courtyard and more period furniture, including a gondola bed in which Céspedes once slept.

This hidden courtyard lies behind the Casa de Velázquez

Catedral► (*Open* usually mornings). A church has stood on this site since the 1520s. However, thanks to earthquake, wind, and fire this yellow edifice, towering over the square on a raised platform, is the fourth to be built and was completed in the 1920s. Its Italianate interior is in surprisingly good condition, with carved choir stalls, an ornately frescoed ceiling, and scroll-pattern pillars.

Hotel Casa Granda► (see also page 201) Featured in Graham Greene's *Our Man in Havana*, and described in the 1960s by the British vice-consul as a "hotbed of revolution, with all the rooms wired for sound," this is the only Santiago hotel that has real style. Named after Don Manuel de Granda, who owned a private mansion on this site, the hotel first opened in 1914, and reopened in 1995 after prolonged restoration. Its terrace bar is a fascinating place to soak up Santiago's beat; a mute magician often performs here. A second bar on the roof offers superb views of the cathedral and bay.

Casa de la Cultura Next to the Casa Granda, this grand old building is in serious need of attention. Art exhibitions are held in the foyer below its sweeping marble staircase.

Ayuntamiento (no entry allowed). Though colonial in style, the blue and white city hall facing the cathedral was actually built in the 1950s. Castro gave his first victory speech on January 1, 1959 from its middle balcony.

Frank

Known affectionately to everyone simply as Frank, Frank País was head of the 26 July Movement in Oriente and was assassinated on July 30, 1957 by the police. Over 100,000 Santiagüeros thronged the streets at his funeral, and the anniversary of his death is commemorated today with a procession from Parque Céspedes to his grave at Cementerio Santa Ifigenia. His former home, the cute little Casa de Frank País▶ at General Banderas No. 226, north of José A Saco, displays a few prized possessions as well as photographs of the funeral and of his corpse lying in the street, blood running into the gutter (*Open* Mon–Sat 9–5. *Admission charge* inexpensive).

El Puerto (the Port) 152A2

Avenida Jesús Menéndez, running along the east side of the bay, is not a place to linger. However, the **Fábrica de Tabacos▶** (*Open* Mon–Fri 7–4. *Admission charge* inexpensive), at the corner of Bartolomé Masó, is well geared to tourists, with the whole cigar-making process on show in one small room and an excellent cigar shop. North of the station, the original Bacardí factory, now state-owned and called the Fabrica de Ron Caney, has a bar and a shop selling every sort of factory-produced rum (*Open* Mon–Sat 9–6; Sun 9–2. *Admission charge* inexpensive).

North of the bay's head, the **Cementerio Santa Ifigenia▶▶** is a beautiful sea of marble (*Open* daily 7–6. *Admission charge* inexpensive). Its significant tombs are close to the entrance. The most revered is José Martí's vast art-deco mausoleum. It is surrounded by the coats of arms of the countries of the Americas and female statues representing the six old provinces of Cuba. Other notable tombs include those of Emilio Bacardí, Carlos Manuel de Céspedes (topped by a classical sculpture), and the armed forces (FAR) memorial, with shells embedded in the surrounding wall. Fluttering above the tomb of *inolvidable* (unforgettable) Frank País, as over many graves, are the Cuban flag and the banner of the 26 July Movement.

▶ Tivolí 152A1

Named after a theater established by early 19th-century French emigrants, the residential quarter southwest of Parque Céspedes is rewarding for aimless wandering. Most visitors, however, make it no farther than the **Museo de la Lucha Clandestina▶▶** at the top of the Padre Pico steps (*Open* 9–5 Tue–Sun. *Admission charge* inexpensive). The restored colonial building in which this Museum of the Secret Struggle is housed was a police station, which the rebels under Frank País attacked on November 30, 1956, to distract from the *Granma* landing. It sheds light on the 1950s resistance movement.

Hilly Tivolí is Santiago's most picturesque district

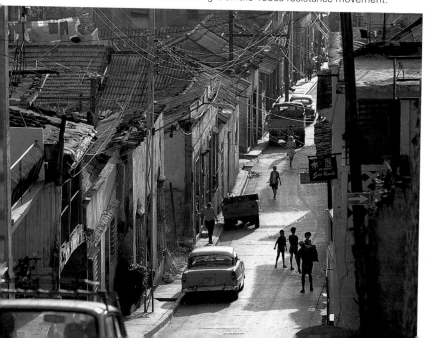

■ **The birthplace of *son*, Santiago is the best place after Havana to find great live music. The fusion of Spanish, French, and African cultures is fully expressed in the city's musical prowess, which reaches a great crescendo in the city's famous carnival.** ■

Santiago's Casa de la Trova It is not much to look at, but this small room on Calle Heredia, with rows of chairs and portraits of famous Santiago musicians, is Cuba's most famous music venue. Daily from around 10:30 AM until 3 PM and nightly from around 9 until midnight, a succession of musicians—ranging from professional groups to solo amateurs—perform every style of Cuban music. The mood can be sedate (when, for example, locals laden with shopping drop in for half an hour) or quite raucous, with dancing in the aisles. Controversially, a small fee was recently levied for tourists. Performers normally have a basket of tapes for sale, and a shop sells music produced by top Cuban bands.

Santiago's Tropicana Santiago's top cabaret, 1 mile northeast of Plaza de la Revolución, begs comparison with its more famous Havana namesake (see page 90). Housed in a large modern complex, it can't compete in atmosphere. But with 100 performers the show (90 minutes long, from 10 PM Wednesday to Monday) is on an equal scale and just as slick. Hotels offer excursions.

Santiago's carnival Cuba's top festival, not held for years due to a funds shortage, has been revived but has not reached its former, riotous heights. Neighborhood groups, or *comparsas*, compete to produce the best floats, and processions take place amid a cacophony of drums, rattles, horns, Chinese cornets, and even electric guitars. The carnival's most famous dance traditions are the Afro-Cuban *conga*, *rumba*, and *tumba francesca* (French drum), the last a combination of African rhythms set to formal French 18th-century *contradanses*. Festivities run for three nights around July 26, and are at their most frenzied beside the port and along avenues Garzón and Libertadores.

Other nightlife options
La Claqueta, a nontouristy late-night hangout just south of Parque Céspedes on Félix Peña, often has live music and dancing. Patio los Dos Abuelos, a more civilized courtyard venue on Plaza de Marte, promises a live band every night around 10:30 PM. La Maison, a classy villa at Avenida Manduley No. 52 and Calle 1 in Vista Alegre, has fashion shows nightly at 10 PM. The swankiest dance club in town is at the Hotel Santiago de Cuba. Noches Cubanas, a mini musical street, festival, takes place on Calle Heredia every evening.

159

Old rum barrels in the Museo del Ron (see page 155)

Cuba's patron saint
In 1608, three fishermen allegedly discovered a statue of a mestizo virgin floating in the Bahia de Nipe off Cuba's north coast. Written on the base was: "*Yo Soy La Virgen de la Caridad*" ("I am the Virgin of Charity"). The statue was taken to Santiago cathedral, but was moved after an earthquake to El Cobre (see opposite), where the virgin became the patron saint of the slaves working in the mines. In 1916, the Pope promoted her to patron saint of Cuba. Part of her appeal to Cubans is that she is identified with Ochún, the important Santería goddess of love and rivers or fresh water. Her saint's day is September 8, when vast numbers gather at El Cobre.

Santiago de Cuba: modern Santiago

▶▶ **Cuartel Moncada (Moncada Barracks)** *153D3*
Off Avenida de los Libertadores
Open: Mon–Fri 9–5; Sat and Sun 9–1. Admission charge: inexpensive
On July 26, 1953, Castro and 125 rebels attacked the country's second-largest military post (see pages 46–47). Despite being a military fiasco, the assault was a publicity coup. The complex was turned into a school in 1961, but a section, whose entrance is peppered with reconstructed bullet holes, serves as a vivid pictorial history of the revolution. Enlarged photographs show Batista's torture victims, Che building homemade rockets, and Fidel doing military training in Mexico, in prison on the Isle of Pines, and making victory speeches in 1959. Among the memorabilia is a copy of the letter from Fidel to Che when the Argentine left for Bolivia, which ends: "I embrace you with all my revolutionary fervor."

▶ **Plaza de la Revolución** *153D4*
A colossal bronze statue of the Santiago-born mulatto General Antonio Maceo (the soldier's nickname was the Bronze Titan) dominates this open space. It is surrounded by 23 girder-size machetes signifying March 23, 1878, the date at the end of the Ten Years' War when Maceo committed himself to continue the armed struggle. The ensemble is particularly impressive when floodlit at night. Underneath the monument is a small exhibition of holograms of some of Maceo's venerated possessions (*Open* Mon–Sat 9–4; Sun 9–1. *Admission charge* inexpensive).

▶ **Vista Alegre** *153D2*
Santiago's upscale, leafy suburb is relaxing after the hassle of the city center, but it has few sights. However, don't miss the **Hotel Santiago de Cuba**▶ (see also page 201). Cuba's most audaciously designed modern hotel is a multicolored 15-story tower block that is the island's answer to Paris's Pompidou Center; its top floor bar has the best view of the city. East off Avenida Raúl Pujol on the eastern edge of the city, there are trenches, cannons, and memorials on Loma de San Juan, where Cuban and U.S. forces, under president-to-be Teddy Roosevelt, defeated the Spanish in 1898 in a bloody battle.

Excursions from Santiago

▶▶ **Castillo del Morro** *152B1*
Open: Mon–Fri 9–5, Sat and Sun 8–4. Admission charge: inexpensive
The misnamed Carretera Turística follows the industrial eastern shore of Santiago's deep harbor for 8 miles to Morro Castle. In a fantastic clifftop position at the entrance to the bay, with a commanding view of the Sierra Maestra, the castle was begun in the 1630s to protect the harbor from pirate attacks. Its enormous battlemented walls and deep moats were designed by the same Italian engineer who built Havana's Morro Castle. There are plans to reopen in its warren of rooms a museum of piracy that spotlights skull and crossbones blackguards and U.S. interference in Cuban affairs.

►► **El Cobre** *152C4*

Open: daily 6:30–6. Admission charge: free

The town of El Cobre, roughly 12 miles northwest of Santiago, is known for having the oldest open-cast copper mines in the Americas (*cobre* is Spanish for copper). But its chief claim to fame is its basilica. The cream and red-domed church, dramatic against the verdant Sierra Maestra foothills, was built in the 1920s to house Cuba's patron saint (see panel, page 160). To reach it from the parking area, you have to run the gauntlet of a mob of kids touting iron pyrites, or fool's gold. You enter a sanctuary at the rear that is packed with offerings to the virgin, from aftershave and locks of hair to model cars and sunglasses. Hemingway placed his Nobel Prize medal here, but it was stolen (and recovered) in the mid-1980s, so is no longer displayed. Walking sticks, crutches, and representations of various parts of the body have been left by supplicants when no longer ill or disabled. The delicate statue of the tiny virgin, draped in a gold gown and holding baby Jesus, is displayed above the sanctuary in such a way that it is also visible from the body of the church.

Every year, thousands make a pilgrimage to El Cobre, Cuba's holiest place

Drive **Santiago to Baconao Park**

See highlighted route on map on pages 148–149.

This 50-mile excursion from Santiago through Baconao Park, a parched strip of land between the sea and the forested eastern end of the Sierra Maestra, offers a full day's sightseeing. It takes in some stunning scenery, half a dozen interesting low-key sights, and the park's top beach. All attractions, unless otherwise stated, are open daily from around 9 AM to 5 PM and admission charges are inexpensive. For recommended hotels in the park, see page 201.

As you leave Santiago, look for the 26 memorials to those who lost their lives in the Moncada assault on July 26, 1953, and its aftermath, standing intermittently at the roadside. After 7 miles, turn left to make the tortuous 9-mile ascent to **Gran Piedra▶▶**. Climb the 440 steps up this 4,000-foot-high massive bare rock for a magnificent 360-degree view of the surrounding forested mountains. The 19th-century coffee plantation *finca*, **La Isabelica▶▶**, 1 mile east down a navigable track, takes its name from the slave mistress of the owner, a Frenchman called Victor Constantin Cuzeau. A musty, atmospheric place, it retains some of its original furniture, a concrete garden where coffee beans were laid out to dry, and a ditch around the house dug to protect Cuzeau from rebellious slaves.

Return to the coastal road and continue east for 1 mile to **Granjita Siboney▶**, the small farm from which Castro and his followers left to make their attack on the Moncada Barracks. It is now a museum, displaying endless photographs and newspaper cuttings. The most quirky piece of memorabilia is the restaurant bill from the Hotel Rex where 20 rebels dined the night before the assault; it shows only three beers—clearly something was up. Reconstructed bullet holes riddle the walls around the building's entrance: it is claimed that after Moncada, Batista's troops brought the bodies of six prisoners they had murdered, laid them on the porch, and fired into the farm to make it look as though a battle had taken place.

The **Valle de la Prehistoria▶▶**, 6 miles east, is the one sight in the park that you really must see. Bizarre in the extreme, it is like a clip from the film *Jurassic Park*. About 250 life-size dinosaur models, some as high as 66 feet, roam the fields and tear at each other's flesh, alongside a colossal club-wielding Stone Age man and Flintstone huts.

Real horses, surreal dinosaurs in Baconao Park

162

163

Playa Cazonal, the park's best beach

A mile farther on brings you to the **Conjunto de Museos y Exposiciones La Punta►**. Many of the half-dozen little exhibitions are dull, but look in on the 2,000 or more miniature cars, mostly donated by a Spanish philanthropist, and admire the full-size classic automobiles, which include Fidel's mother's 1930 Model A Ford and Batista's wife's 1948 Oldsmobile (all for sale, at a price).

Daiquirí fans might consider making the 1.5-mile diversion down to Daiquirí. The beach is lousy and the hotel even worse, but the eponymous cocktail was probably first concocted nearby by Americans working in the mines and acquired its name after U.S. troops landed here in 1898 at the start of the Spanish–American War.

Back on the main road, it is 7 miles on to **Comunidad Artística Verraco►**, a pretty hamlet of painters', sculptors', and ceramicists' studios. The artists may invite you into their homes for a

coffee as they try to sell you their wares. A further 6 miles east, past an odd, defunct fairground where cows graze around giant concrete pineapples and oranges, you come to the run-down **Aquario Baconao** (*Open Tue–Sun 9–5. Admission charge moderate*), only worth visiting if you fancy the opportunity to swim with a pair of dolphins.

Playa Cazonal►, 2 miles east, is incontrovertibly the park's best beach, a stretch of white sand and shallow waters with watersports and a beach bar. The park ends 2 miles farther on at **Laguna Baconao►**, a bewitching lake with a backdrop of mountains. Boat trips are offered from a nasty miniature zoo.

From the lake it is an hour's drive back to Santiago or, if you are feeling intrepid, you could continue east along a drivable dirt track to Guantánamo.

Holguín Province

▶ **Holguín** *148C2*

The fourth-biggest city in Cuba, with over 200,000 inhabitants, cannot compete in appeal with other large provincial capitals such as Santiago and Camagüey, or with the countryside and coastline in the north of its province. Nonetheless, its unrushed and verdant center, laid out on a grid around a row of five squares, deserves exploration, and there are good viewpoints from the hills that enclose it.

A roll call of Cuban patriots in Holguín

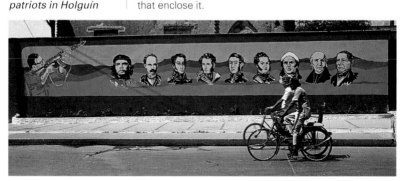

The city center Holguín's hub is **Parque Calixto García▶▶**, named after the locally born 19th-century independence hero whose statue graces the square. On its south side stands a fine art-deco theater, on the west an art gallery with good temporary exhibitions, a *casa de la trova*, and garish *casa de la cultura* with crafts for sale. In the southeast corner, there is a bookshop with an excellent collection of works in English on Cuba, and a couple of intriguing peso department stores worth browsing for inexpensive souvenirs. On weekend evenings, the city's youth descends on the square, clamoring to get into Club Siboney (on the eastern side). The handsome colonial building that dominates the square's northern flank houses the **Museo de Historia Provincial▶** (*Open* Mon–Sat 9–5. *Admission charge* inexpensive). Its vast collection of artifacts relating to pre-Columbian times, slavery, and the 19th-century independence wars includes the province's symbol, an Indian stone sculpture called the Hacha de Holguín (Holguín Axe), found in 1860. Above the fine courtyard lie a dozen rooms full of antiques.

Just south of the square at Maceo No. 129, the **Museo de Ciencias Naturales▶** (*Open* Sun–Thu 9–5; Sat 1–5. *Admission charge* inexpensive), housed in an ornate neo-classical building appropriately guarded by lions, has a wonderful set of brightly colored snails' shells in among a dreary collection of stuffed animals.

One block south brings you to Parque Peralta▶; its cathedral is rarely open, but *bicitaxis* congregate here ready to take you on a guided tour of the city for a dollar. Holguín's other squares lie to the north of Parque Calixto García, the most appealing being **Parque Céspedes▶**, surrounded by colonial buildings, just two blocks away.

Beyond the center The soulless, modernist Plaza de la Revolución, 1 mile east of the center, has a monumental

Loma de la Cruz
There are wonderful views over Holguín from the top of the Hill of the Cross, which marks the city's northern edge. On May 3, 1790 a Catholic bishop commemorated a vision of the Virgin Mary by erecting an enormous wooden cross on the hill, under which many pilgrims celebrate mass every year on May 3. You can either follow their footsteps up the 468 steps, or drive up the western side of the hill.

frieze over Garciá's tomb depicting a roll call of Cuban patriots. More fun is the **Fábrica de Organos▶** (*Open Mon–Fri 7–3:30*), at No. 301 Carretera de Gibara, 1 mile north from the center. The workers at this small organ factory delight in playing their magnificent machines for visitors while plying them with rum. Animal lovers may be disturbed by the beer-drinking donkey at the city's most touristy spot, the Mirador de Mayabe, 6 miles southeast of the center (see page 201).

▶▶ Guardalavaca   149D3

A good choice for a peaceful, stay-put beach vacation, this midsize resort is arguably the best placed on the island, surrounded by gorgeous countryside in which there are a number of interesting sights. Its 2-mile-long sandy beach is lovely at its western end, where cafés and diving and watersports centers are shaded by a little wood of sea grapes. The five hotels behind it are mostly geared to German and Canadian package tourists. The resort does not amount to much more than the beach and hotels. However, unlike some other Cuban resorts, Guardalavaca does not bar locals. Except for La Roca, an open-air disco in a stunning location above the beach's western end, nightlife is all in the hotels.

Some 4 miles west of Guardalavaca, **Playa Esmeralda▶▶** (until recently called Playa Estero Ciego) is a mini-resort with its own helicopter pad for excursions. Its half-mile-long white-sand beach, which is ensconced in palms, sea grapes, and undeveloped headlands and offers beach bars, a full gamut of watersports, and a sophisticated diving center, is every bit as good as Guardalavaca's. Two upscale hotel complexes (see pages 201–202) back onto the beach, and a third is on its way.

Guard the cow
Some say that settlers around Guardalavaca, the last point of land between Florida and Europe, used to farm cattle in order to supply passing galleons with beef. Since the area was protected from marauding pirates by an offshore reef, it acquired the name Guardalavaca, which translates as "guard the cow."

165

There is often a jolly family atmosphere on Guardalavaca beach

A Christian influence
The graves at Chorro de Maíta date from 1490 to 1540, just before and immediately after the first Spanish conquistadors arrived. Some corpses adopt the fetal position traditional in Taíno Indian culture. Others lie outstretched with arms folded across their chests, as is normal in Christian burials, providing visual evidence of how the religious values of the Spanish invaders were rapidly adopted by the aboriginal peoples they conquered. Intriguingly, one corpse is thought to be that of a Spaniard.

Gibara, with Columbus's Silla de Gibara in the background

Excursions from Guardalavaca

Lime-green sugarcane fields and palm-covered hillsides encircle Guardalavaca. This is rural Cuba at its best: thatched peasant dwellings nestle in banana groves, farmers chivvy oxen in the fields, and *campesinos* travel between villages on horseback. Guardalavaca's hotels offer excursions to most of the places described below, but it is more rewarding to rent a car or bike for a day or two.

South of Guardalavaca Chorro de Maíta▶▶ (*Open* Tue–Sat 9–5; Sun 9–1. *Admission charge* inexpensive), 4 miles southeast of the resort, is the largest aboriginal burial ground found in the Antilles. Much of the site is visible, with around 60 corpses arranged exactly as they were when they were discovered (in 1986). Some of the superb tributes and offerings found next to the bodies, such as gold and shell idols and coral necklaces, are on display. See also panel.

You can pursue the Indian theme at the small town of Banes▶, a lovely 21-mile drive south through fertile hills. Its **Museo Indo Cubano**▶, one block from the main square, has a dourly displayed but fine collection of local aboriginal finds (*Open* Mon–Sat 9–5; Sun 8–12. *Admission charge* inexpensive). There are a few simple Ciboney Indian objects, but most—ranging from ghoulish mud and stone figurines to delicate shell necklaces and ceramic bowls showing European influence—were made by Taíno

Indians. Don't leave without seeing the prize exhibit, a 13th-century gold idol of a woman in a headdress. Allow an hour's wandering to take in shabby Banes' old clapboard houses and rustic street life; you might be offered a pork sandwich made with meat sliced off a whole pig's carcass before your eyes. Castro, who grew up south of Banes in Birán, was married in 1948 in the ugly art-deco church on the main square.

West of Guardalavaca The marina on forested, undeveloped **Bahía de Naranjo►**, 5 miles from Guardalavaca just beyond Playa Esmeralda, is the departure point for a five-minute trip out to an aquarium that is beautifully sited on a platform in the middle of the bay (*Admission charge* expensive). Once a day the aquarium has a show with a sea lion and a few dolphins; for an extra charge, you can swim with them.

It has been established with some certitude that Columbus first landed in Cuba at Bahía de Bariay, where two little-visited monuments claim to mark his exact disembarkation point. One, 6 miles north of the scenic sugar mill at Rafael Freyre, stands near Playa Blanca, a sandy beach where locals park their Cadillacs under the palms. A dirt track south of the beach leads to a small, anticlimactic memorial right on the bay's edge. The other, at **Cayo Bariay►►** in the middle of the bay and reached via a long unpaved lane north of Fray Benito, is far more substantial and evocative. Set in a clearing within a vast palm grove near the shore, it consists of reproductions of Spanish and aboriginal architecture that represent the meeting of old and new worlds.

The potholed road west from Fray Benito to Floro Pérez passes the Silla de Gibara, the saddle-shape mountain that Columbus described in his journals. The road improves from Floro Pérez on to **Gibara►►**, a sensationally picturesque little town on a rocky peninsula. The region's most important port last century, it is now the sleepiest of backwaters with dozens of tumbledown colonial houses, many prevented from collapsing only by (rotting) wooden pillars. Services continue amid the rubble in the lovely triple-domed church in the town square. Gibara's grandest house, a 19th-century mansion nearby on the main street, Calle Independencia, is in much better condition. Now the **Museo de Artes Decorativas►►** (*Open* Tue–Sat 8–12, 1–5; Sun 8–12. *Admission charge* inexpensive), it is a treasure trove of overblown antique mahogany furniture and colonial architectural details (see pages 64–65). Before leaving town, climb Calle Independencia to the remains of an old hilltop fort for the fabulous view it commands over Gibara's rooftops. And visit the fishing harbor, where small boys tout bagfuls of shrimps.

167

Priceless, rustic images are commonplace around Guardalavaca

Cayo Saetía
At the entrance to Bahía de Nipe southeast of Banes, this large undeveloped island is part forested, part prairie, and boasts virgin beaches beneath low cliffs. It is home to unexpected wildlife, some of it imported. You can admire zebra, rhea, antelope, buffalo, and wild boar. Day-long helicopter excursions from Guardalavaca and Playa Santa Lucía are popular though expensive (Jeep or horseback safaris cost extra). You can also come via a poor road, and stay the night in one of the six pricey cabañas (tel: 25350).

Goat-and-buggy rides (here in Bayamo) take place in many town squares on the weekend

Granma Province

▶▶ **Bayamo** 148B2

Founded in 1513, this is the second-oldest town in Cuba, but its fame rests with its elemental role in Cuba's struggle for independence in the 19th century. On October 20, 1868, it became the first town to be taken by the rebel troops under Carlos Manuel de Céspedes, only to be torched by its inhabitants months later before being surrendered back to the Spanish forces. Around its two main squares every other building seems to bear a plaque honoring some revolutionary hero. Allow half a day to soak up its atmosphere.

Plaza de la Revolución▶▶ This handsome square is the town's focal point: old men while away the hours on marble benches under a thick swathe of live oaks and on the weekend children take goat-and-trap rides. A statue of Céspedes, mounted on a plinth with bas-reliefs showing significant events in the town's independence history, faces another local patriot called Perucho Figueredo, composer and writer of the national anthem, *La Bayamesa*, in 1868. The score and words, beginning with the stirring, famous cry "*Al combate corred bayameses*" ("Hurry into battle, people of Bayamo"), flank his bust. On the square's north side stands the house where Céspedes was born on April 18, 1819, the **Casa Natal Manuel Carlos de Céspedes**▶ (*Open* Tue–Sun 9–5. *Admission charge* inexpensive). Its cool rooms are packed with mementos of El Padre de la Patria (the Father of the Country), as he is commonly called, and period (but not original) antiques. Next door is the more diverting **Museo Provincial**▶ (*Open* Tue–Fri 8–6; Sat–Sun 10–2. *Admission charge* inexpensive). Its highlight is a guitar made from 19,109 pieces of wood; peek inside it to see miniature replicas of the tools the carpenter used to make it. Look, too, for personal effects, such as the top hat and pen of Cuba's first president, a local man named Tomás Estrada Palma.

Plaza del Himno▶ One block from Plaza de la Revolución, Hymn Square is dominated by the **church**▶ (*Open* usually afternoons 3–5) where the Cuban anthem was first sung in 1868. Despite being gutted by the 1869 fire, it is worth visiting to see the vast painting over the nave depicting a militant Bayamese gathering and a priest blessing the Cuban flag.

Beyond the center A half-mile south in a pleasant little park overlooking the river stands a former barracks that was unsuccessfully attacked on July 26, 1953, in an assault that was planned to coincide with that on the Moncada Barracks (see page 160). Now the small **Museo Nico López**▶ (*Open* Tue–Sat 8–12, 2–6; Sun 9–1. *Admission charge* inexpensive), it displays the boots of the scholarly looking young López, the leader of the attack, and a few jackets and rifles belonging to those who died.

See pages 172–173 for a two-day **drive** from Bayamo to Santiago across the plains of Granma and around the mountains of the Sierra Maestra.

► **Manzanillo** *148B2*

Granma's main port both surprises and disappoints. Overblown Moorish architecture makes its main square Cuba's most unusual. However, the waterfront is largely industrial and worth visiting only on a clear evening to enjoy a sunset from the island's one sizable west-facing coastal town. Few tourists bother with Manzanillo (there is nowhere memorable to stay or eat), with the consequence that those who do are smothered by the attentions of the locals.

The centerpiece of **Parque Céspedes**►► is La Glorieta. Built in 1924, it is a pavilion covered in Arabic lettering, marble pillars, and multicolored tiles. Whimsical Sphinx statues, wedding-cake fountains, and wrought-iron lamps further ennoble the square, as does the Edificio Quirch, with its keyhole windows and a lookout tower, on its north side. Drop in to the Casa de la Cultura, on the west side, to see art exhibitions and two giant tiled murals depicting Columbus's landing in Cuba.

Seven blocks west of Parque Céspedes' southwest corner brings you to the **Monumento a Celia Sánchez**►, a long flight of steps adorned with sunflowers and doves. From the mid-1950s until she died of cancer in 1980, Sánchez was almost certainly the most important figure in Castro's life, everything from secretary to confidante and lover. Referred to as the Most Authentic Flower of the Revolution, she is much loved by Cubans.

Bayamo delicacies
Those with iron constitutions might try a *coctel de ostion*, or oyster cocktail (oysters with lemon in a hot sauce), served at street stalls and in an atmospheric old bar called La Bodega de Atocha in Plaza del Himno. A less potent local specialty is a crunchy sweet that is made from yuca and sold from every other doorway.

169

The Arabic influence in Manzanillo is evident in Edificio Quirch

The Sierra Maestra is only gradually becoming accessible to the outside world

Cuba's biggest and highest mountain range extends from Oriente's southwestern corner 149 miles eastward past Santiago. Hardy *campesinos* do their laundry in mountain streams and live in clusters of thatched huts that share concrete platforms used for drying coffee beans. Motorized transportation is virtually nonexistent, whereas you are quite likely to come across columns of mules on mountain paths. Away from a couple of coastal spots, tourism has not yet taken off. Unless you are on an excursion, it is virtually impossible to get around without a car. See also the Drive on pages 172–173.

Walking The most dramatic and interesting region to explore on foot lies south of Santo Domingo (see pages 172 and 202). It is designated a national park and you need to hire a guide (*Charge* expensive). Ask at the hotel, and try to call in advance, since the whole area is sometimes put out of bounds for scientific and military reasons. With a guide, you can drive from Santo Domingo to the end of a steep 3-mile road. From here, it is a very strenuous trek (8 miles each way) to Pico Turquino, at 6,467 feet, Cuba's highest point. A much easier 4-mile circular hike takes you to Comandancia de la Plata►►, Castro's headquarters in the 1950s. Buildings include a radio station, field hospital, and Fidel's office; no photography.

Resorts Marea del Portillo►, near the mountains' western end, is no more than two all-inclusive Canadian-run hotels on a mediocre black-sand beach. Isolation is offset by a diving school and excursions to an offshore key, an oyster farm, and (on horseback) into the mountains. Chivirico►, 47 miles west of Santiago, is a real community, far less out on a limb. Again, there are two all-inclusive Canadian-managed hotels; both are appealing and offer a range of facilities and excursions. See also page 202.

A propaganda coup
Soon after the débâcle of the *Granma* landing, Batista's government announced that Castro was dead and his contingent had been snuffed out. So, in February 1957, the underground rebel movement smuggled Herbert Matthews of the *New York Times* into the Sierra Maestra to see Castro. To create the impression that his miniscule force was bigger than it was, Castro arranged for his 18 men to arrive at their mountain hideout from different directions and talk of other columns nearby. The result: a story about a large band of rebels on the front page of the influential American paper.

■ **As its most important asset as well as its greatest curse, sugar has defined Cuba's history. A long-lasting reliance on "white gold," as it has been called, has produced great wealth for the country, but also an economic monoculture. As a result, despite the amount of the island's fertile land, Cuba is nowhere near self-sufficient in food.** ■

An unhealthy dependency Sugarcane originated in southeast Asia and was brought to the New World by Columbus. Sugarcane production, and the influx of slaves to harvest the crop, took off on a large scale in the 19th century: by 1860 it accounted for 70 percent of Cuba's revenue. Up to 1960, Cuba found itself increasingly economically bound to the United States, primarily because the U.S. guaranteed to receive most of Cuba's sugar in return for low import duties and taxes on U.S. goods. Immediately after the revolution, Cuba tried unsuccessfully to break the shackles of its sugar dependency by diversifying its economy. But it soon became locked into trade agreements with the Soviet Union, which imported Cuba's sugar in return for arms, food, and above all, oil. In 1970, virtually the whole country was mobilized to produce a 10-million-ton harvest, the biggest ever, but the target was too high and the rest of the economy was brought to a standstill.

The present situation In the 1980s Cuba was the world's biggest sugar exporter, but after the collapse of the Soviet Union production halved due to a lack of machinery and fuel. Since the mid-1990s, matters have improved, with foreign investment resulting in increased mechanization, new spare parts, and the latest fertilizers: Cuba now rates as the fifth largest exporter. The industry provides employment for 350,000 people. Sugarcane, grown on co-operatives of thousands of acres, covers 50 percent of Cuba's cultivable land. There are 156 mills—steaming, rickety factories of cathedral-like proportions with fume-belching funnels for steeples rising out of the plains. Around them cluster little factory towns, complete with hospitals and schools.

Most cane is cut mechanically, though workers can still be seen using machetes

Producing sugar
The *zafra*, or harvest, takes place from January to May. The cane is stripped of its leaves, then carried on conveyor belts to rollers that squash out its juice; the remaining stalks are used for cardboard, paper, and animal feed. The juice is heated and refined to form sucrose crystals, leaving a residue called molasses, which serves as cattle feed as well as the basis for rum.

171

Drive Around the Sierra Maestra

See highlighted route on map on pages 148–149.

This 280-mile drive, taking the long way around from Bayamo to Santiago, explores some historical sights in the plains of Granma and Cuba's grandest scenery in the Sierra Maestra. Allow at least two days for the journey.

From **Bayamo**▶▶ (see page 168), head west across the vast cane-rich plains for 27 miles to Yara, where Carlos Manuel de Céspedes proclaimed independence in his famous speech, the "Grito de Yara," in 1868 (see below). Paddy fields line the road, and the Sierra Maestra's moody outlines dominate the horizon. Head south from Yara for 9 miles to the bustling sugar mill town of Bartolomé Maso. From here, a good quality but often disturbingly steep switchback road ventures into the mountains to Santo Domingo, 12 miles away; locals use rudimentary sledges, *carros de las montañas*, to descend the slopes at speed. You could stop for lunch or the night at this simple walking base (see page 202), and take a guide into the mountains to find the rebels' military base, **Comandancia de la Plata**▶▶ (see page 170).

Drive back down to Yara via Bartolomé Maso, then continue across the plain for 11 miles to **Manzanillo**▶ (see page 169). **La Demajagua**▶ (*Open* Mon–Sat 8–12, 2–5, Sun 8–12. *Admission charge* inexpensive), 6 miles south of the port, is the former sugar estate from which Céspedes freed his slaves on October 10, 1868, and by doing so set Cuba on the long road to independence. The site is moving in its simplicity: the bell with which Céspedes summoned his slaves has been enshrined in a reconstructed wall of the sugar mill and there is a small exhibition, but otherwise there is little to see.

Follow the coast road for 25 miles on to Media Luna, hometown of Celia Sánchez (see page 169). There are billboards of her all over town, and you can visit her pretty clapboard family home on the main street, now an interesting little **museum** (*Open* Tue–Sat 9–12, 2–5. *Admission charge* inexpensive).

Playa Las Coloradas▶, 22 miles farther on, may be one of Cuba's most significant revolutionary sites, but it is also one of its bleakest. The motor launch *Granma* landed (or, as Che Guevara more accurately put it, was shipwrecked) in this remote and godforsaken spot on December 2, 1956. A mile-long boardwalk now traverses the mangrove swamp through which Castro and his followers waded ashore, but there is

nothing to see at its end. On reaching dry land, the bedraggled but ever-optimistic rebel leader is supposed to have said to the first Cuban peasant he met: "I am Fidel Castro and we have come to liberate Cuba."

Retrace the road toward Media Luna, turning off at Montero south-eastward across the mountains. The lush countryside abruptly changes to a dry, scrubby yellow landscape as you reach the Sierra Maestra's southern slopes. After 26 miles you come to the lonely resort of **Marea del Portillo►** (see page 170), where you can have a swim or stay the night.

The brand new 124-mile **road►►►** that clings to the coast all the way to Santiago (until recently large sections were hardly passable dirt track) is the most awesome drive on the whole island. It is possible to reach Santiago in about two and a half hours, but ideally you should allow much longer. Scree-covered slopes topped by forested mountains often shrouded in cloud or mist plunge precipitously to rocky and shingle beaches. Expect to have to stop at roadblocks set up to catch coffee thieves. Save for a few lonesome hamlets where rugged peasants totter along under pails of water, the western half of the coastal strip is virtually uninhabited. Places of interest include La Plata, where a museum recalls the rebels' first military success against a military barracks in 1957, and Uvero, scene of a bloody battle a few months later and now commemorated by a monument. Consider staying at the outstanding Hotel Sierra Mar at Chivirico (see pages 170, 202) before heading on to Santiago.

The view from Marea del Portillo

Guantánamo Province

Street parties
If you have the chance, be in Baracoa around the first week in April, when nightly street parties celebrate General Antonio Maceo's disembarkation at Playa Duaba on April 1, 1895 at the start of the War of Independence.

The incomparable view from the Hotel El Castillo, with El Yunque in the background

▶▶▶ Baracoa   *149F2*

The first settlement established by Diego Velázquez in 1512 and Cuba's capital until 1515, this small town is regarded by many as the most magical place in all of Cuba. Pillared, clapboard houses from colonial times, dazzlingly painted in pink and turquoise, line its streets. The surrounding countryside is amazingly fertile, with hillsides coated in thick swathes of forest and palm, cocoa, coffee, and banana groves. Its remote location—93 miles or a three-hour drive from Guantánamo—means the modern world has largely passed Baracoa by. Locals seem immune from late 20th-century cares and are among the most friendly on the island. Tourists are invariably beseiged with offers to visit their homes, where they are plied with local specialties such as *bacán*, a slab of

pork and plantain wrapped in banana leaves, hot chocolate drink, and *cucuruchos*—crushed coconut, orange, sugar, and honey presented in paper cones. While tourism has firmly arrived here, it has yet to spoil the atmosphere. There is a selection of lovely hotels and good places to eat: come for less than two or three days and you will wish you had stayed longer. Try to be here over the weekend: every Saturday night the town holds a raucous street party in the main square, with live bands and stalls selling cheap rum and food.

Exploring inland For an overview of the town start at El Castillo▶▶, a hilltop fort converted into a hotel. It surveys Baracoa's red-tile roofs, oyster-shaped harbor, tiny airport ensconced in banana groves, and the landmark mountain of El Yunque, called the Anvil because of its flat-topped shape. Don't miss the view at sunset and in the early morning, when trails of mist often hang over the palmy hills.

Steps lead down to the town's little main square. The church▶ (*Open* daily 8–11, 1–5) has a very plain interior (apparently a prerevolutionary priest sold all the furniture), but is worth visiting to see the Cruz de la Parra (see panel, right). Outside there is a bust of Hatuey (see panel, page 178), described as the "first American rebel."

A block west on Calle Maceo stands the pretty pink and lime-green Casa de la Cultura and its theater. Next door at Maceo No. 120, Galeria Yara sells interesting aboriginal art, and its staff are a mine of local information. Directly opposite is a Baracoa institution, the **Casa del Chocolate**. Strange as it might seem in a tropical climate, the specialty is hot chocolate (in truth, it is watery and pretty horrible; the locals brew much better cups). East from the main square down José Martí, the main shopping street, is a quaint **tobacco factory▶** at No. 214 (*Open* Mon–Fri 6–12, 2–5; Sat 6–12. *Admission* free); it sells its home-produced Maguana cigars, but it is just as likely that someone will give you one as a souvenir.

Exploring along the seafront The seaside avenue, the Malecón, stretches eastward to a scruffy beach and the 18th-century **Matachín fort▶**, now a little museum (*Open* daily 8–6. *Admission charge* inexpensive). Interesting exhibits include photographs of Che opening the local chocolate factory in 1963, pieces from 84 types of wood from the nearby forests, maps showing the local Taíno archeological sites, and mementoes of La Rusa (see below). The impressive waterside statue of Columbus outside was erected in 1992 to celebrate the 500th anniversary of Columbus's landing; stalls here often sell *cucuruchos*. A half-mile west, the Hotel La Rusa is named after its former owner, a glamorous Russian émigrée who hosted celebrities from Castro to Errol Flynn before she died in 1978. There are photos of her in the foyer. Her son René Frometa, who lives across the street, loves receiving guests, not least so he can show them his gallery of naïve paintings of Baracoa. Farther west lies the town's third fort (now a second-rate restaurant), overlooking a little port protected by a rusting hulk.

See page 178 for **Excursions from Baracoa**.

Baracoa and Columbus
Despite Baracoan protestations, it has been established that Columbus did not land here in October 1492 but at Bariay near Gibara (see page 167). Baracoans base their claim on the fact that El Yunque looks remarkably like the mountain Columbus described in his notebooks, and that the Cruz de la Parra (or the Cross of the Vine—it was found under the branches of an early settler's vine) was that which the explorer planted in the soil on his arrival. Intriguingly, carbon dating has established that the wood used to make the cross is, in fact, more than 500 years old.

175

The Cruz de la Parra was once much larger, but locals have hacked off pieces as keepsakes

Guantánamo Naval Base

■ Southeastern Cuba is the unlikely territory for the world's last Cold War frontier. Gitmo Bay, as the base has been nicknamed, is a 45-square-mile thorn in Castro's side. The U.S. government has retained it as much for political as for military reasons. To many, the whole situation seems extravagant, given the improvement in U.S–Soviet relations in recent years. ■

The old timers
The only people who are permitted to cross between communist Cuba and the U.S. base are the dwindling number of Cuban staff who began working on the base before the 1959 revolution. There were 21 at the last count. Bussed in and out daily, they are some of Cuba's best-paid workers as they receive their wages in dollars—over $1,000 a month, a fortune by Cuban standards.

Hotel Caimanera
It is theoretically possible to view the base from an even closer vantage point than Los Malones. The small, high-quality Hotel Caimanera (tel: 21 99414) is situated on the western side of Guantánamo bay in Caimanera, a town which is said to have underground bunkers in case of a U.S. attack. However, because of its sensitive location (you have to pass through road blocks to reach it), the hotel has not been accepting reservations from independent foreign vacationers for the last few years. The authorities claim the situation may soon change.

History In 1901, the Platt Amendment granted the United States land on either side of the mouth of this vast natural harbor in an open-ended lease, ostensibly to guard Cuba's recently won independence. The U.S. initially paid an annual rent of $2,000, which was increased to the lofty sum of $4,085 in 1934 when the lease was reduced to 99 years. Understandably, the Cubans were still not too pleased about the deal, and matters deteriorated further when Castro came to power. He refuses to acknowledge the legality of the American presence, and does not cash the peppercorn rent checks.

Life on the base Before the revolution, Guantánamo city and Caimanera had reputations as sex and gambling dens for the U.S. troops. Now the base is cut off from the rest of Cuba—an island within an island, with a population of around 7,000. It is self-sufficient down to its own water supply, radio station, and even McDonalds (the only one on Cuba, of course).

Until recently, a barrier ring of some 60,000 Cuban and American mines surrounded the base in a full-blown no-man's land, but there have been reports of the Americans removing theirs. The Cuban authorities have reported over 13,000 acts of provocation since the revolution, ranging from firing to verbal abuse. Meanwhile, the U.S. attitude is perhaps epitomized by the base's marine colonel played by Jack Nicholson in the film *A Few Good Men*, who says he eats breakfast "300 yards from 4,000 Cubans who are trained to kill me." The last deaths were in the mid-1960s, when two Cuban soldiers were shot.

Recent events In 1992, tens of thousands of Haitian boat people trying to gain entry into the United States were detained at the base. A similar situation occurred in 1994, when over 15,000 Cubans who had tried to make it to Florida on makeshift rafts were, in ghastly irony, transported back to the island and placed in a vast camp on the base. Some, fed up with the camp's conditions, crossed back to Cuba via the bay's waters and minefields. A number ended up in Cuban hospitals with lost limbs. All who stayed were eventually allowed into the United States. In 1995, the U.S. government changed its immigration policy on Cubans trying to enter the U.S. and now returns to Cuba all illegal immigrants (see page 28). One consequence is that Cubans no longer risk their lives for freedom by swimming across the shark-infested waters to the base.

Spying on the base Presently, the only place from which to see the base is Loma Los Malones, a Cuban lookout on a hill on the bay's eastern side. To reach Los Malones, you need Peter Hope, a highly educated, Jamaican-born Cuban guide who speaks near-perfect English; ask for him at the Hotel Islazul Guantánamo (see page 202). His services cost just a few dollars per person. He can arrange transportation, but it is easier and much cheaper if you have your own. Much more expensive tours to Los Malones are also arranged from Hotel Villa Gaviota in Santiago (see page 201).

177

The hour-long drive from Guantánamo city passes through road blocks guarded by "border troops." The destination, a bunker built deep inside a hill, has a quasi-operations room with a two-dimensional model of the base and a camouflaged observation post on top. In the near distance, you can make out U.S. watchtowers draped with the Stars and Stripes, and beyond, by peering through binoculars (Russian-made of course) you can see the two airports, the moored ships, and the communities of drab houses where the Americans live.

Top: Cuban soldiers keep watch
Below: the base's U.S. commander points out the perimeter to the U.S. Navy's Secretary General in 1964

Guantánamera

Cuba's most famous melody, the refrain of which is a tribute to a peasant girl from Guantánamo, was composed by Joseíto Fernández in the 1940s. On his radio show, news items were sung in verse following the *Guantánamera* rhythm. Since the late 1950s, José' Martí's *Versos Sencillos* have been sung to the tune.

Hatuey

The most famous Indian to defy the Spanish conquest fled to Cuba from nearby Hispaniola with 400 Guahaba Indians to try to create unity among the Cuban Indian tribes before the conquistadors arrived. His burning at the stake by Velázquez in 1512 symbolized the swift end to Indian resistance. The story goes that, invited to be baptised before he died so that he could go to heaven, Hatuey asked if Christians also went there. When told that they did, he replied that he did not want to go somewhere where he would have to meet such cruel and wicked people again.

Yumurí's river gorge

Excursions from Baracoa

Baracoa's environs are a lush paradise where everything imaginable seems to grow. Preindustrial scenes are commonplace: women wash their laundry in the shallow, wide rivers, leaving it to dry on the shingle banks or hanging it on cacti outside their thatched huts.

Two miles west of town there is the **cucurucho factory►** (*Open* Mon–Sat 7–3), where you can buy this incredibly sweet concoction of chopped coconut, fruit, and honey, and watch it being made. A half-mile beyond the Río Duaba, an unsigned track leads to **Playa Duaba►►**, a fantastic gray-sand beach with a hidden hamlet of rustic *bohíos* in among the palms whose owners sell *polymitas* (colored snails' shells). Back on the main road, you soon come to another turn off, to **Finca Duaba►** (*Open* Tue–Sun 8–4. *Admission charge* inexpensive), a plantation of exotic fruit trees where a *bohío* has been constructed to show how peasants live, and you can watch cocoa beans being roasted for chocolate. **Maguana►►►**, 13 miles west of Baracoa on a dirt track you can drive down, is one of Cuba's loveliest beaches, with endless palm-backed sands. Children split coconuts and tout magnificent conches. For lunch, head for Villa Maguana (see page 202), right on its own sandy cove.

East from Baracoa, a 19-mile paved road leads (via a military checkpoint; take your passport) to **Yumurí►►**, a ramshackle rivermouth fishing village. While a bridge is being built (over the years three have been washed away), there is a ferry across to the other bank.

Guantánamo   *149E1*

Most travelers to Guantánamo pass through quickly, unless they are visiting the lookout over the U.S. naval base (see pages 176–177). This sprawling city with a large Jamaican population has less to commend it than most other provincial capitals. That said, there are a couple of fine buildings downtown, notably a grand market and the art-nouveau Edificio Salcines, which houses an art gallery.

Packages buying

There is a lot to be said for a package to Cuba. Choose between a stay-put vacation in a resort; a combination of, for example, a week in Havana and a week in a resort; or a cultural bus tour. As public transportation is so poor, this last option is one of the best ways to see most of the island. Havana, Santiago, Trinidad, and Viñales appear on most itineraries, which usually also allow for a few days on a beach. Some companies also offer theme tours, for example to tobacco farms and cigar factories, hospitals and cooperative farms, and meeting with the Committees for the Defense of the Revolution.

Independent travel

There are no restrictions on independent travel in Cuba. You can travel wherever you want, without pre-arranged accommodations, but you also need patience to cope with inevitable administrative hassles. A good compromise is to use a specialist agency in your own country to book some accommodations in advance (in Havana and resorts, for example), for which you will be

Walk down any street in Cuba and someone will stop you for a chat

issued with vouchers. Immigration officials often demand evidence of booked accommodations for your first few nights.

Arriving by air

From the U.K. Cubana, Cuba's national airline, flies to Havana from London three times a week and Manchester once a week; some flights go via Brussels and Varadero; comfort is limited, but rates are usually the cheapest available. Alternatively, fly with KLM via Amsterdam or Iberia via Madrid. There are also charter flights to Varadero, and to Camagüey and Holguín for the island's eastern resorts, but seat-only availability is normally very limited. Direct flights take around 10 hours.

From Canada The only direct scheduled service is with Cubana, operating weekly between Montréal and Havana and Varadero and taking about four hours. There are also many charter flights to seven regional airports across the island, most from Toronto and Montréal, but also from Vancouver, Halifax, Ottawa, Calgary, and Winnipeg; seat-only bookings are possible.

From Germany Apart from charter flights, Cubana flies from Frankfurt and Berlin to Havana, and LTU flies from Düsseldorf to Havana, Varadero, and Holguín.

From the U.S. The U.S. embargo against Cuba means it is against U.S. law for most U.S. citizens to spend money in Cuba, and if caught they are liable to a $50,000 fine. Only those with relatives in Cuba, those on government business, accredited journalists, and academics specializing in Cuba can visit the island officially; licenses are available from the Treasury Department's Licensing Division (tel: 202/622-2480). Direct flights between Miami and Havana were suspended in 1996, but license holders can fly from Miami via Cancún or Nassau; contact Marazul Tours (tel: 201/319-9670) for details. Marazul, as well as The Center for Cuban Studies (tel: 212/242-0559) and Global Exchange (tel: 415/255-7296), also arrange study tours.

Thousands of U.S. citizens annually fly to Cuba via a third country such as Canada or Mexico. Cuban immigration officials help out by not stamping American passports.

Airports Cuba's main international airport is Havana's José Martí, about 16 miles south of the city center. Major construction work resulted in the opening of the new Terminal 3 in April 1998, and services being shunted between terminals. These details were available at the time of press, but check before you travel.

• Terminals 2 and 3 will handle international flights.
• Until late 1998, Terminal 1 will also be used for international flights, while internal Cubana flights will leave from the Domestic Terminal. From late 1998, Terminal 1 should deal with internal Cubana flights.
• Terminal Caribbean will continue to deal with internal charter flights.
• Nine other smaller airports receive mainly international charter flights for tourists on their way to nearby resorts. The busiest is Varadero's, 14 miles southwest of the resort and not served by public transportation.

Havana's skyline from La Cabaña fortress

182

Customs
Duty-free limits into Cuba are:
2 liters of spirit
200 cigarettes, or 50 cigars
Anti-Castro literature may be
confiscated.

Passports and visas
Passports should be valid for six
months from your return date from
Cuba. Most visitors travel on a
"tourist card," best obtained through
an agent who arranges package
tours; it is often included in the holiday price. Otherwise contact the
Cuban embassy in your home country. Though valid for only 30 days, it
can be extended once you are in
Cuba for up to another month at
hotels and immigration offices.
Obtaining a "tourist visa," for those
staying with relatives or friends, and
an "official visa," for those on business, is a much more bureaucratic
process (many visitors in these cate-
gories risk traveling on a tourist card).

When to go
For lying on the beach, any time of
year is usually fine in Cuba, though
cold fronts can sometimes set in
between December and February.
The best months for sightseeing,
being cooler and drier, are November
to April. May to September is often
debilitatingly hot, and you can expect
short, heavy downpours on about a
third of days between June and
October. September and October are
the likeliest months for hurricanes,

which can be very serious: more than
4,000 people died in Hurricane Flora
in 1963, and Hurricane Lili destroyed
over 5,000 homes in October 1996.
   The chart below shows Havana's
average daily maximum temperature
and average monthly rainfall. The
mountains are cooler and wetter, and
the southeast is drier and hotter.
   Tourism on the island has not yet
reached a level where it ever feels
unpleasantly busy. The high season,
when seats on flights are in shortest
supply and hotel rates are highest, is
from December to April and in July
and August.

What to take
Bring medicines, sunscreen lotion,
mosquito repellent, bathroom essentials, toilet paper, a two-pin plug adaptor (current is usually 110 volts),
camera, and film: all are expensive
and often hard to come by in Cuba.
Many tourists also come armed with
ballpoint pens, chewing gum, soap,
and other toiletries to give away to
needy locals.
   It is warm enough to wear shorts
year round, but trousers or longer
skirt will make you look less like a
tourist. You need to dress up only if
you are going to one of Havana's
smart restaurants or a top cabaret.

National holidays
Most offices, shops, and museums
are closed on the following days:

Tobacco farmers, western Cuba

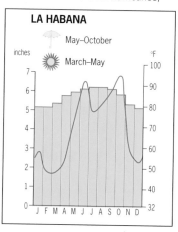

LA HABANA

☂ May–October

☀ March–May

The Capitolio's vast dome lords it over Old Havana's backstreets

January 1: Anniversary of the Triumph of the Revolution or Liberation Day (in 1959).

May 1: International Workers' Day or Labor Day.

July 26: National Rebellion Day (commemorating the attack on the Moncada Barracks in 1953; July 25 and 27 normally holidays, too).

October 10: Anniversary of the beginning of the Ten Years' War (in 1868).

Christmas was celebrated for the first time in Communist Cuba in 1997, but New Year's Eve is generally a far more popular occasion for celebrating.

Time differences
Cuban time is on Eastern Standard Time, GMT minus five hours. Clocks are turned forward an hour in late March or early April and back an hour in early October.

Money matters
Pesos and dollars Cuba's official currency is the peso. Confusingly, Cubans often refer to dollars as pesos, and both peso and dollar prices are marked $ (with "USD" added to indicate greenbacks). The peso has no international value, so Cuba's economy operates ever increasingly with *divisa*, or hard currency, namely the U.S. dollar. Cuba welcomes tourists primarily for their dollars, so, not surprisingly, tourists need to pay for virtually everything in dollars—accommodations, transportation, food, souvenirs. You will also use something called the convertible peso, introduced in 1994, which has exactly the same value as the dollar. This is worthless abroad, so exchange any before you leave.

The only things you are likely to be able to buy with pesos are street snacks, food from farmers' markets, stamps, and trinkets from nondescript peso shops. But as the peso is worth so little compared to the dollar, these items are amazingly cheap for foreigners, so it is worth changing a few dollars (no more than $10) into pesos. Banks offer only one peso to one dollar, but, at the time of going to press, bizarrely you get 23 pesos to the dollar at recently opened official currency exchanges called Cadecas.

What to travel with Take as many dollars in cash as you feel safe with. Small denominations are preferable: large notes can be hard to break and often mean you will be asked to show your passport. Also take dollar traveler's checks, but **note that American Express traveler's checks, or any checks drawn on or cards issued by a U.S. bank, are not accepted** (however, see, as a last resort, Asistur on page 188). The commission rate for changing traveler's checks is normally 4 percent in hotels, 2 or 3 percent in banks, and they can also often be used as direct payment. **Credit cards issued in the U.S. are not accepted anywhere in Cuba.**

demand outstrips supply. The two biggest companies, Havanautos and Transautos, whose prices are virtually identical, have rental centers at locations right across the island, including at Havana, Santiago, and Varadero airports. Rates are significantly lower for longer periods of rental; limited mileage rates are rarely worth taking as Cuba is so big. Be wary of renting Jeeps: rates are high, they guzzle gas and those with soft tops are a security risk. One-way drop-off fees (which allow you, for example, to pick up a car in Havana, drive to and leave the car in Santiago, and fly back to Havana) are very cheap.

Insurance Collision damage waiver (CDW) must be paid locally. Always take full cover (normally called cover B). Havanautos has no deductible, but with some other companies you are liable for the first few hundred dollars' worth of damage if you cannot prove an accident or breakage was not your fault. Despite the hassle, always obtain a report form from the police to help validate your CDW.

Before you set off Have a number to phone if you break down, and a map with locations of Cupet garages (see page 185). Check the water, oil, and tires, establish everything works, and identify existing scratches and dents. You will be forced to pay for a full tank of gas and advised to return the car empty; you may get a refund if some gas is left in the car, but not always.

Driving

There is very little traffic, and main roads are fast and in reasonable condition. Since their cars are usually on their last legs and the prospect of a replacement nonexistent, Cubans are cautious drivers. The main dangers are potholes and bicycles. Driving at night is best avoided, since bikes, horse-and-buggies, and even sometimes cars have no lights. Follow the local practice of honking your horn when overtaking, since most vehicles do not have (or use) rear view mirrors. You are likely to have a flat tire at some point: if so, ask for the nearest *ponchera*, or puncture-repair workshop.

Car rental

Renting a car is expensive and often fraught with hassle, and many vehicles are in poor condition. Nonetheless, it is the best way to explore the country in depth, and as everyone hitches (see page 187), it is a great way to meet local people.

Reservations and costs Because so many problems arise, many agents abroad will not reserve cars. If you have arrived without a booking, reserve as soon as possible, especially in main tourist destinations, where

Driving

Rules of the road Drive on the right.
Speed limits are:
60 m.p.h. on an *autopista* (major
  highway)
55 m.p.h. on the open road
30 m.p.h. in built-up areas.

On-the-spot fines are enforced.

No one in Cuba wears seatbelts,
though it is sensible to do so.

While most road signs are
internationally understood, note the
following: "*pare*" means "stop,"
"*ceda el paso*" means "yield," and a
yellow diamond signifies you have
right of way.

Watch out for railway crossings
(*crucero ferrocarril*) which appear
even across the *autopista* and never
have gates.

Security Rental cars are conspicu-
ously modern and clean (and their

*Spare parts are hard to obtain, so
Cubans are careful drivers*

license plates spell TUR for *turismo*).
Hide all belongings in the trunk at all
times. Virtually wherever you stop,
someone will ask for a dollar to guard
your car. Unguarded cars at night are
liable to lose side mirrors, etc.

Petrol Only 24-hour Cupet and Oro
Negro garages are allowed to sell gas
to tourists. Every major town and
resort has at least one of these
garages, but elsewhere they are few
and far between. Rental cars are
supposed to take only *especial* gas,
but many pump attendants will fill the
car with much cheaper *regular* gas. To
avoid being ripped off, make sure
the pump's dial starts at zero. The
cut-price gas that locals try to sell is
sometimes watered down.

Bicycle and moped rental
Both are possible in resorts; crash
helmets are unheard of. In cities,
locals are only too willing to lend you
their bike for the day for a few dollars.
Some tourists bring their own bikes;
bring all the spares and mending kits
you might need.

Domestic flights

Cubana operates the country's scheduled domestic flights. Though much of its fleet comprises old and rickety Russian planes, its timetable is fairly reliable and fares very reasonable. Flights operate between Havana and Santiago, Baracoa, Bayamo, Camagüey, Ciego de Avila, Cayo Coco, Nueva Gerona, Guantánamo, Holguín, Manzanillo, Moa, and Las Tunas, and between Varadero and Baracoa, Cayo Coco, Holguín, and Santiago. Frequency varies from three times a day from Havana to Santiago or Nueva Gerona, to three times a week from Havana to Baracoa. As planes normally fill up long in advance, book as soon as you know your plans (ideally from home).

Cubana has an office in every major city. Its main office is in Havana at the bottom of La Rampa in Vedado at No. 64 between Calle P and Infanta. It is best to visit in person to make a reservation.

Excursions (see page 196) from resorts to places such as Cayo Largo, Pinar del Río, and Trinidad often use charter airlines such as Aerotaxi, Aerocaribbean, and Aerogaviota.

Trains

Railways connect all of Cuba's provincial capitals. Services are frequent but generally unreliable and

Flying is a sensible option when traveling from one end of the island to the other

interminably slow. Stations are sights in their own right, and the trains are venerable and often fairly comfortable old beasts. But the best reason to travel by train is the ease with which you can obtain a ticket. Dollar-wielding tourists do not have to wait in line, since stations in the main cities have special desks exclusively for tourists run by a company called Ladis. The most useful, comfortable, and reliable service runs daily between Havana and Santiago in both directions, leaving around tea time (check for exact times) and arriving 13–14 hours later. It stops at Matanzas, Santa Clara, Ciego de Avila, Camagüey, and Las Tunas. Heading west, Havana to Pinar del Río takes six hours. See panels, pages 114 and 128 for interesting local services.

Buses

You need a strong masochistic streak to consider tackling a journey by *guagua* (pronounced "wawa"), as buses are called in Cuba. Since the advent of the Special Period, services have reduced dramatically. It can be very difficult to obtain a ticket on long-distance journeys. If you are intent on making such a trip, enlist a Cuban to help make arrangements; dollar-paying tourist often get to the head of the line.

Taxis

The most common way for tourists to get around large cities such as Havana is by taxi. Modern taxis wait for your dollars at hotels and airports, but there is also an enormous black market in providing lifts. Private cars and taxis that are supposed to take only peso-paying passengers cruise around looking for tourists. This way, for the same sort of fare—just a few dollars—you may well get the chance of a ride in an old Cadillac. If they are caught, the owners risk a heavy fine, but tourists should get nothing more than a telling-off. Many tourists hire a Cadillac and driver for a whole day for a very reasonable rate.

Coches and *bicitaxis*

Hard times have led to a massive increase in nonmotorised transporta-

You need to be fairly hardy to face the rigors of public transportation

tion. In many towns and cities, fleets of *coches*—sometimes rustic horse-and-buggies, sometimes fine canopied carriages—ply the main streets. They are legally required to carry a bag to collect the horse's droppings. Some act like buses on set routes, others as taxis. Ironically, in resorts this form of transportation has been turned into a tourist attraction. A recent development has been the arrival of fleets of *bicitaxis*—Cuban rickshaws, made by welding bikes and chairs together; a ride should cost you a dollar.

Hitchhiking

Everyone, from students and nurses to soldiers and policemen, hitches everywhere. In one day's driving you could easily pick up 50 people; while you are not obliged to stop, locals will wave disbelievingly at you if you drive by when you have space in the car. Officials in yellow suits, called *amarillos*, marshall great crowds of hitchers outside towns and wave down state vehicles, which do have to stop. If you are hitching yourself, as a foreigner you will probably go to the head of the line.

187

Police are stationed on street corners throughout Old Havana

Crime

By most standards, Cuba is very safe for travelers. However, its economic crisis and the growth in tourism have led to an increase in crime, and the spate of bombs aimed at tourist sights in 1997 (allegedly by right-wing American-Cubans) should remind visitors to be vigilant at all times. Crime almost always takes the form of petty theft rather than mugging: you can reduce the chances of being a victim by avoiding ostentatious displays of wealth on the streets.

Be particularly careful in parts of Havana (see page 93). At major street festivals such as carnivals, when purse-snatching and pickpocketing are very common, it is best to go out carrying literally nothing for anyone to steal. Most hotels provide safes, though most charge for their use.

Police

Police dress in shades of blue and are heavily armed with pistol and baton. Their presence is so strong in Havana and Varadero at night that it may feel as though you are out during a curfew. Ostensibly the police are there to protect tourists from black marketeers and prostitutes; some tourists find this off-putting, others reassuring. Cuba has a large state security apparatus, with many plainclothes operatives.

You should be very wary about fraternizing with people who openly disapprove of the government, both for their sake and for yours.

Embassies

All foreign embassies are in Havana.
Canada Calle 30 No. 518 at Avenida 7, Miramar (tel: 7 242516).
Germany Calle B No. 652 between calles 11 and 13, Vedado (tel: 7 332569).
United Kingdom Calle 34 No. 702 at Avenida 7, Miramar (tel: 7 241771).
United States U.S. Interests Section, Calzada between L and M, Vedado (tel: 7 333550 to 59). This is an embassy in all but name.

Asistur

If something goes seriously wrong with your trip—if, for example, you have an accident, or your money or passport are stolen, or you lose your luggage or travel documents—consider seeking help from Asistur. This state-run agency provides foreigners with assistance in medical, financial, and legal emergencies, and deals with many big insurance companies overseas. It may be able to arrange anything from having funds sent to you from abroad to repatriation. As a last resort, you can also change American Express traveler's checks here for a 5 percent commission.

Asistur's head office is on the Prado No. 212 in Old Havana (tel: 7 625519). There are also offices in Varadero (tel: 5 667277), Cienfuegos (432 6402), Holguín (24 30148), and Santiago (226 86128).

Emergency numbers

Police 116
Fire brigade 115
There is no single number to phone for the ambulance service.

188

Health

Vaccinations Cuba is malaria-free, but vaccinations are recommended against typhoid, tetanus, polio, and hepatitis A.

Hazards The most common illness among travelers to Cuba is an upset stomach, though as the food is so plain you are less likely to suffer from a bout of diarrhea here than in many undeveloped countries. Nonetheless, be wary of unhygienic-looking hotel buffets, and try to eat only cooked vegetables and fruit you peel yourself. Tap-water quality is not of the best and bottled mineral water is recommended (however much this bemuses Cubans).

Dehydration, another risk, can be avoided by drinking plenty of water (and little alcohol), and wearing a hat or staying out of the sun when it's at its hottest. Cuba's tropical rays can burn in minutes, so you should apply plenty of sunscreen regularly.

Mosquitoes in Cuba do not carry diseases, but they are ubiquitous and can be real pests, especially in summer: take roll-on insect repellent to apply when out and about; you might also want to bring coils or a plug-in electrical device that repels bugs for your hotel room; you cannot rely on buying these locally.

Some resort beaches employ life-guards and a flag system to indicate whether it's safe to swim. A red flag means no swimming, yellow means take care, and green that swimming is safe.

Health care The Cuban health care system is touted as one of the best in the world, but lack of money means medicines are in short supply. Bring a first-aid kit and any medicines you know you may need. Resorts and major cities have an international clinic dedicated to treating foreigners. You must pay for treatment, so medical insurance is vital—check the details of your coverage before leaving home. The clinics have decent pharmacies, but the medicines they sell can be very expensive. Local pharmacies (every town has one that is open 24 hours) are far less well stocked, but prices are much lower.

Large hotels, like this one in Varadero, have a doctor on call

Telephone

A joke going around Cuba is that the antiquated phone system is so bad that if you give someone your phone number it is regarded as a brush-off. Many establishments have a string of phone numbers to improve the chances of getting through, while latest estimates suggest only a quarter of international calls are completed. A new phone company called ETECSA may improve matters.

Where to phone from The easiest place to make a call is your hotel room, though rates are high and you must normally leave a deposit. Sometimes you can dial direct, sometimes you need to go through the hotel operator. You can also make calls with operator assistance from telephone centers, often located in larger hotels. Except for newly installed card phones found in a few top hotels (purchase the cards from the hotel reception), pay phones rarely work.

Making calls Phoning abroad sounds like calling another planet. It is easy, though expensive, to call the U.S. Rates to Cuba from abroad are generally far cheaper, so get someone to phone you back (collect calls from public Cuban phones and hotels are not possible; from a private line dial the collect-call operator on 661212).
• To make an international call from your hotel room add the prefix 88, and from a card phone add 119.
• To call Cuba from abroad, add the country code for Cuba: 53.
• For long-distance calls within Cuba, add zero to the area code (all hotel numbers on pages 198–204 include the area code).
• Many numbers cannot be dialed directly so you must go through the operator (most speak English).
• Note that, ignoring the area code, the digits 33 on numbers in Havana's Miramar district have changed or will change to 24.

Mail

Many Cubans don't trust their postal service and ask foreign visitors to post letters to their friends abroad on their return home. Moreover, mail takes an inordinately long time to reach its destination (3–4 weeks to the U.S.). Mail sent via hotel or airport letterboxes is likely to arrive fastest. Stamps are much cheaper in post offices, where they are sold for pesos, than in hotels.

Radio

Stations worth finding include: tourist-oriented Radio Taíno around Havana and Varadero on 93.3FM, 1100–1180AM; the American Forces Network around Guantánamo on 102.1FM and 103.1FM. Florida-based Radio Martí (wavelengths change) pumps anti-Castro propaganda into Cuba.

Television

Cuba has two state-run TV channels, Tele Rebelde and Cubavisión, which are devoted mainly to sports, soaps, and domestic politics. When a favorite soap or dubbed Hollywood movie is showing, the streets are empty as whole towns gather around their TV sets. Many hotels have

Communications

satellite channels, and some don't even bother to show Cuban TV at all. CNN opened a bureau in Havana in 1997, the first U.S. mass media network to have an office in Cuba for 28 years.

Newspapers

Paper shortages mean newspapers are thin and hard to find. *Granma*, the main newspaper and "official organ of the Central Committee of the Communist Party of Cuba," has as many column inches devoted to Castro's speeches as to proper news. Its foreign editor once said: "The role of this newspaper is not to criticize the revolution." A weekly version, *Granma International*, is published in English, French, German, and Portuguese. Other national newspapers (in Spanish only) include *Trabajadores* ("*Workers*") and *Juventud Rebelde* ("*Rebel Youth*"). See page 93 for listings magazines.

Language guide

Many Cubans speak reasonable English, especially young people, who learn it in school, and old people who dealt with Americans before the revolution. However, you need at the very least some basic Spanish to survive outside the resorts: be sure to take a dictionary or a phrase book with you.

Castilian Spanish is easily understood, though Cuban Spanish is markedly different, with hundreds of special words and a Latin-American pronunciation. For example, ce, ci and z are pronounced "s", not "th" as in Castilian Spanish.

Everyday expressions
Yes sí
No no
Hello hola
Goodbye adiós, ciao
Please por favor
Thank you gracias
Is there any...? hay...?
I don't understand no entiendo
I don't speak Spanish no hablo español

Hanging around the boats in the backwater port of Gibara

Addresses

An address on a street (*calle*) or avenue (*avenida*) is normally indicated as being on the corner (*esquina*, or *esq.*) of another street or between (*entre* or *e/* for short) two cross streets. Many streets have two names: a prerevolution one often still used by locals, and an official postrevolution one.

Camping

Cuban campgrounds are collections of simple huts, rather than places to pitch a tent. Almost all are exclusively for Cubans and are open only in summer. There are presently just two designed for foreigners: Aguas Claras near Pinar del Río (see page 199), and El Abra, a large floral site with good facilities on the coast at Jibacoa, 25 miles west of Matanzas (tel: 692 83612).

Children

Cuba is not a good family vacation destination: picky kids will moan about the food, and excursions can be hard work. The best family option is perhaps two weeks in package beach hotel. A few have children's activity programs, such as the new Club Med in Varadero (tel: 5 66 8288), the Delta Las Brisas in Guardalavaca (see page 201), and the Sierra Mar west of Santiago (see page 202).

Departure

A departure tax ($15 at the time of writing) is payable at the airport. Havana and Varadero airports have reasonable selections of basic souvenirs such as rum, cigars, and T-shirts.

Electricity

Current is normally 110 volts, 60 cycles, though you will also find 220 volts in newer hotels. Some sockets take two flat pins, others, even in the same hotel room, two round pins, so bring an adaptor and a converter.

Etiquette

Walk down any street in Cuba and you will encounter lots of smacking of the lips and "pssts" (an insistent

CONVERSION CHARTS

FROM	TO	MULTIPLY BY
Inches	Centimeters	2.54
Centimeters	Inches	0.3937
Feet	Meters	0.3048
Meters	Feet	3.2810
Yards	Meters	0.9144
Meters	Yards	1.0940
Miles	Kilometers	1.6090
Kilometers	Miles	0.6214
Acres	Hectares	0.4047
Hectares	Acres	2.4710
Gallons	Liters	4.5460
Liters	Gallons	0.2200
Ounces	Grams	28.35
Grams	Ounces	0.0353
Pounds	Grams	453.6
Grams	Pounds	0.0022
Pounds	Kilograms	0.4536
Kilograms	Pounds	2.205
Tons	Tonnes	1.0160
Tonnes	Tons	0.9842

MEN'S SUITS

U.K.	36	38	40	42	44	46	48
Rest of Europe	46	48	50	52	54	56	58
U.S.	36	38	40	42	44	46	48

DRESS SIZES

U.K.	8	10	12	14	16	18
France	36	38	40	42	44	46
Italy	38	40	42	44	46	48
Rest of Europe	34	36	38	40	42	44
U.S.	6	8	10	12	14	16

MEN'S SHIRTS

U.K.	14	14.5	15	15.5	16	16.5	17
Rest of Europe	36	37	38	39/40	41	42	43
U.S.	14	14.5	15	15.5	16	16.5	17

MEN'S SHOES

U.K.	7	7.5	8.5	9.5	10.5	11
Rest of Europe	41	42	43	44	45	46
U.S.	8	8.5	9.5	10.5	11.5	12

WOMEN'S SHOES

U.K.	4.5	5	5.5	6	6.5	7
Rest of Europe	38	38	39	39	40	41
U.S.	6	6.5	7	7.5	8	8.5

Other information

"excuse me"). It can all be great fun, but visitors can find it exhausting, too. Cubans perceive themselves to be, and almost always are, very poor in comparison with tourists. While some simply want to strike up friendships with foreigners, many are pursuing some economic agenda. With beggars (a recent phenomenon), street kids, black-market cigar sellers, and overt prostitutes, this is immediately obvious. However, often Cubans will subtly befriend you in the hope of a free meal or a few dollars. Some may offer just to show you around town, while others try to strike up a more intimate relationship. Treat any seemingly romantic overtures with caution, as many unfortunate foreigners have found themselves targets of a *jinetera*, or prostitute. The simplest advice is to try to befriend people on your terms rather than theirs.

Topless sunbathing is acceptable only at hotel pools and on beaches where there are large numbers of tourists.

Films
Our Man in Havana (1960), starring Alec Guinness, was largely shot in Havana. Much of the *The Godfather Part II* (1974) is set in the seedy clubs and Mafia hotels of late 1950s Havana. *A Few Good Men* (1992) tells the story of life in Guantánamo Bay Naval Base. *Strawberry and Chocolate* broke down barriers in 1995 (see also panel, page 142).

Gay travelers
Because of Cuba's political and social outlook, people rarely express homosexuality in public. Nonetheless, gay people are not persecuted as they were in the early years of the revolution. See also page 15.

Maps
Detailed large-scale road maps do not exist. For driving, try to obtain Freytag & Berndt's 1:1,250,000 map of Cuba (for sale abroad only) in

Like many others, this mansion in Trinidad has a sumptuous interior

193

The oldest house in Havana, Calle Obispo

combination with more up-to-date but smaller-scale road maps that are for sale in Cuba. Hotel shops also often sell city maps. Do not attempt to drive around Havana without a detailed city map.

Opening hours
Shops for local people keep loose opening hours, depending on whether they have anything to sell, but tourist-orientated stores usually open daily from about 10 until 6. Banks open typically weekdays 8:30–3 with maybe a break for lunch; those in resorts keep longer hours. As a rule, most museums close on Sunday afternoons and Monday, but times vary and are given in this guide. Tourist restaurants stay open late; locals' restaurants tend to run out of food by mid-evening.

Photography
Photo service shops stock ordinary color print film. Cubans are normally happy to have their photo taken, but may ask for a dollar in return, or to be sent a copy of the picture. Many museums forbid the taking of photographs or charge a fee; ask first.

Reading matter
Much has been written on Cuban history and politics, especially the Cuban revolution and communist Cuba. Many one-sided works, translated into English, are for sale on the island. For a more balanced picture, however, read some of the books listed below, virtually none of which is available in Cuba.

For light but informative reading, try *The Land of Miracles* by British journalist Stephen Smith (Little, Brown, 1997), a most insightful account into Cuban daily life, and *Cuba and the Night* by Pico Iyer (Vintage Books, 1996), a romantic novel set in 1990s Cuba. *Marita— From Castro to Kennedy: Love and Espionage in the CIA* by Marita

Lorenz and Ted Schwarz (Thunder's Mouth Press, 1993) is a bizarre kiss-and-tell yarn of a lover of Castro recruited by the CIA.

For the most detailed account of Cuba's history read *Cuba, or the Pursuit of Freedom* by Hugh Thomas (Da Capo Press, 1998), part of which has been reprinted as *The Cuban Revolution* (Weidenfeld and Nicolson, 1986). *Cuba—Between Reform and Revolution* by Louis A Pérez Jr (OUP, 1995) is also readable and considerably shorter. Of the many biographies of Castro, one of the more digestible is *Castro* by Sebastian Balfour (Addison Wesley, 1995). The best and most exhaustive biography of Che Guevara is *Che Guevara: a Revolutionary Life* by Jon Lee Anderson (Grove Press, 1998). *Cuba in Focus* by Emily Hatchwell and Simon Calder (Interlink Publishing Group, 1998) provides a concise account of the contemporary political and cultural scene.

Havana: Portrait of a City by Juliet Barclay (Sterling Publications, 1996) is a beautiful, interesting coffee table book on Old Havana. For everything you could possibly want to know about cigars, buy *The Cigar Companion* (Running Press, 1997). *The Exile – Cuba in the Heart of Miami* by David Rieff (Vintage, 1994) looks at Cuba and Cubans from a different geographical perspective.

See also Cuban literature on pages 142–143, and works by Ernest Hemingway on page 81 and by Graham Greene on page 74.

Tipping
The chief reason why so many Cubans want to work in tourism is the dollar tips. It is easy to overtip in Cuba: remember that one dollar is a lot of money for Cubans. Nonetheless, a dollar is expected by parking lot attendants and roving musicians; in taxis round up the fare to the nearest dollar, in restaurants add 5–10 percent to the bill, and in bars leave any coins from your change.

The whimsical tower of Havana's Gran Teatro, a theater that lives up to its name

Toilets
Public toilets are scarce in Cuba, but you can go into a bar or restaurant to use the facilities without buying anything. Only upscale establishments provide toilet paper, so it is a good idea to carry some at all times.

Travelers with disabilities
The only facilities in the country for travelers with disabilities are in a couple of the top hotels: ask your travel agent or tour operator for details.

Women travelers
Machismo is alive and well in Cuba, but less acute than in other Latin-American countries.

Foreign women receive much unsolicited attention, but no more so than local women and foreign men do, and on the whole most of it is playful rather than threatening. See also page 14.

Tourist offices in Cuba

There is no such thing as a tourist office in Cuba. Instead, state-run travel agencies such as Havanatur, Cubanacán, Gaviota, Rumbos, and Cubatur often have walk-in offices in the main cities and resorts, and run information desks in hotels. Their purpose is to sell excursions. Ask about anything involving independent travel and you will almost invariably get a blank response; local people are much more helpful and better informed. Nonetheless, tourism desks should all have a copy of the annual *Directorio Turístico de Cuba*, which lists addresses and phone numbers for hotels and restaurants and museum opening hours.

Cuban tourist boards abroad

Canada 55 Queen Street East, Suite 705, Toronto, Ontario MC5 1R6 (tel: 416 362 0700).
Germany An der Hauptwache 7, 60313 Frankfurt (tel: 069 288322).
United Kingdom 167 High Holborn, London WC1V 6PA (tel: 0171-2406655).

Tours

Organized tours or excursions cocoon you from the realities of Cuba, and are often slow, bureaucratic, and expensive. Moreover, they are conducted by guides who undergo extensive psychometric tests to make sure they tell you politically correct information and won't crack under probing questioning.

However, given the difficulties of making independent travel arrangements, they are the most popular way of exploring the island. From Havana and from every resort, tours are offered to virtually every major place of interest on the island. Some involve long bus trips, but there is often the option to pay extra and take a flight instead. Others take you to sugar plantations or cigar factories, which may be either hard to find or not open to independent travelers. And usually the only way to reach beaches on offshore islands is on a charter flight or boat trip.

The sun sets on one of Varadero's marinas

HOTELS & RESTAURANTS

HOTELS AND RESTAURANTS

ACCOMMODATIONS

Expect truly comfortable accommodations only in Havana and Santiago, and in resorts where there has been a recent proliferation of snazzy, all-inclusive hotels. These are geared almost exclusively to package vacationers; rates, which cover all meals and drinks, are prohibitively expensive for independent travelers on a budget.

Elsewhere, almost all cities have one massive Soviet-style monstrosity of a hotel on their periphery. These, at least are normally clean and have reasonable facilities, including restaurant, bar, and swimming pool. Moreover, they are so big there is hardly ever a problem getting a room. In the city center, you can usually find cheaper, more characterful but often very basic hotels (frequently with no hot water, for example) geared primarily to Cuban travelers.

Make advance reservations throughout the year for hotels in Old Havana, and in high season (December to April and July and August) in resorts and popular destinations such as Viñales, Trinidad, and Baracoa. Elsewhere, at any time of year, you would be extremely unlucky not to find a room on the spot.

As it can be difficult getting through to phone numbers in Cuba, for reservations from abroad you would be wise to use a specialist agency in your own country. For reservations from one hotel to the next, ask the receptionist to telephone ahead for you (you will be charged for the call).

Prices drop by as much as a third in low season. You will always be expected to pay in U.S. dollars. Almost all hotels take traveler's checks as long as they are not issued by a U.S. bank. U.S. credit cards are not accepted (see page 183). Bargaining does not work, as all hotels are government owned and use official rates.

In the last few years, many Cubans have started to let out spare rooms to foreigners to earn dollars, and many impecunious independent travelers stay in private homes (called *casas particulares*). In 1997 these casas particulares were legalized and owners are now forced to pay punitive taxes. This means that far fewer homes are offering rooms and prices have risen dramatically (mostly to around $25)—still good value. Note that no one can rent rooms legally in any beach resort in Cuba, including Varadero, Guardalavaca, and East Beaches. There are still rooms for rent illegally, at much cheaper rates, across Cuba (around $15 in Havana and $6–10 elsewhere). The only way to find out about rooms is by word of mouth—no problem in popular tourist destinations, where foreigners are swamped with offers for rooms. Always ask to see the bedroom and bathroom (normally shared with the family) first, and don't leave valuables lying around in temptation's way.

For the following accommodations, the $ symbols are a rough price guide for a standard double room per night in high season. Breakfast is normally optional, quoted separately from room rates: add around $3–7 per person.

- **budget** ($) = under $30
- **moderate** ($$) = $30–65
- **expensive** ($$$) = over $65

HAVANA

The phone code for Havana is 7. For more details on where to stay in Havana, see pages 86–87.

Old Havana

Ambos Mundos ($$) Obispo and Mercaderes (tel: 669530). Reopened in 1997 after a facelift. Ideally placed 1930s hotel, with colorful lobby, rooftop bar, and classy restaurant. Small but comfortable bedrooms (avoid interior-facing ones).
Caribbean ($) Prado No. 164 and Colón (tel: 338233). Havana's best-located budget option, and guests can use the nearby Sevilla's pool. However, the lobby/bar is a prostitute's hangout and rooms are dingy.
Hostal Valencia ($$) Oficios and Obrapía (tel: 623801). 18th-century mansion close to Plaza de Armas with a gorgeous courtyard. Twelve simple but individual and often large bedrooms, an appealing bar, and decent Spanish restaurant. Good value; book well in advance.
Inglaterra ($$) Parque Central (tel: 338593). Cuba's longest-serving hotel, opened 1875. Bustling, central location, ornate bar and restaurant, lively rooftop bar. However, the overpriced bedrooms are mostly pokey or noisy (ask for one facing Calle San Rafael).
Plaza ($$) Agramonte and Neptuno (tel: 338583). Elegant, restored early 20th-century building. Restaurants, attractive lobby bar, and good bedrooms (ask for one with a balcony).
Convento Santa Clara ($) Cuba and Sol (tel: 669327). Nine large, plain bedrooms (once monks' quarters) around a courtyard of a serene former convent (see page 69).
Santa Isabel ($$$) Plaza de Armas (tel: 338201). Former 18th-century palace stunningly converted into a small, peaceful luxury hotel. 27 romantic bedrooms, 10 of which are suites.
Sevilla ($$$) Trocadero between Agramonte and the Prado (tel: 338560). Revamped 1920s hotel with a sumptuous lobby, stuccoed rooftop restaurant, good dining, attractive bedrooms and, unique in Old Havana, a large pool.

Centro

Deauville ($$) Galiano and Malecón (tel: 628051). Monstrous tower block, right on the seafront, 10 minutes' walk from Old Havana. Many bedrooms are big and have ocean-facing balconies.

Lido ($) Consulado No. 210 between Animas and Trocadero (tel: 627000 and 622046). No frills but quite peaceful accommodations in a modern block close to the Prado.

Vedado

Meliá Cohiba ($$$) Paseo and Malecón (tel: 333636). Havana's swankiest hotel is a massive 21-floor modern high-rise geared to businesspeople, but in a poor, isolated location for tourists. Superb buffets, a cigar bar, and the city's top disco.
Nacional de Cuba ($$$) Calle O and 21 (tel: 333564). Far and away the most atmospheric hotel outside Old Havana; ordinary bedrooms, but wonderfully grand public areas, stylish bars, good food, two pools, a cabaret, and attractive gardens.
Riviera ($$$) Paseo and Malecón (tel: 334051). This revivified 1950s Mafia haunt is a giant, waterfront, turquoise tower block. Spacious bedrooms and the city's top venue for live music (see page 90).
Victoria ($$) Calle 19 and M (tel: 333510). Classy, small peaceful hotel catering primarily to businesspeople, with excellent bedrooms and a small pool. Close to Vedado's main street, La Rampa.

Miramar

Comodoro ($$–$$$) Calle 84 and Avenida 1 (tel: 245551). Miramar's most characterful hotel has a tiny beach sheltered by a bizarre metal breakwater and a popular disco. Choose between stylish bungalow accommodations and simple bedrooms with balcony and sea view.

Playas del Este

Villa Los Pinos ($$–$$$) Avenida de Las Terrazas No. 21 between calles 5 and 7 (tel: 2591). Not really a hotel, but rather 27 well-furnished prerevolution holiday homes with two to four bedrooms. Some have a private pool.

WESTERN CUBA

Pinar del Río Province
Viñales

La Ermita ($–$$) (tel: 8 936071 or book through 334238). Modern low-rise complex with fine valley views and pool. A short walk from Viñales town, but less appealing than Los Jazmines (see below).
Los Jazmines ($–$$) 1 mile from Viñales (tel: 82 93205). Serene, colonial-style mansion with a seductive pool and plain but attractive balconied bedrooms. The view across Viñales valley is a strong contender for being Cuba's most memorable.
Cayo Levisa ($$) A tiny island with nothing but 20 plain, thatched bungalows (with hot water), a restaurant, and a fabulous beach. Rates include all meals. No phone; reservations can (in theory) be made via Havana on 7 331162; or contact a travel agent.

Península de Guanahacabibes
María La Gorda ($$)

Small hotel with diving school and simple en suite rooms right on the pristine beach. Rates are full board. Best booked through Marasub in Havana (tel: 7 333055).

Pinar del Río

Globo ($) Martí No. 50 (tel: 82 4268). Wonderful, decaying 1917 mansion on the main street. Spartan (no hot water), but big airy bedrooms with refrigerator and balcony.
Pinar del Río ($) (tel: 82 5070). Large, noisy, characterless modern block with a full range of facilities, on the outskirts of town at the start of the *autopista*.
Villa Aguas Claras ($) 5 miles north of town on the Viñales road (tel: 82 2722). Simple chalets around a big pool in exotic grounds; a lovely rural spot. Horseback riding available.

Soroa

Moka ($$) Las Terrazas (tel: 85 2996). Imaginative new complex with stylish bedrooms in the lush Sierra del Rosario foothills. Bike and horseback nature tours. 10 miles east of Soroa (turn right off *autopista* at 51km mark (32 miles) from Havana).

199

Archipiélago de los Canarreos
Isla de la Juventud

Colony ($$) (tel: 61 98181). Very isolated, large diving enclave by a fetching beach, 26 miles southwest of Nueva Gerona. Comfortable rooms, reasonable facilities.
Villa Gaviota ($–$$) (tel: 61 2 3290 and 61 2 4486). Small, cheerful riverside hotel with spacious bedrooms and pleasant pool. Off the *autopista* just south of Nueva Gerona.

Cayo Largo

Isla del Sur Resort ($$) (tel: 5 48159). Five low-rise hotel complexes spread along 1 mile of beachfront. Isla del Sur itself is the busiest, with a full activities program and disco. Villa Capricho is the most romantic, comprising vaulted, thatched bungalows with hammocks, but no pool. The classiest is Villa Coral, its bedrooms in colonial-style villas around an appealing pool.
Pelicano ($$) (tel: 5 48333). Large, soulless complex of Spanish-style villas amid modern sculpture. Next to a better stretch of beach and with better bedrooms than the Isla del Sur Resort.

Matanzas Province
Varadero

The telephone area code for Varadero is 5. For more on where to stay in Varadero, see page 112.
Club Varadero ($$$) 2 miles east of the center (tel: 667030). Cuba's first all-inclusive hotel, part of a Jamaican hotel chain, is rather snooty, taking only guests over 15 years old. Pretty grounds and bedrooms. Watersports included in the rates.

HOTELS AND RESTAURANTS

Cuatro Palmas ($$$) Avenida 1 between calles 61 and 62 (tel: 667040). Varadero's most central large package hotel faces a lovely, busy section of beach and has a good palm-lined pool. Ask for a room facing or close to the beach.
Dos Mares ($$) Avenida 1 and Calle 53 (tel: 62702). Reasonable budget option: a small-scale Spanish-style building in the center of town that doubles as a hotel school. Cramped, plain bedrooms.
Internacional ($$–$$$) ½-mile east of the center (tel: 667038). Varadero's most charismatic and best-value hotel, built in 1950 for high-rolling Americans. One of the few large complexes in walking distance of the resort's center. Roomy apartments in the grounds, and classy rooms.
Kawama ($$–$$$) Reparto Kawama (tel: 667156). Pre-revolution and modern villas spread around palmy grounds near the resort's western end. Lively bar, and direct beach access but no pool.
Meliá Las Américas ($$$) 2.5 miles east of the center (tel: 667600). This big Spanish-run complex is one of Varadero's most sophisticated and pricey. A cornucopia of facilities, pretty bedrooms, classy restaurants, and right on a great slice of beach.
Pullman ($) Avenida 1 and Calle 49 (tel: 667161). Overpriced but cheapest hotel in Varadero; a guesthouse ambience (rocking chairs on the terrace) in a modest 1940s turreted villa in the resort's center.
Riu Las Morlas ($$) 1 mile east of the center (tel: 667230). Mid-size complex centered on a palm- and banana-fringed pool and facing a beautiful section of beach. Good value
Sol Palmeras ($$$) 3 miles east of the center (tel: 667009). Varadero's biggest hotel is Spanish-run and can house 1,100 guests. Enormous pool and a great stretch of palm-shaded beach. Many bedrooms in bungalows in tranquil, verdant grounds.

Matanzas
Louvre ($) Plaza de la Libertad (tel: 52 4074). 19th-century hotel epitomizing decaying grandeur. Some antique-furnished bedrooms with balconies overlooking the city's main square; cold water only.

Península de Zapata
Villa Playa Girón ($) Playa Girón (tel: 59 4110). Large beachside complex used mainly by Canadians. Some 300 rooms in spacious, plain bungalows under palms, and a big pool.
Villa Playa Larga ($) Playa Larga (tel: 59 7219). 50 roomy yet simple bungalows with sitting rooms, set in grassy parkland by a decent beach. Canadian clientele.
Villa Guamá ($) Laguna del Tesoro (tel: 59 2979). Thatched huts, each with refrigerator, air conditioning, and balcony, spread over interconnected islands in a swamp. Mosquito repellent essential.

CENTRAL CUBA

Western Central Cuba
Trinidad
Ancón ($$) Playa Ancón (tel: 419 4011). Hideous, giant, and dated multicolored high-rise, hovering over a fabulous beach. Every facility, including excellent watersports. Ask for a room in the new block.
Costasur ($$) Playa María Aguilar (tel: 419 6100). Visually less offensive and smaller than the Ancón (see above), but next to a slightly poorer section of beach. Best accommodations are in bungalows.
Las Cuevas ($) (tel: 419 4013). Over 100 spacious bungalows spread across a hillside, a 15-minute walk up from the town center. Pleasant pool.
Finca Dolores ($) (tel: 419 3581). 18 cheap, very basic and small chalets in a lovely rural spot next to a river, 1 mile west of Trinidad. Tacky cabarets some evenings, and cockfights and riding competitions some weekends.

Sierra del Escambray
Hanabanilla ($) Embalse Hanabanilla (tel: 42 491125). Big unattractive block in a lovely lakeside setting with cheap, balconied bedrooms. Fishing and boat trips available. Popular with Cuban vacationers.

Cienfuegos
Faro Luna ($–$$) Playa Rancho Luna (tel: 48 162). Peaceful small hotel with a salt-water pool and excellent bedrooms, in a rocky, waterside position 1,000 feet from Playa Rancho Luna's sands.
Jagua ($$) Punta Gorda (tel: 432 3021). Large, ugly 1950s building, but comfortable bedrooms and well sited; just south of the city center in Punta Gorda, right on the bay.

Remedios
Mascotte ($) Parque Martí (tel: 39 5481). The only place to stay in town. Extremely basic (water only at certain times) but some grand rooms in an historic colonial building on the main square.

Sancti Spíritus
Zaza ($) Embalse Zaza (tel: 41 26012). 6 miles southeast of town, a Soviet-style block pleasantly sited by a lake. Good food and a pool.

Santa Clara
Santa Clara Libre ($) Parque Vidal (tel: 422 27548). Landmark 11-story high-rise with small bedrooms, but a decent 10th-floor restaurant and an ideal location on the city's main square.
La Granjita ($$) (tel: 422 26051/2/9). Pretty, tranquil complex surrounded by orange groves, 2.5 miles northeast of the center. Above-average rooms in thatched-buildings, and appealing pool.

Eastern Central Cuba
Camagüey
Colón ($) República No. 472 (tel: 322 83368). Bargain-basement 1920s hotel with lots of atmosphere and simple rooms (no hot water) around a lovely fern-filled courtyard with a bar and restaurant.
Gran ($) Maceo No. 67 (tel: 322 92093). Recently renovated neocolonial hotel in the city center. Beautiful airy restaurant, secluded small pool, and nice but noisy balconied bedrooms.
Maraguan ($$) Circunvalación Este (tel: 322 72017). Former country club in rural surroundings 6 miles northeast of Camagüey. Good bungalow rooms and inviting pool.

Cayo Coco
Tryp Cayo Coco ($$$) (tel: 33 301311). Cuba's most attractive beach hotel: palm-lined gardens, a dazzling beach, luxurious rooms in pastel-colored colonial-style villas, freeform pools, excellent food in six restaurants, and first-rate shops.
Tryp Club Cayo Coco ($$$) (tel: 33 301300). Swanky, modern, massive, and all-inclusive hotel. Not as attractively landscaped as the Tryp Cayo Coco, but like its neighbor offers every conceivable activity.

Cayo Guillermo
Club Cayo Guillermo ($$$) (tel: 7 667171). Boisterous, all-inclusive, used almost exclusively by Italians. Next to a seductive stretch of gently shelving beach.
Villa Vigía ($$$) (tel: 33 301760). Slick all-inclusive complex. Impressive pool and bungalow rooms, but a less appealing beach than other Coco and Guillermo hotels.

Morón
Morón ($) Avenida Tarafa (tel: 33 3076). Large hotel school that delivers tasty food and attractive, well-functioning bedrooms; an excellent choice as a pit stop.

Playa Santa Lucía
Club Caracol ($$$) (tel: 32 36302). The resort's prettiest, most peaceful hotel is all-inclusive. Palm-filled gardens, a fetching pool, and bedrooms, all with balcony and sitting area, in rose-colored villas.
Cuatro Vientos ($$) (tel: 32 335533). The resort's largest hotel has some 400 bedrooms in thatched units ranged around landscaped gardens. Good buffets, and a panoply of activities alongside the best section of the beach.

EASTERN CUBA

Santiago de Cuba
The phone code for Santiago and Parque Baconao is 226. For more details on where to stay in Santiago, see page 153.
Casa Granda ($$) Parque Céspedes (tel: 86600). The best place to stay in town;

a revamped neocolonial mansion on the main square with attractive rooms, a wonderful terrace bar, and good, refined restaurant. See also page 157.
Gran ($) José A Saco No. 312 (tel: 20472). A good bet if all you want is a simple, large, cheap bedroom right in the center—the hotel, under gradual restoration, is on Santiago's main street.
Santiago de Cuba ($$$) Avenida de las Américas and Calle M, Vista Alegre (tel: 42612). Far and away the city's snazziest hotel; a postmodernist tower block with six bars, a fantastic pool, and indulgent buffets. Very affordable out of season.
Villa Gaviota ($–$$) Avenida Manduley No. 502 between calles 19 and 21, Vista Alegre (tel: 41368). A lovely secluded pool and good roomy accommodations (especially superior rooms in old villas) in a very peaceful location in leafy suburbs.
San Juan ($$) (tel: 86602). Tranquil, woody setting by a park 3 miles from the city center on the road to Parque Baconao. Rooms in villas set under trees and around a big pool.

Parque Baconao
Bucanero ($$) Arroyo La Costa (tel: 22 5224). Large, rustic, and isolated package vacation complex on a rocky shoreline with its own pretty sandy cove.
Los Corales ($$) Playa Cazonal (tel: 226 86177). German-managed package hotel at the eastern end of Parque Baconao next to the park's best beach. Pleasant gardens and a good pool.
Villa La Gran Piedra ($) (tel: 22 5224/5913). Amazing views from simple but spacious bungalow rooms under the summit of La Gran Piedra.

Holguín Province
Holguín
Pernik ($) Avenida Jorge Dimitrov (tel: 24 481011). Soulless, large modern block on the outskirts of the city, but comfortable and with a huge pool.
Mirador de Mayabe ($–$$) (tel: 24 423485). On a hilltop 6 miles southeast of the city; a popular open-air restaurant, pool, and beer-drinking donkey, plus simple chalets and four outstanding luxury rooms.

Guardalavaca
Delta Las Brisas ($$$) Playa Guardalavaca (tel: 24 30211/8/9). Sophisticated, Canadian-run, all-inclusive, popular with families. Right on the beach, good choice of restaurants, very attractive pool.
Sol Club Rio de Luna ($$$) Playa Esmeralda (tel: 24 30030/1/2/3). Sensitively designed, peaceful low-rise beachfront complex with good-quality, balconied bedrooms. Spanish-managed and all-inclusive.
Sol Rio de Mares ($$) Playa Esmeralda (tel: 24 30035). Large complex not quite as attractive as its neighbor, the Sol Club Rio de Luna, but not all-inclusive; good value.

201

HOTELS AND RESTAURANTS

Villa Guardalavaca ($$) Playa Guardalavaca (tel: 24 30212). Overpriced, but cheapest option in the resort. Comprises just a bar, restaurant and two dozen good-size but simple rooms. 492 feet from the beach.

Granma Province
Bayamo
Sierra Maestra ($) Carretera Central (tel: 23 481013). Charmless large Soviet-style complex with decent facilities 1 mile from center.

Manzanillo
Guacanayabo ($) Circunvalacíon Camilo Cienfuegos (tel: 23 54012). Ugly, noisy, large modern hotel on the town's western outskirts. Bearable for a night or two.

Sierra Maestra
Farallón del Caribe ($$–$$$) Marea del Portillo (tel: 24 5301). Canadians dominate this attractive, Canadian-managed all-inclusive hotel 650 feet from the beach.
Marea del Portillo ($$) (tel: 23 594201). Older, far less attractive option than the Farallón del Caribe, but right on the beach, cheaper, and not all-inclusive.
Los Galeones ($$) Chivirico (tel: 22 26160). Intimate, all-inclusive Canadian venture in a great position—on a hilltop isthmus separating a gray sand beach and inlet. Use of sister hotel Sierra Mar's facilities.
Sierra Mar ($$–$$$) 8 miles east of Chivirico (tel: 24 6336). Arguably Cuba's best beach hotel and certainly its most dramatically sited—tiered into a hillside above a long stretch of dark sands. Superb facilities, great staff, outstanding value (all-inclusive).
Villa Santo Domingo ($) (tel: 23 375). Remote mountain trekking base 12 miles south of Bartolomé Masó. Simple huts and a restaurant in a gorgeous riverside spot.

Guantánamo Province
Baracoa
El Castillo ($) (tel: 21 42103). Hilltop hotel converted from one of the town's old forts, with memorable views, lovely pool, good food. Two minutes' walk from the center.
Porto Santo ($) (tel: 21 43590). Low-rise modern waterside complex 1 mile from the town center near the airport, with pool, tiny beach, and terraced bedrooms.
La Rusa ($) Máximo Gomez No. 161 (tel: 21 4 3570 and 21 4 3011). Basic, small seafront hotel with a popular locals' bar, once run by a Russian émigrée (see page 175).
Villa Maguana ($) Playa Maguana (tel: 21 43570). Magical spot next to an amazing beach, 13 miles northwest of Baracoa. Four comfortable rooms and a tiny restaurant.

Guantánamo
Islazul Guantánamo ($) Ahogados and Calle 13 Norte (tel: 21 381015). Basic, big Soviet-style hotel on the edge of the city; departure point for trips to view the American naval base.

RESTAURANTS

See pages 34–35 for more on eating in Cuba. Proper restaurants are very rarely full, and at *paladares* you are expected to wait for a table. The only places where it is possibly worth bothering with reservations are Havana's and Varadero's best restaurants (for which phone numbers are given below). At any sit-down eatery, tourists are always expected to pay in dollars. Only top city restaurants and resort establishments are likely to accept credit cards. Use the following price bands for the cost of a full meal without drinks (and excluding shellfish, which are invariably the priciest dishes on the menu).
- **budget** ($) = under $6
- **moderate** ($$) = $6–15
- **expensive** ($$$) = over $15

HAVANA
For more details on where to eat and drink in Havana, see pages 88–89.

Old Havana
La Bodeguita del Medio ($$) Empedrado No. 207 near Plaza de la Catedral (tel: 618442). One of Havana's most celebrated and longest-running bar-restaurants. Down-to-earth place famous for graffiti décor, *mojitos*, and pork dishes. Head for the rooftop terrace.
La Divina Pastora ($$) La Cabaña (tel: 338341). Decent seafood (including paella) in a magical waterside setting—an old battery with a lovely terrace under La Cabaña fortress.
Doña Eutimia ($$) Callejón del Chorro, off Plaza de la Catedral (tel: 615163). Old Havana's finest *paladar*: antiques, modern art, and carefully presented dishes from an extensive menu.
El Floridita ($$$) Obispo No. 557 at the corner of Bélgica (tel: 631060). Thanks to Ernest Hemingway, the city's most famous bar-restaurant. Very expensive seafood platters of inconsistent quality are served in its formal muraled dining room, or just stop by for a daiquiri.
D'Giovanni ($–$$) Tacón No. 4 at the corner of Empedrado. Passable pizzas and pasta in a gorgeous 18th-century mansion. Informal dining in the courtyard, fancier upstairs.
Al Medina ($$) Oficios No. 12 between Obispo and Obrapía. Arab and Cuban dishes in a Middle Eastern setting above a gorgeous colonial courtyard. Belly dancing on week-end evenings.
La Paella ($$) Oficios and Obrapía. The Hostal Valencia's restaurant (see Accommodations): good paellas and fish dishes in a lovely beamed dining room decorated with Spanish bullfighting posters.
La Mina ($$) Obispo and Plaza de Armas. Two touristy 24-hour cafés offering snacks and energetic live music, plus an ice-cream

parlor and a beautiful courtyard restaurant serving cheap, mediocre Creole meals mainly to tour groups.

El Patio ($$) Plaza de la Catedral (tel: 618504). Creole meals and more elaborate fare served in a fabulous romantic colonial courtyard. Good value.

La Torre de Marfil ($) Mercaderes No. 111 between Obispo and Obrapía. Chinese music and cuisine in a fine colonial building. Palatable meals; good value.

Vedado

Cafetería La Rampa ($) La Rampa between calles L and M. Cheap sandwiches, burgers, and pasta in a busy, well-staffed modern fast-food joint near the Hotel Habana Libre.

Don Agamenón ($$) Calle 17 No. 60 between calles M and N. Everything from lobster pizzas to Creole cuisine and an open-air barbecue in a stylishly furnished neoclassical villa.

Le Chansonnier ($$) Calle 15 between calles H and I (tel: 323788). A *paladar* with pretensions: *foie gras* and quiche *lorraine* in an antiques-filled old villa in a leafy back street.

Los Amigos ($) Calle M No. 253 between calles 19 and 21. A homely, untouristy *paladar*, with excellent Creole fare.

El Rápido ($) Linea and Calle M. This interesting outlet of Cuba's ubiquitous fast-food chain is a drive-in, full of burger-munching Cubans sitting in Cadillacs.

Miramar

La Cecilia ($$$) Avenida 5 between calles 110 and 112 (tel: 241562). Classy, large open-air restaurant and grill house in a lovely garden full of palms and *jagüey* trees. Cuban and international dishes, and cabaret shows most nights.

La Ferminia ($$$) Avenida 5 No. 18207 between calles 182 and 184 (tel: 336786). Havana's most formal restaurant: private dining rooms, antiques, fine art, international cuisine, and vintage wines.

Tocororo ($$$) Calle 18 and Avenida 3 (tel: 242209). Probably Havana's best restaurant. Art-nouveau lamps and art in a leafy villa owned by the Cristal beer magnate before the revolution. No menu: expect anything from sea bass to veal, and good wines.

Southern Havana

Las Ruinas ($–$$$) Calle 100 and Cortina de la Presa, Parque Lenin (tel: 443336). A bizarre place—a vast, modern yet antiques-filled pavilion built around the licheny ruins of a plantation mansion. Costly, well-regarded formal dinners, as well as lunchtime snacks.

East of Havana

La Terraza ($$) Cojímar (tel: 653471). Founded in 1925, an evocative waterside seafood restaurant and bar once frequented by Hemingway. Expect lunchtime tour bus parties. See page 83.

WESTERN CUBA

Pinar del Río Province
Viñales

Valle-Bar ($). *Paladar* on Viñales' main street is the town's social center; excellent live music nightly and good food, especially shrimp. Just down the road is the much quieter **Casa de Don Tomás** ($–$$), a beautiful wooden mansion built in 1889. At the **Cueva del Indio** and **Mural de la Prehistori**a there are lunchtime restaurants (all $–$$) geared to tour groups.

Pinar del Río

Paladar Don Miguel ($), on a terrace overlooking the cathedral at Gerardo Medina and Ceferino Fernandez, is run by a talented chef and highly recommended.

Rumayor ($$), a decent state restaurant in a vast wooden barn decorated with Afro-Cuban crafts ½ mile from town on the Viñales road, doubles as a cabaret spot most nights.

Soroa

Castillo de las Nubes ($). Turreted villa above Soroa with extensive views and a short bar menu. Open to 5 PM.

Archipielago de los Canarreos
Isla de la Juventud

The friendly **El Cochinito** ($) at calles 29 and 34, Nueva Gerona's best restaurant, produces edible pork dishes; it can run out of food in the evening. **La Casa de los Vinos** ($), at calles 20 and 41, serves peculiar wines made from fruit other than grapes.

Matanzas Province
Varadero

For more details on where to eat and drink in Varadero, see page 111.

Las Américas ($–$$$) Avenida Las Américas (tel: 667750). The former Dupont mansion (see page 112) serves inexpensive snacks on its terrace during the day, and expensive, ambitious, and not always successful dinners in its palatial dining rooms in the evening.

Boulevard 43 ($) Avenida 1 and Calle 43. A reasonable bakery-cum-cake shop next to a passable fast-food joint.

El Bodegón Criollo ($$) Avenida Playa and Calle 40. Spin off of Havana's La Bodeguita del Medio (see above), with similar Creole food and graffiti décor, but no atmosphere.

La Casa de Al ($$) Villa Punta Blanca. Paella is the specialty at this prerevolution villa where Al Capone stayed in the 1920s.

Mi Casita ($$) Camino del Mar between calles 11 and 12 (tel: 613787). Right over the beach; tiny, intimate, and long-established serving prix fixe.

Parque Josone A clutch of themed restaurants lie around the park. **La Casa de Antigüedades** ($$$) (tel: 667329) is possibly the best in Varadero: romantic, small dining rooms are treasure troves of antiques, and

203

specialties (no menu) include shellfish and steak. Lakeside **Dante** ($$) is a small, upscale trattoria. **La Campana** ($$) serves decent, inexpensive Creole meals.

Matanzas
Café Atenas ($) Plaza de la Vigía. 24-hour café in a cool colonial building; cheap sandwiches, chicken, and mini pizzas.

Península de Zapata
The two large tourist restaurants at **La Boca** ($$), sometimes serving crocodile steak, and open daytime only, have better reputations than Guama's thatched restaurant ($$).

CENTRAL CUBA

Western Central Cuba
Trinidad
There is a host of *paladares* on the streets near Parque Central and the road up to the Motel Las Cuevas: try homely, popular **Ines** ($) at Martí 160. Trinidad's half-dozen state restaurants, all in lovely colonial buildings, mostly offer indifferent, overpriced food and are geared to lunchtime groups. The only one open in the evening is **Santa Ana** ($$) (see page126), serving plain, decent fare. For lunch only, try **El Jigüe** ($$), a gorgeous painted house specializing in chicken and spaghetti one block north of Plaza Mayor.

Cienfuegos
Finca La Isabela ($$) Simple open-air Creole restaurant 2 miles outside the city on Carretera Rancho Luna, popular with locals. Holds cockfights and discos.
Palacio Valle ($$–$$$) Punta Gorda. A grand dining room in a dazzling Moorish palace (see page 130). Eccentric pianist, reasonable seafood, good ice cream.

Eastern Central Cuba
Camagüey
Try the **Gran Hotel**'s grand restaurant ($$) (see Accommodations), or, on Plaza San Juan de Dios, the touristy **Campana de Toledo** ($$): pretty colonial courtyard, decorated with *tinajones*; the specialty is *chorizo* rolled in beef.

Playa Santa Lucía
Lobster House ($$) La Boca. Memorable, seafood dishes cooked in a waterside shack and served under an almond tree in the ramshackle hamlet next to Playa Los Cocos.
El Paraiso ($$) Villa Coral. Grilled fish on a tiny platform 250 feet out to sea. Closes 5 PM.

EASTERN CUBA

Santiago de Cuba
The best food can be found at the two top hotels. The **Casa Granda**'s elegant, formal restaurant ($$) offers Creole meals, at excellent value, while the **Santiago de Cuba** has fabulous buffets ($$). Otherwise:

Ereddy ($) Calle 8 No. 202 on the corner of Calle 7, Vista Alegre. A *paladar* in a very private mansion (no sign). Good home cooking presented on a serene terrace.
Las Gallegas ($) Bartolomé Masó No. 305. Relaxed *paladar* offering good lobster, shrimp, and pork dishes in an elegant vaulted dining room.
El Morro ($$). Clifftop, vine-covered terrace next to El Morro castle; specialties are horsemeat and fish stuffed with shrimp.
Plaza de Dolores. This square is something of a gastronomic emporium. Its most salubrious establishments are three adjacent and little frequented tourist restaurants on the north side, which serve indifferent Creole, Chinese, and Italian food in fine surroundings (all $–$$).
Restaurante 1900 ($$) Bartolomé Masó No. 354 between Hartmann and Pio Rosado. Come for the floral courtyard and terraces of this former Bacardí mansion as much as for the mediocre Creole food.
Zunzun ($$–$$$) Avenida Manduley No. 159 and Calle 7, Vista Alegre. Tranquil, stylish villa with private chandeliered dining rooms, a lovely terrace for cocktails, and modern cuisine. No menu.

Holguín Province
Holguín
Everyone eats in the many *paladares* off the main squares: try **Adecuado** ($) at Miró No. 114 for its moody atmosphere as much as its very cheap food. For a drink, head for **La Begonia** ($), a flowery outdoor café on Parque Calixto García. See also **Mirador de Mayabe** under Accommodations, page 201.

Guardalavaca and around
El Ancla ($$) Playa Guardalavaca. Friendly, waterside fish restaurant 650 feet beyond the beach's western end.
Pizza Nova ($$) Playa Guardalavaca. Pricey but impressive pizzas near the resort's western end.
El Faro ($$) Gibara. Lobster and fish in an airy waterfront restaurant. Good value

Granma Province
Bayamo
Restaurante 1513 ($–$$) General García and General Lora. Filling, traditional Cuban fare in an untouristy, family setting.

Manzanillo
Las Américas ($) Parque Céspedes. Cheap lobsters and steaks in a fine colonial building. Food often runs out by 8 PM.

Guantánamo Province
Baracoa
The Hotel El Castillo (see Accommodations) serves delicious coconut-flavored fish, rice, and ice cream ($$). Otherwise, try one of the half-dozen *paladares*: the best is tiny **El Moro** ($) at Maceo No. 110 just off the main square, with seafood and live music.

Index

Principal references are shown in **bold**

205

INDEX

INDEX

208

Acknowledgements

The Automobile Association would like to thank the following photographers and libraries for their assistance in the preparation of this book.

BRIDGEMAN ART LIBRARY, LONDON 143 Untitled (Havane), 1944 by Wilfredo Lam (b 1902). Private collection
GETTY IMAGES Cover, 44/5, 44b, 45, 177
MAGNUM PHOTOS 12, 26a, 29, 32a, 37b, 46a, 49, 50b, 53, 85, 176/7
MARY EVANS PICTURE LIBRARY 38/9, 38, 39, 40a, 40b, 41b, 43b, 105
FRED MAWER 2, 6/7, 9b, 14a, 18a, 27b, 33, 41a, 52b, 57, 60, 75, 83, 92, 106, 107, 108, 109, 116, 116/17, 122, 144, 145, 146/7, 151, 162, 163, 164, 165, 166, 167, 170, 172/3, 174, 175, 178, 190/1
MIAMI CONVENTION & VISITORS BUREAU 28b
NATURE PHOTOGRAPHERS 16 (PR Sterry), 17 (EA Janes)
REDFERN MUSIC PICTURE LIBRARY 91
REX FEATURES 74b
TROPICANA CLUB 90
MIREILLE VAUTIER 84a, 142a, 142b
WORLD PICTURES 159b

The remaining photographs were taken by Clive Sawyer, who was commissioned for this publication, and are now in the Association's own Photo Library (AA Photo Library), with the exception of page 28a, which was taken by Pete Bennett.

The author, Fred Mawer, is grateful to both Cubana and Havanatur for the assistance given in the preparation of this book.

The photographer, Clive Sawyer, would like to thank the following for their help in making this assignment one not to be forgotten: Christina Gibbons at Regent Holidays Bristol; Carmen Mendiz Acosta, representative for Havanatur; Hector del Valle Urizarri and his family in Old Havana, and John Lois who guided me through Pinar del Río.

Contributors

Copy editor: Sue Gordon   **Designer**: Jo Tapper
Verifier: Diana Williams   **Indexer**: Marie Lorimer